S0-BJR-172

T.L.S.

ESSAYS AND REVIEWS FROM
The Times Literary Supplement · 1966

5

T.L.S.

ESSAYS AND REVIEWS FROM

The Times Literary Supplement · 1966

5

London
OXFORD UNIVERSITY PRESS
NEW YORK TORONTO
1967

Oxford University Press, Ely House, London W.1

GLASGOW NEW YORK TORONTO MELBOURNE WELLINGTON
CAPE TOWN SALISBURY IBADAN NAIROBI LUSAKA ADDIS ABABA
BOMBAY CALCUTTA MADRAS KARACHI LAHORE DACCA
KUALA LUMPUR HONG KONG TOKYO

PRINTED IN GREAT BRITAIN IN THE CITY OF OXFORD
AT THE ALDEN PRESS

CONTENTS

NOTE

During 1966 the *T.L.S.* published three special numbers on 'New Ways in History'. The first of these included the review article 'Back to the Sources'. Henry Treece, who died on June 10, is commemorated in the article 'Henry Treece, Lament for a Maker' written for the autumn Children's Books Number. Evelyn Waugh's revised one-volume edition of his war trilogy was his last published book before his death on 10 April.

The year ended for the paper and its readers with a controversy about the Arts Council's policy of awards and bursaries for literature, conducted under the heading 'The Panel Game'. This began with a leading article on 20 October and largely filled the correspondence columns throughout November and December. As the arguments were far too copious to anthologize we have reprinted all the year's reviews of books by the bursary winners. It is important to realize that the books in question are not always representative; none the less the reviews may be found to add a missing element to the debate.

I

DIZZY HEIGHTS

A PROSPECT OF BEACONSFIELD

EVERY READER MUST make up his mind about Disraeli, adventurer or statesman, charlatan or genius, cynic or romantic, and the answer is bound to be subjective. But at least since Mr. Robert Blake's admirable biography it will no longer be necessary to decide in ignorance of the facts. It is indeed astonishing when one considers Disraeli's career, with its roots in the eighteenth century, with its domination of English public life in the nineteenth century and with its influence continuing almost to our time, that hardly any book of any value has ever been written about him. The official biography begun by Monypenny and completed by Buckle is rightly described as a quarry and a classic but such an assignment enforces reticence and discourages objectivity; apart from this and Professor B. R. Jerman's *Young Disraeli*, which is marred by an opening chapter of a brashness and vulgarity which would have made its subject wince, no book has yet been written about Disraeli of more than anecdotal interest. Perhaps the state of the Hughenden archives must bear some responsibility for this; until Mr. R. W. Stewart (whose help Mr. Blake acknowledges) took them in hand they were less a quarry than a haystack; all honour then to Mr. Blake who with scholarly persistence and a serendipity of his own has given us a book that people will still be reading in fifty years' time and long after.

* * *

When Disraeli retired from the House of Commons Sir William Harcourt wrote to him from the Front Opposition bench 'To the imagination of the younger generation your life will always have a special fascination. For them you have enlarged the horizon of the possibilities of the future', and Disraeli's is still in the history of Parliament a unique achievement. Nevertheless his early life has been

---

ROBERT BLAKE: *Disraeli.* 819 pp. 15 plates. Eyre and Spottiswoode. £4 10s.

hidden in a romantic mist, much of it of his own later manufacture, and Mr. Blake has done well in getting the facts on record. His family were respectable and respected, but the extravagant claims to a background of splendour in Venice which he made in a memoir of his father published in 1849 have no foundation. His father was a man of letters of repute and his house Bradenham is to the modern eye infinitely more desirable than Disraeli's machicolated villa at Hughenden. Disraeli himself was baptised at the age of thirteen, and was destined for Winchester, the school that his younger brothers both attended. He refers in an unpublished autobiographical fragment written later to his 'often being described as an alumnus of that public school'. He went to an unimportant private school instead; in no part of his career can he be said to have conformed to conventional Wykehamist standards, but it is an engaging fantasy none the less. The Duke of Argyll, who was a hostile witness, said much later, but with enough justice to sting:

> It is really nonsense to talk of a man in such a position as a mere 'Jew Boy' who by the force of nothing but extraordinary genius attained to the leadership of a great party. The only impediments in his way were not in any want of external advantages but his own often grotesque and unintelligible opinions.

* * *

It is fairer to say that many of the impediments were of his own devising. He lost a fortune in wild stock exchange speculations which he did not have the slightest hope of repaying. He made an ass of himself and of John Murray, too, in attempting in his early twenties to start a newspaper. Worse still, he then proceeded to caricature Murray in unmistakable terms in Vivian Grey, thus forfeiting goodwill earned through his father. (Mr. Blake points out that obvious references to Murray's drunkenness were removed from the revised edition of the novels published in 1853 when he was leading the Opposition in the Commons, but the damage had been done.) Finally his love affair with Lady Sykes and the ambivalent relationship between the pair of them and Lord Lyndhurst, with his stinking reputation for lechery, did him great harm for many years and not only among his constituents in Buckinghamshire. None of this is touched on in the official biography; Professor Jerman brought the Lady Sykes episode to the light of day and Mr. Blake has added his own researches and made a coherent story of it all.

* * *

Max Beerbohm once described Disraeli as a dandy who later adopted a less demanding occupation, but he was certainly not a dandy in the Baudelairean sense and was far too overdressed to be acceptable in the company of Brummell. The literary salons that he frequented had no connexion with Holland House and opened no door to better things. Then as now the 'romantic novelist' was held in no great esteem. Ambition took him into politics, his choice of party being purely idiosyncratic. The Reforms Bill had not broken, it had in fact strengthened, the power of the Whig oligarchy—he saw no future for himself in their ranks and turned to the Tories, to whom his radicalism made then as now a special appeal.

A whole volume of Monypenny is devoted to the start of Disraeli's parliamentary career and there is little new to add to it. But Mr. Blake does well to rescue from the comparative obscurity of a twenty-seven-year-old back number of the *Journal of Modern History* the story of Disraeli's entanglement in 1832 with Henry Stanley, younger brother of the fourteenth Lord Derby. Although he came out of Stanley's scrape honourably and reasonably discreetly the incident must have shown him to Lord Derby as being altogether too intimate with the seamy side of London life to be acceptable as a colleague. There was no compelling reason for Peel to take him into his Ministry in 1841, and of his letter asking for office Mr. Blake comments, with an acuteness gained no doubt from his previous study of Bonar Law, on

> those who imagine that politicians regard office in the same way as schoolboys are supposed to regard selection for the first eleven, an honour to be won on merit and to be lost without complaint. No one who has studied the political papers of any Prime Minister will suffer from that delusion.

Of course if Peel had given him a job history would have been quite different, but the hindsight of the historian added to Disraeli's natural optimism and his skill as a correspondent has given a wholly imaginary importance to his political life up to 1846. Young England was a joke although it earned him the lifelong support of that paragon Lord John Manners: it was his personal unimportance as much as his reputation as a trouble maker that cost him the Conservative whip in 1843. His career was transformed by Lord George Bentinck's acceptance of him as spokesman for the protectionist Tories in the bitter session of 1846 and the only real criticism to be made of Mr. Blake is that he tends to underrate the effectiveness of that demonic and ruthless character. Much later Disraeli was to refer in a letter to the Queen to 'the most singular species in Your Majesty's dominions, the Bentinck', but he had every reason to be grateful for it at the time and it must be admitted that he never overlooked his indebtedness.

* * *

Peel's decision to repeal the Corn Laws was announced while Disraeli was wintering in Paris and he did not even hurry home. He was personally unknown to Bentinck, who had in fact readily turned him down as a possible running-mate for the King's Lynn constituency in 1834, and he would not have expected to find many friends among the protectionist county squires. All this was changed by a single speech. The debate was opened by Peel with a long, boring statement stuffed with seemingly irrelevant detail. Russell's reply was even more unintelligible and there seemed to be a feeling that the defence of the Corn Laws had been conceded by default, when Disraeli stepped in. He spoke for three hours—rather long even in those days for an impromptu—and still today his speech, as Mr. Blake says, makes marvellous reading. Parliamentary speakers who attack their own leaders get much applause, albeit spurious, from the opposite side of the House. Disraeli for the first time in his parliamentary career enjoyed the intoxicating music of the sustained applause of his own supporters. The story of the long battle is a thrice told tale but if it was Disraeli who made the speeches it was Bentinck who got the votes. The instinct of parliamentary *frondeurs* is to return to the haven of their own party as soon as they have salved their consciences and their election pledges. It was not Disraeli's eloquence but Bentinck's passion that got the protectionist block to accept the harsh and bitter logic of the judgment that 'Peel must be punished'. The Corn Laws were repealed, but Bentinck would not allow the Protectionists to swallow their defeat and return to the Tory lobby, much as most of them would have wished to do so. It was he and not Disraeli who whipped them into the Whig lobby to vote against the second reading of an Irish Coercion Bill the first reading of which they had supported, thus destroying Peel's power for ever. When it came to the crunch only about seventy Tories voted with Bentinck and Disraeli in the fatal division, but it was enough: in spite of Disraeli's encomium on the County members study of the division list shows how painfully obscure for the most part they were.

Nevertheless, and however unknowingly, a future Prime Minister was made by their vote. Defeat in that division would have been the end of Disraeli's political career; victory made him a party leader and it was Bentinck who won that victory for him.

For the following thirty years Disraeli sat on the front bench and was his party's chief parliamentary spokesman. Indispensable he may have been, accepted he was not; and Mr. Blake's researches show what intrigue there was against him in the party even up to 1874. On the sudden death of Lord George Bentinck in 1848 the fourteenth Earl of Derby became leader of the Tory party, and as Disraeli was in fact leading the party in the Commons close association between them should have ensued naturally. This was not the case. The Tory Whips who acted also as party managers tended to bypass Disraeli and took their instructions from Derby. The Whips, who act as a self-perpetuating secret police, do not take kindly to rebels or ex-rebels and Disraeli's own appointment to their office of Frank Villiers ended abruptly in ruin for the appointee and tears for his family and friends. Lord Derby established a working but arm's length relationship with Disraeli—he never came to Hughenden and Disraeli was not invited to Knowsley till 1853, some eighteen months after his appointment to Derby's first government as Chancellor. Derby could have sat for Trollope's Duke of Omnium; he was a much more forcible character than historians usually allow and not the least of Mr. Blake's services is to have disinterred his memory. The same can be said of his son the fifteenth Earl, who starting as Disraeli's firm supporter ended up after his resignation as Foreign Secretary in the Gladstone camp. On him Mr. Blake comments: 'Derby surely must be the only Foreign Secretary in British history to reveal the innermost secrets of the Cabinet to the Ambassador of a foreign power in order to frustrate the presumed intentions of his own Prime Minister'. Lord Salisbury on the other hand, having been a bitter and uncompromising critic both by word of mouth and by pen, became a loyal and accomplished Foreign Secretary in Derby's place. Where such great men led, can it be doubted that the jackal pack would follow? Tadpole and Taper did not cease to exist when Disraeli gave up novel-writing, but quite how their machinations were foiled does not come out. All one can conclude is that judging by Disraeli's correspondence with his one-time secretary Ralph Earle the machinations were not confined exclusively to one side.

* * *

When Disraeli first sat on the front bench in 1846 it was not by invitation or co-option but by successful assault, and it was not until half a lifetime later in 1874 that he found himself there not on sufferance but by virtue of the leadership of a parliamentary majority. During that time he had sat in three caretaker governments and for a year led one—the rest of the time was spent in opposition. It is an astonishing feat of stamina, especially when the assiduity of his attendance is borne in mind. (He vetoed Gathorne Hardy's appointment to lead the Commons on the grounds of his uxorious tendency to dine at home.) Like Attlee in 1931 he benefited tremendously from being for many years and for obvious reasons virtually his party's sole spokesman in the Commons. Unlike Attlee he did not gain correspondingly in popularity. He was not elected to Grillions—a contemporary equivalent of the Other Club—until 1865, i.e., twenty-five years after Gladstone joined it: Mr. Blake opines that their dislike of Disraeli was the chief reason of the former Peelite ministers for not joining any of Derby's caretaker governments. Recognition was slow in coming and had to be earned. His triumph was getting the Reform Bill of 1867, with much of which his party were in disagreement, through a House of Commons in which he did not command a majority. It was done by the judicious use of what racing men call 'all the aids' and mastery of detail was not the least of these. This was a far cry from the day when Derby overcame his demur at the offer of the Exchequer with the famous words 'They give you the figures'.

Perhaps the feature of Mr. Blake's work that will most appeal today is his assessment of the influence of Disraeli on modern Conservative thinking. Disraeli's radicalism was temperamental and sympathetic rather than philosophical. He studied the detestable poverty of the working class in the 1840s, was sympathetic to the Chartists and embodied his conclusions in *Sybil*; legislation had to wait until he had a parliamentary majority. In fact the session of 1875 produced two important Trade Union Acts, the Public Health Act (echoing the famous Disraelian phrase *Sanitas sanitatum*), a Factory Act, an Act to safeguard the funds of Friendly Societies, an Agricultural Holdings Act, an Artisans Dwellings Act (albeit ineffective) and most important of all the Foods and Drugs Act which lasted in effect until quite recently. Mr. Blake comments that taken together they constitute the biggest instalment of social reform passed by any one government in the nineteenth century but he questions whether they went further than merely redeeming the party's election pledges and denies that they were the product of a fundamentally different political philosophy from that of the Liberals or that they had anything to do with the paternalistic Tory Democracy that Disraeli had preached in the 1840s. This is not a point that is liable to be settled once for all; what is undeniable is that these measures were the fulfilment not merely of 1874 election pledges but also of the aspirations of Young England thirty years earlier. Such constancy is rare in politics and its proponent deserves the benefit of the doubt. Nevertheless Disraeli summed up his views in a crucial letter to Lord Stanley in 1848: 'The office of leader of the Conservative party at the present day is to uphold the aristocratic settlement of this country', and in this too he remained consistent.

In foreign policy Mr. Blake makes the valid point that not until Palmerston's belated death was it open to Disraeli to adopt the aggressive line for which his last administration is chiefly famous and by which he earned his enduring popularity with the working class and with his sovereign. Salisbury made the apposite comment that much of the trouble came from British statesmen using maps on too small a scale and Disraeli's Near Eastern policies owed more to Sidonia (Disrothschild as Philip Guedalla aptly termed him) than to any more up-to-date appreciation of British interests. It is rather engaging to think of Argyll urging Gladstone as late as 1876 to turn to *Tancred*, first published thirty years before, for light on the ideas underlying the government's foreign policy, much perhaps as more recent British ministers were adjured to read *Mein Kampf.*

So, unbelievably, Vivian Grey's dreams came true and the young man who startled Melbourne by saying he intended to be Prime Minister brought it off. How was it done? Mr. Blake has assembled the facts conveniently and comprehensively at last but he has left plenty of clues that others may care to follow up. Considerations of patronage and the goings on of society played a much greater part in Disraeli's life than in the lives of men of comparable eminence, and full account is taken of them. His emotional life, however, is still a mystery. Compensating a real or imagined rejection by his mother he was always especially at ease in the company of older women. Byron complained that when he was in Venice two dowagers of sixty made love to him, but there is no suggestion of an amorous relationship between Disraeli and Lady Cork, Lady Londonderry or even Lady Blessington, to name a few of his early patronesses. The only passionate liaison of which we have certain knowledge is that with Lady Sykes, and she was certainly no younger than he was. She addressed him as her child and signed one letter at least as 'your mother'. Mary Ann was twelve years older than himself, Mrs. Brydges Willyams who left him her money was also substantially older. True the Queen was younger but the intensity of his homage caused him to treat her as one vastly his senior—the flirtatiousness, if it is appropriate to use such a word, was on her side. Granted that Lady Bradford and Lady Chesterfield were his juniors, it is permissible to suppose that passion really was spent by the time he became enamoured of them. Intense school friendships feature in his novels and his early male friends were mostly on the raffish side; it is one of his most endearing characteristics that he never lost his taste for the frivolous, as his appointment of Corry as secretary shows. Perhaps a modern psychologist could make something of this, perhaps not. What cannot be denied is that there was never a breath of scandal against him from the time of his marriage. He had too many enemies and they were likely to be too well informed for him to have any real chance of getting away with the sort of matrimonial imbroglios in which so many of his parliamentary colleagues seemed to get involved.

* * *

Students of the nineteenth century enjoy the advantage of immersing themselves in a period when so much was written down and so much of what was written down has been preserved. While many of Disraeli's letters, as has been said of a later Prime Minister, were written for brighter eyes than those that peer through politicians' spectacles, his correspondence as a whole makes absorbing reading and taken in conjunction with the Hughenden archives provides an incomparable record of a unique and still unfathomed personality. Perhaps the best tribute that can be paid to Mr. Blake is to say that people will want to know more about his hero after they have finished his admirable biography.

2

POLITICIANS IN PROSE

(*a*) HAROLD MACMILLAN

PRIME MINISTERS of the past used to appear complex and enigmatic to their biographers. It is arguable that they were not really more so than other people, only their inconsistencies were more minutely studied. But since the habit of writing reminiscences in retirement grew up in the present century they have come to seem less inscrutable. Lloyd George, Churchill and Lord Attlee, thanks to their own writings, are much more intelligible personalities than Asquith, Baldwin or MacDonald. Even Lord Avon is no exception, for although the final episode of his political life still remains baffling in spite of his autobiography, what is baffling about it is that he should ever have thought it could succeed.

Mr. Harold Macmillan, on the other hand, may well prove an exception. True, this is only the first volume of his autobiography, ending in 1939, before he had ever held office. But if it is anything to judge by, his personality may possibly seem even harder to assess at the end that at the beginning. Not that the book is obscurely written, nor that its story is deviously told. On the contrary, it is lucid, readable, and distinguished stylistically in a manner that places the author second only to Churchill among prime ministers as an autobiographer, without any attempt to imitate the surge and thunder of Churchillian prose. It is a masterly and assured summary of the author's first forty-five years, beginning with a superb evocation of Victorian childhood and Edwardian schooldays. But as a self-portrait it is still tantalizing, and to some it will seem exasperating.

There were from the first, it seems, two Harold Macmillans. There was the self-made aristocrat, and there was the tribune of the people.

(*a*) *Winds of Change, 1914–1939*. 664 pp. Macmillan. £2 15s.

(*b*) *Erinnerungen 1945–1953*. 589 pp. Stuttgart: Deutsche Verlags-Anstalt. DM. 24.80.

He graduated into the aristocracy by marriage, but he has naturally retained a keen pride in his ancestry of Scottish crofters and publishers who built up a great firm from penniless beginnings. He was often accused of posing as a foppish, intellectual aristocrat interested only in a past age. If it was a pose, it is at least consistently sustained throughout the first volume of his autobiography. The characteristics of it are constantly impressed on the reader: the novels of Trollope, house-parties at Chatsworth, the world of nannies and preparatory schools, the exclusive friendships of Eton, Oxford and the Brigade of Guards. Even in his political life, he seems to be uneasy with those who do not share this background. Apart from the gigantic exceptions of Lloyd George and Churchill, the rest seem scarcely to count. It can hardly be an accident that in a volume which gives copious character-sketches of his political contemporaries, the name of R. A. Butler is never once mentioned.

Mr. Macmillan's historical hero is Disraeli. He shows the same flair for the spectacular and the exotic, but above all the same conviction that the Tory party should rest on the two pillows of the aristocracy and the working classes. Hence the second role of the self-made aristocrat as tribune of the people. Hence also his deliberate preference for a marginal constituency in the industrial north rather than a safe seat in the home counties. By far the most substantial part of the present volume is devoted to domestic problems of the 1930s—unemployment, housing, health, rates—and these at the human and humble level of his own constituents. These chapters are full of his own direct experience: the speeches he made, the pamphlets he published, the doctrines he pioneered. They make impressive reading thirty years later. By contrast, his chapters on foreign affairs and defence are an historical résumé rather than autobiography, for he took little part in debates on these subjects. It is paradoxical, nevertheless, that when he resigned the Conservative Party whip in 1936, it was on an issue of foreign policy.

How is Harold Macmillan's career to be assessed up to this point? It is clear how he wishes it to be assessed—not the precise verdict, but the way of arriving at it. He sees his career as a seamless web, continuous and consistent throughout. The second volume will show how the lessons of the first volume were to be applied, just as the first is full of pre-cognitive hints and echoes of the second.

The title itself is a case in point. 'Winds of Change' at once recalls the celebrated speech at Cape Town in 1960, though it is interesting to find the words almost anticipated in a speech by Baldwin on India in 1934:

> There is a wind of nationalism and freedom flowing round the world and blowing as strongly in Asia as anywhere in the world.

As in many other instances that could be quoted, Mr. Macmillan is arguing by implication that what he was trying to carry out in the postwar period was what could already be seen to be necessary and inevitable in the 1930s—only he was one of the few to see it.

The same impression is even clearer in the domestic and economic field than in the foreign and imperial. Mr. Macmillan has solid grounds for maintaining that he was one of the first Conservative politicians to see the practical value of Keynesian economics. Keynes himself wrote approvingly of his pamphlet, *The Next Step*, in 1932. Unfortunately, although all parties now accept the doctrines of Keynes in theory, they have never been applied in practice in this country except by accident; and Mr. Macmillan himself shares part of the blame. The doctrine that public expenditure should be increased in a period of depression was only accepted when it was almost too late in the 1930s: in fact it was the war which completed the process as a by-product. The obverse and equally essential aspect of the Keynesian doctrine—that public expenditure should be cut back in a period of boom—has never been applied at all. For this deficiency few political leaders are more directly responsible than Mr. Macmillan. His first volume contains several passages of anticipatory lamentation over the problems of over-full employment, but it remains to be seen how he will account for his failure to deal with them.

In anticipation it might be suggested that Mr. Macmillan's consistency throughout his political career was almost too determined and thorough-going. In this respect he is comparable to Eden rather than Churchill. It is hard to recognize Churchill as the same man at different stages of his career. Eden and Mr. Macmillan, on the contrary, remained the men they were even after circumstances had changed. Just as Eden fought the battles of Appeasement again with Nasser in place of Hitler as an entirely inappropriate opponent, so Mr. Macmillan fought the Depression over again long after it had disappeared for ever. It is ironic to recall that this was the true significance of the grossly misinterpreted speech in 1957 which contained the luckless phrase 'You've never had it so good!'.

Yet *Winds of Change* is for all that a portrait of a distinguished and original mind, operating acutely and cogently in the fields of economic and political theory and with a humane rebelliousness in practice, if still only at the lower levels of practice. It will annoy some readers and please others to find these characteristics combined with an instinctive preference for government by the aristocracy—a preference which is one of the indisputable elements of continuity throughout Mr. Macmillan's career.

(*b*) KONRAD ADENAUER

Dr. Adenauer, upon leaving the government in 1963 at the age of eighty-eight, settled down to write his memoirs in three volumes, with a fourth volume of documents. This middle volume, the first to appear, is Dr. Adenauer's account of the military government of postwar Germany, the restoration of political life, the founding of the Federal Republic, and the steps by which it attained independence. He does not attempt to survey the whole scene or bring all the actors on stage. He narrates what he did, what happened to him, what he said, what his intentions and his reasons were, the negotiations he conducted and the political conversations he had.

Occasionally a personal assistant is mentioned, even more rarely a political colleague. His tragic opponent, Dr. Kurt Schumacher, is allotted a distinct if invariably negative part. One by one, the allied military governors and high commissioners, their heads of government and foreign ministers, make their appearances as interlocutors. There is no turning aside for character sketches, anecdotes, scene-setting, colour or atmosphere. Here is the story of how the Federal Republic of Germany was hammered into existence, told strictly from Dr. Adenauer's point of view, and it is like its author: spare, limited, unrelenting, dry, simple, prosaic and lucid. As reading matter it is not entertaining, but it is an invaluable contribution to history.

Dr. Adenauer always had the advantage over his opponents that he formed his opinion on a matter early, formed it in simple terms, and stuck to it untroubled by doubt or distracting considerations. Though he was not necessarily right, he was usually effective. He has never been much of a theoriser, nor wished to be; just as in conversation he will habitually dismiss some critical fellow as 'an intellectual', so he selects for his Socialist opponent on one occasion the dismissive adjective: 'Dr. Schumacher's point of view was very theoretical'.

Where now is the controversy about the Occupation Statute? Who remembers what it was? In July, 1948, following the London conference at which the procedure was laid down for bringing a west German state into existence, the ministers-president of the west German Länder were much concerned that the new state should not be called a state, that its constitution should not be called a constitution (it still is not), and that whatever was done should appear to be an expression of the will of the allied powers, who should promulgate the occupation statute of themselves, without waiting until a west German government was in existence to accept it—all so that no representative German could be said to have accepted the division of Germany.

This kind of high-principled equivocation meant nothing to Adenauer. He saw what the others did not, that the Occupation Statute was a mere form of transition. Thus he did not much care what was in it, and on one occasion told the Allied High Commissioners so; not did he care when it was promulgated, or by whom. Not that he was incapable of interesting himself in matters of form, so long as they had implications of fact. Thus he relates, with one of the gleams of severely controlled humour that do relieve his book every fifty pages or so, how when he went to the High Commissioners on the Petersberg to present the first federal cabinet and receive the Occupation Statute at their hands, the three commissioners received him standing on a carpet, which he was supposed to set foot on only when he had been handed the document; but, advancing in a natural way to greet the chairman, M. François-Poncet, he got his feet on the carpet and kept them there, and nobody was prepared to ask him to step back. He was not troubled when, later, he found that the document handed to him was, through an oversight, unsigned. His assistant, Herr Blankenhorn, took it home and had to be asked to dig it out three years later to be put, still unsigned, in the archives.

As early as October, 1945, Adenauer told two foreign journalists that the Soviet-occupied part of Germany was lost to Germany for an indefinite period; what the remaining western parts had to do was to confederate and to integrate their economy with the economies of France and Belgium, whose security requirements would be better met in that way than by carving out the separate Rhine-Ruhr state they were talking about at the time. Within a few weeks he had elaborated this into the outline of a union of western Europe. All this was six months before Churchill's Fulton speech. Several unproductive conferences of foreign ministers were needed before the western occupying powers began to act on the conclusions which he formed then. He was intolerant of their efforts to keep open the possibility of an East-West agreement and a settlement for all Germany. He was even impatient with the speech of Mr. Byrnes, then Secretary of State, at Stuttgart in September, 1946, for all that it represented a turning-point in American policy to Germany—because he could not see why Byrnes should say that it would not be in the interest of world peace to have Germany on one side or the other in the East-West conflict.

Adenauer took the East-West conflict for an accomplished fact and had no doubt that West Germany must be on the western side. This amounted to the same thing as setting the West on Germany's side. Speculation about any other outcome would have seemed to him 'very theoretical'. Granted this, the hesitant steps of the western powers towards uniting the western zones and setting up an autonomous west German state were inexcusably sluggish to him, their insistence on dismantling the industry of a country to which despite themselves they were giving economic aid was farcical as well as dishonest, and their endless talk of re-education, democracy and denazification was empty prating. He says of the British military government, 'Democracy was much preached at us, but little acted upon.'

What was it that went wrong between Adenauer and the British? There were a few years in the early 1950s when Dr. Adenauer seemed to have put out of his mind his bitter but, after all, transient misfortune at the hands of British Military Government in Cologne in 1945. His later political conduct has shown that his grudge against the British was in fact not forgotten, and his book documents the fact. In recounting the circumstances of his dismissal as Mayor of Cologne in October, 1945, he does mention that he had been instructed to allow the felling of his beloved trees in the Cologne green belt for winter fuel, and that he had refused—an attitude which a British brigadier might indeed at that time have been disinclined to tolerate. Dr. Adenauer makes plain his belief that his dismissal was caused by Social Democratic intrigues with the British Labour Government, with a view to barring him from politics. But, as he relates, his exclusion from political activity lasted only a few weeks;

before the year was out the British authorities not only permitted but encouraged him to get on with organizing the Christian Democratic Union. The episode may suggest some political innocence among the British soldiery, but who—given the time and the place—finds that hard to believe? Dr. Adenauer does, evidently, to this day. Mr. Macmillan's government felt the consequences, many years later.

Dr. Adenauer's narrative suggests that the real misfortune from the British point of view may well have been simply that his city of Cologne, his home, Rhöndorf, and his field of political activity in the years of hardship happened to fall in the British Zone. He blames the British for the fuel shortage in the winter of 1946 (cutting down trees would have been no use, he points out even now; what was required was that the British authorities release some coal), for the ruthless timber-cutting that all European countries went in for during those years of scarcity, for the food shortage in 1946 and 1947 and especially for the cuts in the fats ration, and for the dismantling policy—although the British, if only because they were in possession of the Ruhr and had to think seriously about what to do with it, took the most liberal position of the four Powers in the crucial debates about the level-of-industry plan. The snail's pace (as it seemed to him) at which German self-government was approached he usually blamed on the British, if only because he was chairman of the Christian Democrats in the British Zone before his party had a national organization, and it was to the Advisory Council of the British Zone that he, as a leading politician, belonged. As he remarks himself (June, 1948), 'Up to now England has had the sole power of decision in by far the greatest part of western Germany'; to him it was British rule, more than American rule or French, that had to be wound up.

In his political speeches in those years he used to attack dismantling as an expression of British (not French, or American) commercial aggressiveness. French policies in Germany were throughout this period more restrictive and more suspicious than British, but for this he has understanding; the long history of Franco-German strife accounted for it, French political leaders had their domestic public opinion to think of, and so on. That British politicians had to manage their public opinion, too, he knew, but he was less inclined to allow it in extenuation. Among his talks with foreign statesmen, those with the British, Labour and Tory alike, seem usually to have consisted of his inquiring about Britain's possible part in a European union and being told that the British were far too interested in other parts of the world to think of joining in. At times it may be suspected that he was not totally unwilling to be told this; all the same, his account is melancholy comment on the British national myopia in the 1950s.

3

WRITERS IN POLITICS

(*a*) ANDRÉ MALRAUX

TOWARDS the end of 1923, the Minister of Culture in the present French Government, already at twenty-two a rising star in the artistic and literary world of postwar Paris, went to French Indochina. His object, and that of his associate Louis Chevasson, was to explore some of the still largely abandoned architectural treasures of the Cambodian jungle, and to take home with him examples of Khmer sculpture.

André Malraux's ambition was at the time perfectly legitimate, and until a few years earlier it could have been fulfilled without any difficulty. There had, however, recently been several 'particularly flagrant expropriations of Cambodian antiquities'. Under the prodding of the French School of the Far East, the foremost French society in this field, the colonial government was on the lookout. M. Malraux was warned by the school that objects found in the jungle must be left *in situ* pending its own decision on their disposal, but the legal position was not clear. To be protected by law a monument had to be officially *classified.* It was at least questionable whether the school or the government could legally stop the removal of sculpture from unclassified ruins in the Cambodian jungle.

The monument in the depth of the jungle which M. Malraux and M. Chevasson intended to visit, and from which they proceeded to remove a quantity of sculpture, had been recorded by archaeologists but it had not been *classified.* Nevertheless, the two young men, who had made no attempt to conceal what they had done, were arrested and put on trial. The affair was widely and deliberately misrepresented as a dastardly theft of art treasures from Angkor itself. The trial was administrative rather than judicial—to say the least—and in July, 1924, M. Malraux was sentenced to three years in prison and his companion to eighteen months.

(*a*) Walter G. Langlois: *André Malraux: The Indochina Adventure.* 259 pp. Pall Mall Press. £2 2s.

(*b*) *Uscita di Sicurezza.* 241 pp. Florence: Vallecchi. L.2,000.

The amateur archaeologists appealed. By the time the Saigon appeal court had reduced the sentences at the end of October, a furore over the case had arisen in France, and M. Malraux was bitterly at odds with the editor of the semi-official newspaper in Saigon whose reporting of the case would have come close to contempt of court in this country. A further appeal was lodged with the highest appeal court in Paris which, in July, 1925, set aside the Saigon court's decision because of a drafting irregularity, and here for all practical purposes the matter ended.

But M. Malraux, outraged by the way in which he had been treated, had by now taken up the cudgels against what he considered to be the fantastic corruption of the colonial government and against its oppression of the governed. There was no question yet of a nationalist rebellion. The mood of the Vietnamese intellectuals was still for reform rather than revolt. They believed, said one of the most distinguished among them,

> that collaboration between Frenchmen and Indochinese is possible. But if the colonials stubbornly continue to deny elementary liberties to the Vietnamese, they cannot blame the masses for any violence. Let France remember all this repressed power.

These were also M. Malraux's views. Conversely, the little sympathy he met in Indochina for his personal plight came from the Vietnamese and the few Frenchmen who were already agitating against colonial injustice. The group decided that the most effective weapon would be an opposition newspaper. M. Malraux made most of the preliminary arrangements in Paris and the journal *Indochine* appeared for the first time on June 17, 1925. It was constructively critical of the colonial administration in Cochin China; it investigated some of the major cases of oppression and uncovered some sordid stories of corruption: it exposed the governor himself and the editor of the semi-official newspaper; when the former had failed to terrify it into silence, the latter bought out its printers; it had lasted just over eight weeks.

Its enemies made all the capital they could out of the closing of *Indochine*. Failing to find another printer the editors decided to print it themselves. They bought the type from Hongkong. When the first consignment was confiscated by the Indochinese customs they ordered a second, and an austerity version of their newspaper, *Indochine Enchaînée*, appeared from November 17, 1925, until its presses broke down in January, 1926. But by then M. Malraux had left for home. His object had been to secure reform in the colony itself; he and his group now realized that the important thing was not the removal of the governor and his cronies but the re-education of opinion in France towards a reformulation of the fundamental principles of colonial government. 'We are going to appeal', wrote M. Malraux in his last editorial, which he addressed to the Vietnamese,

> to all those who, like yourselves, suffer. The people—in France—will not permit the sufferings whose marks you bear to be inflicted in their name. . . . This is why I am leaving for France.

Having related this story, and documented M. Malraux's side of it in 222 pages of his book, Dr. Langlois, who is associate professor of French at the University of Kentucky, devotes the remaining thirty pages to a consideration of what in fact M. Malraux did after his return home to further the cause he had espoused so energetically abroad. The conclusion is that M. Malraux's Indochina adventure turned him from the elegant and gifted dilettante of the early 1920s into the fervent reformer and anti-Fascist of the 1930s. There was nothing direct that he could do; the Indochinese tragedy was already rolling towards its inevitable end. Only twice did he write on a specific Indochinese subject between 1926 and 1935. But the three novels he wrote between 1926 and 1930, *Temptation of the West*, *The Conquerors* and *Man's Fate*, arose directly out of his experiences in Indochina, and his two subsequent anti-Fascist novels, *Days of Wrath* and *Man's Hope*, owed much in their way to the first three. So far from forgetting the Vietnamese, his adventures among them informed his work—and brilliantly effective work it was—for the next thirteen years.

Dr. Langlois is a scholar and he has done his work well. In the author's evident devotion to his subject and in M. Malraux's own lovingly quoted polemical eloquence, however, there lies a danger that the book may be read as an attack on the French colonial record in Indochina as a whole. Such an interpretation would of course be invalid. M. Malraux's words, none the less, have an occasional prophetic ring. In 1935 he wrote a preface for a friend. In Indochina, she had said:

> They indiscriminately label as communists not only nationalists who want to see the democratic principles they have learnt from us applied to their country, but also the destitute, who plead for someone to come and help them, and all those who—for one reason or another—don't have the

talent for pleasing the administration or the police. These people accept that epithet and take pride in it.

But repression was not the answer; 'cutting off people's heads', wrote M. Malraux,

> is not a permanent way of keeping them from using them. . . . Nationalists, communists, liberals—there is one thing you all know: that a people will become tired of anything, eventually—even of being murdered for nothing.

(*b*) IGNAZIO SILONE

All that Ignazio Silone has written is part of a whole. More than most writers he is judged (inevitably, considering how he writes) on himself, his personal standards, his own sincerity and wisdom. There has never been a strict division between his novels, his essays, his satirical writing, between straight autobiography and autobiographical narrative involving fictional characters: all is coloured by a single moral attitude that has developed, but not radically changed, throughout his life. Not long ago he said: 'The only subject that has ever exercised me [is] man's condition in society. If I were to start writing about incest and prostitution, in the current fashion', he went on, 'I'd lose my self-respect. I'm not interested in fashion.'

'I'm not interested in fashion' might have been his lifelong motto. His progress as writer and thinker has all the way exemplified his total independence of fashion, not just in externals and in detail but in a basic way that has made him enemies by showing up the (relative) fashionableness and insincerity of others. Flag-wagging is something of which he is temperamentally incapable, not through any lack of warmth (all his writing is suffused with humanity, with the feeling of man for man), but through what you might call a temperamental lack of orthodoxy. Now that it is orthodox to be outspoken, for instance, he is unorthodox enough to be thought old-fashioned. And so it was always. Because he has never done what seemed the thing to do at that particular moment, but has followed his instinct and sure moral sense instead, he has always been politically and socially ahead of his time, even of his enlightened contemporaries.

From its earliest days he saw the evils of Italian fascism; in the late 1920s he broke with the Communist party, having seen what Stalinism implied long before most of his contemporaries; in the 1930s he already knew, as Orwell was to know, the tyranny of the far left; in the postwar Marxist euphoria he was an odd man out, noticeably cold-shouldered on his return from exile to Italy—famous elsewhere, unknown or ill-considered at home, the man history had proved right all along and foreigners mysteriously overrated. A political and social moralist whose judgments always ring true is an uncomfortable man at times to have about; and people have shrugged off discomfort by making the face-saving point that, since the official end of fascism and of his official exile, Signor Silone has lacked a cause to espouse, an enemy to whack, a stirring war cry.

This really has little bearing on his writing as a whole. Of course persecution and exile make for more dramatic conditions than (relative) peace and prosperity; but it is absurd to consider him *merely* as an opposition voice in a particular time and place and to a particular regime. His is a voice of sanity and liberalism in any world, the voice of anti-cant in a world where cant is much more insidious than it was in the days when politics were much blacker or much whiter than they now seem. 'I have always felt committed in the strictest sense of the word', Signor Silone said recently. 'I'd almost say pledged in the pawnshop sense.' (The Italian word for artistic commitment is *impegnato*, which means literally 'pawned' as well.) But, he went on to say, novels like *Fontamara*, which are labelled political, are in fact anti-political: for in dealing with men caught in the machinery of politics, it is the men they back, not the machinery. In fact, Silone is committed to people, not to politics, still less to any one party.

Uscita di Sicurezza ('Emergency exit') is a record of this commitment throughout his life, in essays and in what might be called short stories but are really extensions of the autobiographical essay. It is an important book; for anyone interested in Silone a crucial one. For it shows his thought at its most concentrated, his judgment at its most characteristic, his entire development: from the instinctive democracy of childhood that made him find friends among the peasants rather than among the more prosperous; through communism, which then seemed to offer the only means to fight fascism; through long exile, outside communism and outside even a feeling of identification with the Allies, to his postwar return to an Italy that was hardly welcoming, and to thoughts on the present world. The long title essay is already known in English and is part of the book called *The God That Failed*, in which Arthur Koestler, Gide, Stephen

Spender, Richard Wright, Louis Fischer and Signor Silone gave their reasons for breaking with communism. In a shorter essay he describes the situation of ex-communists, men who have lost a whole way of life with their belief, who look back even with a certain nostalgia to the days when they 'belonged', when things were more companionable and more secure. People ask how they ever bore the 'prison' of party membership. 'Who would be ready to admit our good faith?' Signor Silone asks. 'Perhaps only an ex-monk.'

The parallel between the communist and the religious believer is implicit in much that he writes; indeed in a broad sense his preoccupations are religious, in that they ask the fundamental, not the materialistic, questions. In the book's final essay, a recent one as long as 'Uscita di sicurezza', called 'Ripensare il progresso', which might be translated as something like 'New thoughts on progress', he questions what has happened to the people he has seen freed from the poverty and oppression they suffered from in the years he wrote *Fontamara* and *Bread and Wine* about them. Italy is now a relatively prosperous country, many of the abuses he once saw have gone, and things on the face of it are incomparably better. Signor Silone wastes no time regretting the lost picturesqueness and has no sneers to make about television aerials and washing machines. What worries him is the spirit that seems inextricably linked with affluence: a spirit that is greedy and mean and unmanly and unneighbourly, that relies on official help whenever anything goes wrong, that refuses to act unless paid for every action, that keeps up with the Joneses to what seems an hysterical degree.

As he faced what to some were unfaceable truths in the 1920s and 1930s, Silone now faces what the progressive liberal finds, perhaps, hardest of all to take: the paradox of material advance bringing spiritual retreat. The men he knew in his early political days were poor in money and leisure, yet they worked long hours unpaid for what they believed in: today, with leisure and money then undreamed of, even the boys who distribute political handbills in the streets expect payment. Characteristically, after a survey full of gloomy examples, Silone refuses the easy comfort of disillusion: his final hope for the future of this materially cushioned society is tentatively mystical.

4

NOVELS OF 1966

(*a*) PATRICK WHITE

The Solid Mandala

The Solid Mandala is the latest of Mr. Patrick White's journeys into the ulterior, a landfall in a spiritual Thule so remote that it can be reached only by metaphor and symbol. Yet even armchair stay-at-homes who do not know how to navigate by stars or parable can read it simply at surface level, marvel at the likeness and the strangeness of the traveller's tale, and put it down at last with a feeling that they have been given a notion of something beyond knowledge. They may not have seen eternity like a great ring of endless light. But they have seen Mr. White see it.

On the surface, this is a novel about two twin brothers, Waldo and Arthur Brown, brought as small children by their immigrant English parents to live in a rural suburb of Sydney, that Sarsaparilla which Mr. White in his earlier novels has created and peopled for us and which by now has acquired the quasi-reality we concede to Trollope's Barchester or to Hardy's Wessex—perhaps the first such colony the imagination has made in Australia.

The novel opens with a bus-ride from Barranugli to Sarsaparilla in which a gossip between two neighbours, Mrs. Poulter and Mrs. Dun, gives the essential preliminary facts about the Brown family and creates the Australian social ambience in which the Browns—too sensitive, too genteel, and too set—have not been able to find acceptance. The parents by now, it appears, are dead, and the twins eccentric and concentric, aging, queer. And then, from the bus

---

(*a*) *The Solid Mandala*. 317 pp. Eyre and Spottiswoode. 25s.
(*b*) *Despair*. 222 pp. Weidenfeld and Nicolson. 25s.
(*c*) *The Anti-Death League*. 352 pp. Gollancz. 30s.
(*d*) *Le Déluge*. 285 pp. Paris: Gallimard. 15 fr.
(*e*) *The Time of the Angels*. Chatto and Windus. 25s.
(*f*) *Das Einhorn*. 489 pp. Frankfurt: Suhrkamp. DM. 24.

window, the twins themselves are descried, out on their daily walk with their two decrepit dogs, elderly and hand-in-hand, a spectacle shocking in that masculine land where men may shake hands but never hold them, unless they be the hands of women and even then not in public.

In the second section we read through Waldo's eyes and move forward and backward over the chessboard of his life, following a game in which, a pawn always, he has fancied himself both queen and king and has met stale mate at the end. He is a clever boy at school and, impressed with his own control of words and his superiority to Arthur and to others, plans to become a writer. He gets a job at the Municipal Public Library, reads endlessly and makes notes for a novel he will never finish, *Tiresias a Youngish Man*. He brings himself to propose to Dulcie Feinstein, only to find she is already engaged to Leonard Saporta. His nature becomes more and more intricately suspicious, rejecting all the normal human overtures. His parents die, two wars pass hardly noticed, like his own life, and he has become an old man, his only companion his half-witted brother Arthur. He knows little of Arthur's real life and hates him as a drag and a burden and a humiliation. He indulges fantasies of the dissipation he would enjoy if Arthur would die and allow him to escape. Yet he obscurely knows that Arthur is also his last access to living and the only outlet for his faint impulse of human feeling. Hatred wins at the last, however, and he dies, as Mrs. Poulter later says, 'of spite like a boil must burst at last with pus', but clinging to Arthur's wrist with the fierce grip of a man drowning.

Waldo's death ends the second section. The next opens with Arthur a child at sea, trying to climb the rails of the ship and reach 'the red gold disc of the sun'. And at night there are the icebergs he cannot see by day. 'Only in sleep the icebergs moaned, and jostled one another, crunching and tinkling. The moons of sky-blue ice fell crashing silently down to splinter into glass balls which he gathered in his protected hands.'

Arthur's recapitulation covers the same time-span as Waldo's, the same events and characters appear, but seen through Arthur's mind which though confused and inarticulate, reaches outwards with love and the desire to understand. His simplicity and his warmth give him access to the lives of those around him and evoke a response, a resonance, in all those who, like him, are naturally good and capable of truth and love.

Because his perceptions are inarticulate his family think him a simpleton. Thus, when his father reads Greek myths to the boys, Arthur

was only surprised they didn't notice how his heart was beating when Zeus rewarded Tiresias with the gift of prophecy and a life seven times as long as the lives of ordinary men. Then there was that other bit, about being changed into a woman, if only for a short time. Time enough, though, to know he wasn't all that different.

As a schoolboy Arthur acquires a special treasure of four marbles to which he constantly turns for comfort and contemplation. One day he chances on a passage in an encyclopedia about the word mandala. It is a symbol, he reads, of totality. It is believed to be the 'dwelling of the god'. Its protective circle is a pattern of order superimposed upon psychic chaos. Sometimes its geometric form is seen as a vision (either waking or in dream) or danced.

He instantly relates this to the marbles and feels he has had a glimpse of deeper knowledge, 'if only the curtain on his mystery hadn't stuck halfway up'. Inquiry of his father about the meaning of 'totality' proves useless and he realizes that 'It was himself who was, and would remain, the keeper of mandalas, who must guess their final secret through touch and light'.

To one whom he loves, that Dulcie who rejected Waldo, he gives his blue marble. For another, his young childless yet fruitful neighbour, Mrs. Poulter, he is inspired to dance a mandala: a dance of four corners—the four corners of the compass and his world—in which he enacts a totality which contains his love of them and of himself. After the dance he gives Mrs. Poulter a marble, 'the gold one, in which the sparks glinted, and from which the rays shot upward whenever the perfect sphere was struck by its counterpart'.

The third of his marbles is one with a knot in it, a knot that temporarily dissolves in light. This is the marble that symbolizes his relationship and tie with Waldo and it is to Waldo, when their mother is dying, that he offers it for comfort. But Waldo rejects the marble as he rejects the union it symbolizes, without understanding.

Arthur blames himself for the failure in understanding, the rejection, his failure to be able to give Waldo more than a little comfort, to redeem him from dryness and sterility. And when Waldo dies in hatred Arthur blames himself for the death and runs from the house despairing.

At this point the fourth and final section begins and we see with the mind of Mrs. Poulter. Because of her husband and Waldo's fear of what the neighbours might say and his jealousy, she and Arthur have long since stopped going for walks but 'the bonfire of Arthur's head had never quite gone out for Mrs. Poulter'. And one day on an impulse of dread she crosses the road—Terminus Road—and through the window sees Waldo lying dead and being gnawed by the dogs on the bed the brothers shared.

While she is waiting for the police, Arthur returns from wandering in the city, where he has lost Waldo's marble, and Mrs. Poulter comforts him. The police take him away. Her husband comes home. She gives him his supper. 'Then she turned, to do the expected things, before re-entering her actual sphere of life.'

On this phrase, loaded with the suggestion of a life left at birth and resumed at death and a totality in which all life is one, the novel ends. The deliberate cliché resounds with Arthur's red gold disc of sun, his mandala, the wheel-tree which he saw with Mrs. Poulter glorying in its fiery wheels, and we are left to feel that it does not matter that her life has been barren and that his will end in the lunatic asylum known to him as 'Peaches and Plums': for there is a wholeness somewhere in which all life and all suffering have a meaningful part and a power to love beyond the self is a condition of its entry.

So bald an account of the novel can give only a faint notion not only of what Mr. White is trying to do but also of what he succeeds in doing. Our curtain, like his, is stuck halfway up. The emphasis on his use of symbols to communicate the ineffable has to be made since they lie at the core of his novel. But their abstraction does not prevent the novel from moving, or the characters from living. The details of their day-to-day life are hard and firm, the characters who are not informed by love have their own fierce, mean and sterile life frighteningly clarified. The ultimate religious preoccupation is prevented from becoming maudlin because the sounds and sights of the uglier physiological life on which all aspiration must be founded are if anything overstressed, and the flowers of language are always seen in the earth of life.

Mr. White's style is indeed perhaps over-stern to the idle of perception. His meanings have to be worked for. One has the impression that in his revisions he must labour over his prose, paring his sentences and whittling them to favour elision, asyndeton, parataxis, elimination of pronouns, all in the interest of harshness and abruptness, so that when a sentence rises in sudden flight we shall be aware that it is intentional and not rhetorical self-indulgence. But the consequent occasional ambiguities and obscurities of sense are microcosmic warnings of the difficulty of the whole pattern he is trying to convey, a meaning that in the end takes flight above the words, transcending them.

(*b*) VLADIMIR NABOKOV

Despair

The textual history of *Despair*, the latest of Mr. Nabokov's Russian novels to appear in the uniform edition, is even more roundabout than usual: the book was written in 1932, serialized two years later, and finally published complete by an émigré firm in 1936. An English translation by the author appeared here in 1937, but the stock of this was destroyed in the war. A French version came out in 1939 and was reviewed by Jean-Paul Sartre (to whose notice Mr. Nabokov alludes in an acid footnote). The present text is a wholescale revision of the original. We thus have a narrative in Mr. Nabokov's early manner, resembling particularly *Laughter in the Dark* (1933) and to a lesser extent *The Defence* (1930), refurbished with some of the stylistic trimmings more characteristic of a recent work like *Pale Fire*. The author points out that the narrator of *Despair* is a 'neurotic scoundrel' like Humbert Humbert of *Lolita*, but this amounts to no more than a similarity of tone.

At its surface level, *Despair* is a crime story in which Hermann, an objectionable German businessman who deals in chocolate, accidentally meets his split image—a tramp called Felix. Hermann proceeds to evolve a scheme whereby this unwitting double, dressed as Hermann and thinking he is being used to establish an alibi, is actually to be killed off. Hermann, who thus becomes technically dead, can then collect the insurance on his life, through the collusion of his 'widow'. To his fury, however, his plan to exploit his newly acquired double identity is frustrated by some unforeseen contingencies. This 'plain structure and pleasing plot', as the author calls it, is very neatly organized—even if its relative simplicity involves rather leisurely exposition—and the trumping twists at the end are expertly dealt. But even though this is all what Mr. Nabokov calls 'great fun' it is not, as one might expect, the whole story. As is common in Mr.

Nabokov's *pièces noires*, the reader is tempted to chase after fugitive suggestions of more occult meanings. These tend, like the butterflies to which this author is so devoted, to be iridescent, unpredictable in flight, and fragile enough to be easily broken by clumsy handling.

Just as *The Defence* plays with the idea of human movements which reflect the formal relations of chess pieces, so here the notion of a double or alter ego (to be developed in *The Real Life of Sebastian Knight* and *Pale Fire*) is sustained by the frequent use of the image of the mirror. The relationship of star to understudy or stand-in is another variant. Mr. Nabokov mentions the kind of film (had he seen *The Student of Prague*?) in which the split screen technique allows the same actor to appear simultaneously in two roles, such as twin brothers—and indeed Hermann at one point pretends to Felix that he is a film actor. Hermann's imagination is said to 'hanker after reflections, repetitions, masks', and he even produces, in the (futile) hope of placating the Soviet authorities, a little allegory of his resemblance to Felix in Marxist terms—a characteristically Nabokovian parody of dialectical 'correctness'. There is too a curious passage where Hermann finds his conjugal pleasure enhanced by dissociation: one self performs while the other seems to watch. (This is presumably the scene which the publishers rather absurdly say 'could not have been published' before *Lolita* broke up 'rigid puritan standards'.)

However, by the end of the book Hermann cannot bear mirrors, and this fear of his own reflection seems to be related to the miscarrying of his crime. He more than once claims his whole murderous design as a work of art, and bolsters up the case by mocking references to novelists of crime—Conan Doyle, Dostoevsky, etc. The wrong construction put on his crime by blundering police is likened to the obtuse missings of the point critics fall into when faced with the new works of genius. Hermann keeps the reader continually aware, even if in a fatuously complacent way, of the problems of literary form, and one of the titles he considers for his book is *Portrait of the Artist in a Mirror*. He reflects, perhaps, the baffled vanity of the artist. It would be interesting to discover how far this layer of meaning, in which the narrator's story is made to serve as a model of the artistic process, has been sharpened in the recent revision.

It must of course be added—if this line of thought is correct—that Hermann is clearly a monstrous character and can only represent the kind of artist of whom we are to disapprove. The whole book turns out to be, as it were, at his expense. Mr. Nabokov is always at his most exuberant when writing scornfully of human vanity (the tone of his recent prefaces is ineffably contemptuous), and his treatment of Hermann is exhilaratingly disdainful. This relationship between author and hero is the only one of which, as in other novels of Mr. Nabokov's, we have any acute sense. However, this aristocratic detachment should not always be taken at face value. Perhaps—a last twist of the resemblance theme—Hermann is in the final analysis a kind of *hypocrite romancier*, the hated reflection in the novelist's own glass, a disturbing double-ganger distanced and contained.

Mr. Nabokov, however, is never easy to pin down, and it is wise to heed his refusal to have anything to do with the vulgarities of 'message' or self-revelation. The preface to *Despair* refers to his work as 'a derisive mirage organized by my agents'. Certainly, in this fascinating novel, he takes a heartless Olympian glee in the fact that, if a work of art *is* a mirror, then what it chiefly shows the eager, trusting reader is himself.

(*c*) KINGSLEY AMIS

The Anti-Death League

Something horrid is going on in the secluded army camp which Mr. Amis has made the scene of his new novel. Not until near the end do we know what it is, and there is a surprise twist awaiting us when we do. Though his structure is conventional enough, Mr. Amis seems to have absorbed a stimulating fall-out from many characteristic writing forms in our time—spy story, suspense novel, psychological thriller, technical handbook, a dash of science fiction, all mixed with a strong flavouring of double bluff.

The atmosphere is at once boring and malign; the suspense is a cross between a yawn and a yell of outrage—like war or what we call peace, like life itself. It is a more sombre book than we might expect from this writer, and it generates a strong air of protest. There are few deliberate jokes, though sometimes the ingredients click so that a joke comes out like a small word-prize. ('Could I be a repressed heterosexual, do you suppose?') One or two comic situations are extensively deployed, such as the security man who considers it sophisticated to work without cover and even to talk about his job, or the psychiatrist who interprets everything in terms of concealed homosexual tendencies. But most of the humour is anything but a laughing matter.

As far as the message goes, the argument of the anti-tract which is evidently meant to be a significant part of Mr. Amis's allegory, this would be an easy book to knock. The rebellion against the facts of pain and death seems rather juvenile, like kicking God's ankle for doing such things to people. But he takes the argument to more audacious and hopeful lengths. God leaves the means of suffering lying about for man to inflict on himself and his fellows, and man demonstrates his superiority by refraining—a heartening act of self-control which puts him morally a cut above God. All this would make a jolly good telly-argument with a broadminded bishop, but Mr. Amis is entitled to be judged by different standards—lower ones, no doubt, but more the true concern of a novelist and his critics.

What is going on in that heavily-guarded Block D4? What is the nastiness about to be perpetrated in Operation Apollo? Do we care about the people involved? The characters can be divided into agents and victims—the plotters and counter-plotters on behalf of death and its antidote, and the young officer and his girl-friend whose love for each other is the only armament they possess against the biological powers, cosmic and human. Put like that it may appear too portentous for words, anyway for words in a novel. Yet Mr. Amis carries us along with him. We do care about his creatures: the agents intrigue us and the victims concern us. The handling is vastly less pompous than the theme: oracular, yes, but eloquent and earthy and even moving. If one may switch the image to a more familiar one in the Amis world—and large quantities of drink are consumed in this book—it is not the pub sign that matters so much as the quality and flavour of the drink and the talk. Here he scores well. Surprisingly, the fact that theme and style are rather at odds is an advantage. The friction invigorates, and Mr. Amis settles into a morose yet mischievous kind of mood that suits him very well.

Having accepted his book thus far, which is indeed most of the way, one can stop to goggle a little at Mr. Amis's apparatus. He has a near-Gilbertian talent for all-out paradox, which is used effectively right at the heart of his theme. In a society that lives on death, any life-promoting intervention is treason. But again, characteristically, the handling is far less ponderous than the idea itself. The security services at work in this sinister camp are far from Kafka-like or Koestler-like; they are British and above-board and slightly absurd. It is here that Mr. Amis's preoccupation with double and treble negatives is given full play, as well as his addiction to military and psychological jargon. You feel he must once have belonged to a crack corps of trick cyclists known as the Bluffs.

Just as Aldous Huxley used to travel with an encyclopedia, it is hard not to believe that Kingsley Amis automatically packs a technical handbook or two with his toothbrush. He adores phrases like 'schemata-data divergence', and builds himself alarming elaborations such as 'maximally destructive self-terminating improvisation'. He takes a jaunt into science fiction by inventing what he calls 'lethal nodes' of special peril, existing in time and fatal to enter. Back on earth, he even goes into the techniques of trio-sonata playing. Music is apparently one of the tokens of man's superiority to God.

(*d*) J. M. G. LE CLÉZIO

Le Déluge

In *Le Déluge* M. le Clézio has opted very gracefully for the dark, but luckily his is a young man's darkness, liable to be lit up now and again by the headlights of an Alfa-Romeo, or a flashing Martini sign. He proves in short that he is one of those modern stylites who play safe and erect their pillars not in the wilderness but within easy transistor range of the Golden Gate or, in this case, the Promenade des Anglais.

Le Déluge is quite a muscular piece of Pop-Mysticism. The first forty pages and the last twenty together elaborate one of those extreme states of mind which interest M. le Clézio more than anything else, where the brain and the world fuse in a series of hallucinations. What he writes here is easy to admire but hard to understand, since the stable objects of common reference are few. But there is no doubt about what the message is: Down with eyesight. At the start we have a Creole proverb, to the effect that the eyes have no frontiers, and since it is frontiers he seems above all else to want M. le Clézio comes forward, at least partly seriously, as the champion of blindness. Because we can see we are involved in a false and disturbing communion with the material world; sight turns things into ideas and thereby knocks down the proper walls between one thing and the next, or one man and his neighbour. What is recommended is a return to the blind reign of the mineral, before the vegetable leap into consciousness which destroyed the wholeness of things. Blindness then is a step on the road to reconciliation with matter.

These are extreme views which the hero of *Le Déluge*, François Besson, has to be made to share. He finds his environment to be a hell and the eyes of another human being an unbearable torment. He has had a very shattering experience; one January afternoon a siren blows and a girl goes past on a powered bicycle. The sound of the siren and the appearance of the girl are so completely synchronized that Besson is overwhelmed by the possibilities of sensual exchange. From this moment on he sees death everywhere; things are in motion. He comes down from his lonely bedroom and walks the streets of the town, making a quick round of the activities which for most people cloak the truth of their mortality, but it is all in vain. Finally, in an act of sacrifice, he offers up his offending eyes to the sun, which blinds him.

This central section of the novel is plain picaresque, even down to the simple-minded synopses of events at the head of each chapter. The philosophy is limited to the beginning and end. Besson, the empty, passive vessel, waiting to be filled, visits those parts of his home town whose vitality is most calculated to confound him; the market, the bus-station, a breakwater during a storm, a building site, and so on. He also has a banal series of encounters with various men and women, that serve to eliminate the chances of salvation through work, or love. During these he is nothing more than an unobtrusive interviewer, his presence so hollow that one begins to wonder just what the novelist is up to. There are moments indeed when Besson is surely nothing more than an excuse for some good old-fashioned set pieces, such as the description of a sunrise or a storm at sea.

Where M. le Clézio is most himself is in the way he conveys a sense of the town as an organism. Besson has a sewer-fixation which matches his concern with the biological activities of his own body. *Le Déluge* is excellent and original at the times when it establishes these arterial connexions between the inside of our bodies and the outside of our environment. The simple moving of a chair, for example, takes on a new menace when it is described in terms of glandular disturbance within the mover. And this exchange is often taken further, to an extreme point where there is full identity between the watcher and the movement he is watching, be it only that of the ball on a pin-table machine, about to disappear down a hole which suddenly yawns open like the entrance to hell.

Whatever doubts one may feel about the integrity of M. le Clézio's fashionable flight from consciousness there is plenty to admire as usual in the fun and vitality it involves him in. His books are always full of charming moments of anarchy and eccentric typography, where the words are suddenly asked to do double duty and become ideograms. And there is entertainment to be had, too, in the impressively negative capabilities of hero Besson. When he finds himself kneeling in the confessional, for all his apparent lack of belief, he manages to repent of an extraordinarily complete list of sins.

The ultimate problem of a book like this of course is the playful paradox it rests on. What worries Besson is the impossibility of coming directly into touch with the material world. He is thus bound to reject language as a basic form of rhetoric which conjures things away rather than reveals them. *Le Déluge* is dedicated in a sense to the death of verbal communication, but it has to deliver this message as a verbal communication. M. le Clézio, let us say, is not wholly to be trusted in what he would like to have us believe about a possible return to the mineral state. But there is a wholesome imagination and intelligence in his books that could well help us to reconcile ourselves for another day or two to the torments of our conscious, seeing life.

(*e*) IRIS MURDOCH

The Time of the Angels

This is Miss Murdoch's tenth novel since *Under the Net* (1954), and one may be tempted to echo Byron's sardonic, 'Another poem by Mr. Southey in the Spring'. Her most faithful admirers must be beginning to feel Miss Murdoch's ease and fertility of invention a source of mingled wonder and misgiving, and it must be said that *The Time of the Angels*, intelligent, technically adroit and compulsively readable, cannot be cited with satisfaction as evidence of more than an original and entertaining minor talent.

Yet the early books seemed to promise so much more, and *The Bell* (1958) partly redeemed these promises. What has gone wrong since then? Or have we, dazzled by her possession of some of the novelist's skills to an extraordinary degree, expected too much of her? One persistent source of trouble for the reader is her uneasy wedding of fable and realism—although when she dropped the yeast of fable and laboriously manufactured the 1916 Easter Rebellion background in *The Red and the Green* (1965) the book did not really rise at all and became in some parts nearly indigestible.

Even in *The Red and the Green* the obsession with 'incest discovered' persisted—there was the black-comic-opera scene where Andrew and his aunt Millie are surprised in bed by other interested parties. In *The Time of the Angels*, the Reverend Carel Fisher, an unsettling Nietzsche-like figure who refuses all visitors, makes paper darts and lives in a darkened room playing records of Tchaikovsky's *Swan Lake* and 'Frère Jacques, dormez-vous . . .', is discovered in bed with his ward, Elizabeth, who is ostensibly his niece but is in fact his daughter by his brother's wife. Elizabeth, an enigmatic girl, with the long fair hair of a princess in a fairy-tale, is an invalid who wears a surgical corset because there is something wrong with her back. The pair are seen reflected in a mirror by Carel's other daughter, Muriel, when she peeps into Elizabeth's room through a crack in the wall.

Miss Murdoch's bizarre sexual 'figure in the carpet' is associated on this occasion with Carel Fisher's role as the tortured victim of lost faith. 'The death of God', he says, 'has set the angels free. And they are terrible.' Since he had earlier taken as his mistress his illegitimate, half Irish, half West-Indian servant, Pattie O'Driscoll, a gentle, bewildered but resilient person, it appears that Elizabeth and Pattie stand in some way for the different forces pulling him apart—he commits suicide with Muriel's stolen sleeping-pills when Pattie, who has hitherto felt herself as closely identified with Carel as Cathie Earnshaw with the demonic Heathcliff, finally leaves him because she cannot endure his betrayal of her with Elizabeth. Again 'in some way', a Russian icon showing the Trinity represented as sorrowing angels has a bearing on the novel's statements about the consequences of the death of God. The icon is the last precious possession of the porter at the Rectory, a sad aging Russian émigré, Eugene Pleshkov, whose twenty-year-old son Leo appears to be an amalgam of Verkhovensky in *The Possessed* and the stock delinquent of the more 'serious' type of B.B.C. documentary. The icon's appearances and disappearances—it is stolen from Eugene in the first place by his son—constitute one of the novel's many dispiritingly perplexing bits of symbolism. The demolished Wren church (bombed during the war) of the parish to which Carel Fisher has recently moved is, on the other hand, rather too *simpliste* a device, and so too is the deep fog which hangs round the Rectory for most of the story.

Some sort of normal focus for the strange goings-on at the isolated Rectory is provided by three remaining characters, who are all intensely curious about what is happening, and constantly try to get into the house or to offer advice to those of its occupants whom they can reach. They stand, in effect, for representative modern attitudes to the ethical and religious problems posed by the book. The regretful non-believer is Carel's brother Marcus, a headmaster on sabbatical leave who is writing a philosophical treatise on morality in a secular age designed to be as epigrammatically brilliant as Nietzsche's *Birth of Tragedy*. Although co-guardian of his niece Elizabeth, he has seen neither her nor Carel for some years—when he does eventually get into the Rectory, it is by way of the coal-hole and at a moment when the electricity has failed, so that his interview with his brother is conducted entirely in the dark. The forthright rationalist of the old school is his friend Norah Shadox-Brown, a teacher who has no regrets about the breakdown of Christianity but recognizes that 'it hasn't worked out as we thought when I was young. This sort of twilight-of-the-gods atmosphere will drive enough people mad before we get all that stuff out of our system'. The third character is Anthea Barlow, a psychiatric social-worker who is seen at intervals throughout the story knocking at the Rectory door, and, like Marcus, always being rebuffed.

Carel emphasizes the 'blind accident' that brings us into being, but it is hard to tell how much value his creator attaches to what he says or how sympathetic she is to the Kierkegaardian notion that passionate ideas are more real than others. This difficulty breeds confusion. Too many signposts point in too many directions. The artist 'sets the problem and need not solve it', but this should not be taken to mean that a confusing problem should be set confusingly. Iris Murdoch's intricacies appear to run nowhere but into the sand. What lifts the book is its way of realizing a sad but far from depressing quality of the human spirit—it is felt in the two misfits, the dispossessed Russian émigré and the West Indian girl who has never possessed anything, both of whom are muddled and lonely but still generous and unselfish—and its satirical portrait of the blandly modernistic Bishop which captures the tone of a John Bird impersonation, but the total effect of the rest is rather unhappily that of a superior Gothic extravaganza, a 1966 version of (say) *Melmoth the Wanderer* which seems to bid rather pretentiously for more attention than it really deserves.

(*f*) MARTIN WALSER

Das Einhorn

In his earlier novels, short stories and plays Herr Martin Walser was preoccupied with social criticism, though the vehemence of that criticism sometimes suggested that his real quarrel was not so much with the west Germany of the *Wirtschaftswunder*, or indeed with any specific social and economic set-up, as with the depravity and conformism of anybody, anywhere, who was prepared to play the power game. His novels *Ehen in Philippsburg* (1957) and *Halbzeit* (1960) were powerful and brilliant in parts, but they were less satisfactory as works of art than some of the short stories in his first book, *Ein Flugzeug über dem Haus*.

In many respects Herr Walser's new novel is even more ambitious than its two predecessors. The hero and narrator, Anselm Kristlein, has been taken over from *Halbzeit*, just as Beumann has been taken over from *Ehen in Philippsburg*; but the main emphasis has been shifted from social satire to a number of themes that are closer to Herr Walser's dominant concerns. Kristlein, once a copywriter, has become a novelist. A Swiss woman publisher commissions him to write a book about love. Kristlein, a married man with children, goes out to collect material, some of which is provided by an affair with the publisher herself. While staying at the villa of the industrialist Blomich, a friend of his employer, he falls in love with a girl who is camping nearby with her Dutch boy friend. At the beginning and end of the narration Kristlein is back in his Munich flat with his wife and children, literally prostrate and utterly self-estranged.

The analysis of love, of different varieties of love, is only one of the themes that hold this book together. The unicorn of the title is symbolic not only of the erotically questing male, but also of the outsider—among other things. Kristlein's exploration of love is organically related to his social status and his ambitions as a writer. Since he is at once writing a book and presenting the raw material for the book, another principal theme is the discrepancy between truth and fiction, experience and memory. It is this discrepancy that defeats Kristlein, but gives Herr Walser ample scope for a critique both of love and of fiction. His sketches of the *Wirtschaftswunder* and its accompanying *Kulturwunder* are more devastating than ever in this larger context. The two parties, in Munich and at the Lake Constance villa, stand out from the more subjective sections of the narrative, with their neo-Joycean streams of consciousness in several languages and dialects, their discursive interpolations and digressions, their flashbacks and deliberate criss-crossing of references. Though Herr Walser has found a distinct manner in this book, at once rich and vigorous, expressive and ironic, some of his verbalizing does tend to obscure the narrative line. This reader, for instance, is not quite sure whether Kristlein did or did not adhere to his resolution not to make Orli his mistress; a single statement towards the end of the book seems to contradict all that we have been told about his painful abstinence. Yet elsewhere, too, we are warned about Kristlein's occasional reticences; and his fantasies are as essential to the story as his actions and his failures to act.

Das Einhorn is by far the most successful of Herr Walser's major works to date, because all his remarkable gifts have been applied to a structure large and intricate enough to accommodate them. If even this work calls for a sequel, it is for reasons not strictly literary. Kristlein's wife, Birga, is only one of the female characters who remain somewhat vague, and not only because she is overshadowed by Orli, the dream girl. It is significant that Kristlein's passion for Orli takes him back to his childhood—in a way just a little too reminiscent of the novels of Günter Grass. Kristlein's final self-estrangement has to do with his failure to make the past and the present coalesce; and this failure suggests the need for a further development not only in his personal relations but also in the novel's analysis of love and, incidentally, of memory. Herr Walser has written a passionately truthful account of certain stages of love, but Kristlein's reticences about his married life mark its limits and its limitations. The fusion, in his mind, of Birga and Orli at the end of the book indicates the direction which a sequel might take.

5

PROSE OUT OF AFRICA

(*a*) LEWIS NKOSI

Home and Exile

THERE IS NO SHREWDER test of original intelligence nowadays than to write about race without either boring or repelling the reader. This test Mr. Nkosi passes triumphantly in his book of essays *Home and Exile*. Starting his journey with the stenuously multi-racial parties of the 1950s, held in the plush white suburbs of Johannesburg, he chronicles the gradual disillusionment of the South African intellectuals, their final withdrawal from a social and political position based on compromise and mediation, daily belied by a regime which permitted of neither. The old *Drum* of Anthony Sampson was a part of that world; its collapse cannot be better measured than by looking at the same magazine today. There is no one now to challenge the 'pop' magazine stereotype as Can Themba, Bloke Modisane, Henry Nxumalo, Casey Motsisi, Ezekiel Mphahlele, Todd Matshikiza and Lewis Nkosi himself did, each in his different rhythm, so that the result became something unpredictable and alive, something far removed from the given formula of crime, sex and hair-straighteners. The first section of Mr. Nkosi's book shows the break-up of this whole group under the remorseless, steadily-tightening grip of apartheid. Of the writers just listed, four at least are now in exile and one is dead, murdered by the *tsotsis* a benevolent government forced him to dwell among. And yet the time of which Mr. Nkosi is writing is barely ten years ago.

(*a*) *Home and Exile*. 136 pp. Longmans. 18s.
(*b*) *A Man of the People*. 167 pp. Heinemann. 18s.
(*c*) *The Beginners*. 488 pp. Weidenfeld and Nicolson. 30s.
(*d*) *Iska*. 222 pp. Hutchinson. 25s.
(*e*) *The Late Bourgeois World*. 160 pp. Gollancz. 21s.
(*f*) *Prelude to Independence*. Foreword by Ian Smith. 219 pp. Capetown: Nasionale Boekhandel. London: Bailey Bros. and Swinfen. 26s.

Lewis Nkosi himself moved to Harvard and exile in 1961. The second section of his book offers a highly personal and inspiriting impression of New York and lays bare both the evident similarities and the fundamental differences between the situation of the urban industrialized Negro in South Africa and in America. Above all, he appreciates how much the American Negro, though condemned to be in a perpetual minority, has acted as a cultural peacemaker within the whole texture of society there:

> And I saw—and this is what seemed to set the younger generation apart—a young Negro walking down Lennox Avenue in a kind of rolling gait, which was later translated for me into a taunting, mischievously arrogant jazz phrasing by Miles Davis. . . . Miles and the younger jazz musicians seem to be expressing all the colour, subtleties, the mocking arrogance, and the defensive qualities of the life of a people who live on the fringe of a colour-bar society. There was a painful, though touching irony, when I saw the sons and daughters of white middle-class families desperately trying to appropriate this style, while the Negro was forever moving further 'out'—way out—in order to evade definition.

It is this ability, rare among African writers, to enter with imagination and sympathy into the American Negro dilemma that enables Mr. Nkosi to observe that what happens in American society in the next few years is intimately involved with what happens in Africa itself. This interaction, which began to be significant after the war, has grown steadily more so with the mounting importance of Africa in international affairs and the answering intensification of the Civil Rights struggle. Experience has taught Mr. Nkosi to be wary of liberal white allies and to look to the black man, everywhere, for the resolution of his own problems. In the book's most challenging essay he argues that

> only when the black world is powerful enough to neutralize the camouflaged but hideously menacing power of the white nations of the West will it be possible for black and white men with a humanistic, conciliatory vision to share an identity of interests across the colour-line.

At first sight this reasoning summons up a dismal vision of African nations frenziedly amassing nuclear weapons and the other paraphernalia of 'power', in the belief that this and only this will enable them to speak to East and West as equals, but perhaps Mr. Nkosi would not wish to push his case that far. Mexico, to cite only one example, has notably improved its international status in recent years without joining in the nuclear race. The development of a vigorous economy has more to do with it than power in the conventional sense. Too much reliance on foreign aid cannot fail to perpetuate a psychology of dependence, with all its attendant evils. The argument certainly has the merit of testing the easy liberal assumption that real human relationships can be established in total isolation from the surrounding social, political and economic arrangements. For, 'when the chips are down in Harlem or Notting Hill Gate', the Negro intellectual will soon find that 'none of his liberal white friends . . . is likely to be out there in the streets with him'.

(*b*) CHINUA ACHEBE

A Man of the People

According to one observer, Chinua Achebe's first novel, *Things Fall Apart*, is probably one of the biggest 'factors in the formation of a young West African's picture of his past and of his relation to it'. One might add that for many non-Africans this book is almost the only picture of that past they have seen. A remarkable situation, and without disrespect to Mr. Achebe, perhaps not entirely due to the merits of the work. *A Man of the People* stands fair to reach a similar status as an eloquent, acute and convincing anatomy of the strange period just ended in Nigeria. Not that the book speaks of 'Nigeria', nor is its capital called Lagos or its politicians Ekoti-Eboh. But then Mr. Achebe's situation when he began to write it was rather as if the director of the British Council should undertake to predict the Chinese occupation of London, so one is only surprised that the disguise is so casual.

Odili is a young African, educated mainly into rueful puzzlement, who is suddenly offered the bountiful hand of his tribesman and former teacher, the eponymous Minister (of Culture), Chief The Honourable Dr. M. A. Nanga, M.P., LL.D. A stay in his residence (' . . . the double bed that seemed to ride on a cushion of air . . . the beautiful furniture . . . the gleaming bathroom. . . . I had to confess that if I were at that moment made a minister I would be most anxious to remain one forever') ends when the great man poaches Odili's girl friend with typical benignity. Bent on vengeance, he decamps to a lawyer friend conveniently about to form a revolutionary party. Then a national *crise de scandale* forces a general election, and Odili decides to contest Nanga's seat among their own people. He will not be bribed or intimidated out, so he has to be beaten up and hospitalized until safely after nomination day. But the regime over-reaches itself, the worm turns and the army takes over. Odili has his satisfaction in full. Nanga loses his head to the people and his intended 'parlour-wife' to our hero.

Matter like this implies a texture removed from the prematurely aged *gravitas*, the over-exertion towards a kind of Ibo Homerics in the previous novels. By comparison, this one is scabrous, unbuttoned, reckless—a black fabliau. Odili has no *chi* by which to align his conduct. The village gods are dead, and their translation into 'the will of the people' provides, at the crunch, no guide-lines at all, because, so Achebe says, the people have no will. Nanga *is* their man and they deserve him. So everyone, and especially Odili himself, is motivated by chance, not forewill, greed not social good, sexual pique rather than honour. Even Cool Max, the leader of the reforming Common Peoples' Convention takes dirty money, and although he dies a martyr, his style is unheroic.

A Man of the People clearly fills out the argument of the earlier novels in presenting the inglorious results of a weak indigenous culture hustled into an unreal modernity by a colonialism calculating and insensitive, and by a transitional generation of its own people which could not help being hesitant and quisling; but this is not the book's chief interest because Achebe's political thinking is misty and ambiguous, fatally dependent on a harness of shaky western abstractions and Ibo proverbial analogizing (although much of the latter has happily gone out with the Homerics). What he has in fact achieved is an essentially and admirably *journalistic* triumph of documentation. Nearly all the most telling and odious features of recent Nigerian life are here, intelligently observed. The frustrated 'Standard Six intellectual' ('it is equal to B.A. today—if not more'); the devouring American wife more knowledgable about Lagos history than her African lover is, the eternal lunch-time radio commercial for a ring-worm expeller, the Italian shoes and Levis which the 'been-away' adolescents sport when they come home to their bush village for Christmas. Above all, it is in the rotund complexity of Chief Nanga, his roguery as bottomless and impenetrable as his outrageous plausibility, that a central clue to this pathetic, quizzical epoch is uncovered.

(*c*) DAN JACOBSON

The Beginners

The Beginners is nothing if not panoramic, and the frequent shift of focus from ranging sweep to sharp detail is an essential part of Mr. Dan Jacobson's method in this novel. Yet if writers were divided into hawks and doves, Mr. Jacobson would be a dove; as distinctive a species as the ones he describes in the South African region where the greater part of his novel is located: 'the small, pearl-grey Namaqua doves with long bills, whose cooing echoed among the stones'.

These carefully composed descriptions of settings, artfully selected details of landscape and townscape ranging from South Africa to Israel and finally to the self-absorbed, gossipy drawing-rooms of intellectual London, are the strength of the book. They are done with a superb yet always unobtrusive skill. A less fastidious writer would have given them more emphasis, thus taking the weight off the characters which are by no means so well realized. In fact they seem rather conventional and as undistinguished as most panorama populations. In a book that travels so far in time and space it would no doubt take a Tolstoy to bring them off completely. Mr. Jacobson often gets down to detail and for long enough to set himself a human challenge he has hardly succeeded in meeting.

The story is of three generations of an emigrant Jewish family, concentrating on the third. Since its sweep carries us through the Hitler era and into the hardening period of apartheid, nobody can accuse Mr. Jacobson of piling on the agony. Indeed, his chosen family could be accused of coming through rather too smoothly. True, as well as doves there are dragons—not only scaly, heraldic creatures like the *likkewaan* which also have a place in his stony landscape, but more dangerous flashes of menace as when the South African police break up an anti-apartheid meeting.

But these things are symptoms, mere embroideries of a theme which is hinted at with a modest lack of stress. If Mr. Jacobson were a preaching sort of novelist he would no doubt be telling us in as many words that these are the sort of anguished contortions that have to be gone through in the detribalization of man. Instead of ranting at us, he makes his best-realized character end up in London, married to a gentile who is also another man's ex-wife, rather than on the kibbutz where he worked earlier in the book. This is not presented as either a forward or a backward march. But a sort of uprooted happiness has been achieved, and the old cohesive, God-centred clan life has taken another knock.

This ending, like the beginning, is admirable. For the rest, a novelist whose centralizing drive is to be found in dispersal and whose characters—if they are to be made airborne at all—have to be lifted in a complicated family flight, has clearly set himself special problems. Mr. Jacobson was right to give himself space. Unheroic, unsentimental, shot through with a feeling intelligence about the problems and prospects of the total human tribe, here for once is a book that could profitably have been longer still. As it is, the price he pays for his method and pattern seems unnecessarily high. His most valuable gift as an artist is under-used. We pay calls, so to speak, on too many different privacies and are briefly admitted to an excessive number of innermost feelings. This is not the same thing as the true penetration, the ultimate intrusion into private grief or love or triumph, which is ideally the novelist's special privilege.

(*d*) CYPRIAN EKWENSI

Iska

Mr. Ekwensi's new novel is the story of Filia Enu, an Ibo girl brought up in Northern Nigeria who is rash enough to marry a Hausa Civil Servant. There are predictable objections from both families on evasively tribalistic grounds. 'We have our pride and must do as our fathers did', says Filia's father. This sounds to her like the benighted talk of a fading generation, but when her new husband is killed in a brawl between Ibo and Hausa thugs, she decides the North cannot hold her any longer. Liberation and adventure await her in the capital. In Lagos she becomes a successful model, ubiquitously pursued but sexually aloof, disaffected and unappeased by any of the city's ingenuities. She is briefly fascinated by Piska Dabra, a beach Messiah, and then naively repelled at discovering how unspiritual his appeal actually is. Ultimately she finds her first lover reembodied in a young political journalist but she is too withdrawn and fastidious to come to terms with the frank jobbery of his world. Filia Enu dies of a mysterious sickness, definitely if tortuously self-wished.

Mr. Ekwensi is the original West African urban novelist. As

against Achebe, who is, or was, characteristically preoccupied with the educated African coming to terms with what he has grown from, Mr. Ekwensi is interested in watching gifted, wily individuals sink or swim in the new shambling metropolis. 'The city attracts all types and the unwary must suffer from ignorance of its ways', runs the epigraph to his first book. Mr. Ekwensi's heroes are not out just to survive. They want (or their creator wants them) to stay afloat with their consciences intact—a hard option in Lagos where Piska Dabra's followers do not pray for grace but for power, position, an increment, or to have their picture in the papers often, 'because life is short'. Mr. Ekwensi's Breughelesque vision of Nigerian life with its dedicated avarice and cancerous vitality is, if anything, rather less sharp-edged here than in that first novel, *People of the City*, now no longer listed among his works and published twelve years ago when this kind of scabrous canvas was more of a literary novelty. Piska Dabra is hardly an advance on Soyinka's Brother Jero, and the pot-pourri of lecherous politicians, good-time girls having a bad time, mothers from the bush tracking down errant children, and the pervasive sense of intention without purpose is all too extraordinary *and* too commonplace for the rather tenuous complexity of Mr. Ekwensi's design. The symbol of 'Iska', the wind which comes and goes 'like magic', is merely evoked casually whereas it needs to be properly integrated into the book's imagistic structure, since it implies an idea obviously crucial to Mr. Ekwensi's reading of Filia Enu and her society. There is also an unfortunate ambivalence about Filia herself. From one point of view, perhaps the crucial one, she is any pretty girl come to make her fortune in town, but Mr. Ekwensi would also have us accept (or half accept, since the notion is conveyed deprecatingly) that she is an *obanje*, 'a delicate child and you come and go from the world just as you please'. There is no reason why both aspects should not be present but it will not do if the reader is uncertain what weight to give to each. Filia Enu remains so indefinite that it is difficult to give any meaning to her strange death.

Iska is very readable and abounds in compact vignettes ripe for the anthologist of African Prose, but it contains relatively few echoes of the very self and voice of contemporary Nigeria.

* * *

Heinemann Educational Books wrote (29 September) to point out that *People of the City* is still in print.

(*e*) NADINE GORDIMER

The Late Bourgeois World

When Nadine Gordimer's short stories first began to appear she seemed to be the very best kind of *New Yorker* writer. That is to say, although these stories tended to be constructed to a recognizable pattern, her sensibility and perception were already such that one was sure she would eventually burst the bonds. She did in fact achieve freedom and real stature with her novel *A World of Strangers* eight years ago. Its themes, the African tragedy, the cruelty and injustice of apartheid, were those which had already been, and still are, central to her thought. Her psychological insight engendered a gentleness of style that proved both fresh and effective.

Since then the stories as well as the novels have taken on new dimensions, though continuing to explore the same areas of experience. Those in *Friday's Footprint* are faultless in technique, sharper in irony than the earlier ones, but no less controlled. Miss Gordimer improves steadily and excitingly from book to book: *The Late Bourgeois World* is probably her finest yet. It is a short book, and the events it describes, or rather the reactions to an event, take place over one weekend. Elizabeth learns by telegram that her husband, from whom she is separated, has killed himself by plunging his car into Cape Town harbour. He was the son of a respectable politician, had shocked his family by going into left-wing politics, but had finally found himself engaged in lone political action. He had planted a home-made bomb somewhere, been arrested, tried, imprisoned, and had eventually turned state witness and implicated several of his former colleagues. And he had finished up in Cape Town harbour. Elizabeth, since their separation, has been having a fairly uninvolved affair with a solicitor who specializes in defending political prisoners. There are, though, the beginnings of involvements elsewhere, moral, political, probably sexual.

There is very little plot and what there is is simply seen in retrospect. There is only the situation, and the beautifully created characters who are engaged in it: the widow Elizabeth, the dead Max, the solicitor Graham Mill, Elizabeth's son Bobo, and Luke, the African who finally puts her values to the test.

The title of the book can be taken in two ways: for its simple and deadly irony and for its promise or threat that, sustained though she has been throughout the years of her husband's political activity by her own bourgeois routine, Elizabeth is now about to abandon it and plunge into something just as deadly to the personality as Cape Town harbour to the body. Despite its background of the horror of life under an oppressive regime, this is in no sense a political novel. Only incidentally, and after one has put down the book, does one reflect on the situation out of which so fine, compassionate and exquisitely written a work has emerged.

(*f*) A. SKEEN

Prelude to Independence

'I was accosted by the usual throng of journalists to whom I had little of importance to say'—so Brigadier Skeen describes his arrival at Salisbury Airport on the eve of the visit by Mr. Harold Wilson. The comment would serve as a fitting summary of this whole book. Brigadier Skeen has little of importance to say. His comments on the political and diplomatic scene are naive in the extreme. Furthermore, his style is reminiscent of a school magazine. He is addicted to verbless sentences and misrelated participles.

As a volume of diplomatic memoirs and as a literary work, this account by the Rhodesian High Commissioner in London in the immediate pre-U.D.I. period is hardly worth noticing. It certainly has nothing of the interest of Sir Roy Welensky's book, though Brigadier Skeen invites a comparison by his subtitle 'Skeen's 115 Days'.

It does have an interest, however, as an illustration of the mentality of the people close to the present centre of power in Rhodesia. It is a depressing illustration. Brigadier Skeen shows himself to be totally out of tune with the modern world. Among the many trivialities which fill his pages there are several references to the dreadful experience of washing up (which he had escaped since 1947). People who disagree with Mr. Ian Smith and demonstrate their disagreement in Britain are long-haired and unwashed louts. The London School of Economics is 'that hotbed of left-wing intrigue'. Participants in the teach-ins on Rhodesia are 'the left-wing and the Communist fellow-travellers'. Brigadier Skeen prides himself—among many other things—on having made a good assessment of public feeling in

Britain. One wonders quite how close his contacts with the real public were. He gives a clue when he writes:

> August was the month when armed with bowler, umbrella and regimental tie, a protective camouflage for the colonial I now had become, I was able to assess public opinion. . . .

His bowler hat plays an important part in his life, and indeed he appears to be obsessed with his and his wife's wardrobe. After several chapters one feels that every change of clothes has been recorded. He records with glee a prank he played on some African politicians visiting London, assuring them of the importance of the bowler hat to such effect that they bought some to wear on return to Rhodesia.

It would be unfair to criticize Brigadier Skeen for writing a book that is both stupid and tedious, but that is not the end of the matter. He shows himself also to be insensitive to the normal demands of good taste, and as he does not hesitate to blunder into judgments of others it is reasonable that this lack should be underlined. There are several examples.

One is his description of the non-denominational church service held to mark the Commonwealth Arts Festival. He mocks it throughout and comments that:

> the African personality cult had been ignored, and there would be shrill complaints from the African members of the Commonwealth because a witch-doctor complete with bones and wildebeest tail, and clad in ochre and skins, had not been invited to join the officiating clergy.

Another is his ill-mannered description of the way of life of diplomatists from other African countries: he finds it hilarious that they should want to grow maize in their London gardens, but presumably sees nothing funny in a white Rhodesian's wish to have an 'English' garden in Africa.

One cannot rely on him to get his facts right. There are many small errors. More important is his comment that the incoming Labour Government in 1964 'completely ignored' the result of Mr. Smith's *indaba* of chiefs, as if this was surprising. In fact, the outgoing Conservative Government made it quite clear throughout that the *indaba* was unacceptable, and the new Government simply confirmed this fact which Mr. Smith had chosen to ignore.

If this book demonstrates anything it is that diplomacy, as well as war, is too serious a matter to be left to soldiers.

6

PSYCHE OR SOMA?

DOCTORING THE EVIDENCE

This disease manifests itself not so much by any particular signs which are never found in any other Distemper, as by the complication of a great many, several of which are likewise observed in other Distempers; but a Person is properly enough said to be Hysterick who has four or five: otherwise the Catalogue of Symptoms belonging to it is so large that it is impossible one woman should show them all.

BERNARD DE MANDEVILLE, who wrote this of hysteria in 1730, was one of a long line of physicians, stretching from the Hippocratic College to post-Freudian psychiatrists, who have found hysteria to be unmanageably diverse. In the past hundred years many have concluded, petulantly or regretfully, that it is not a disease at all. They expressed their conviction vehemently: Steyerthal predicted that:

within a few years the concept of hysteria will belong to history; there is no such disease, and there never has been. What Charcot called hysteria is a tissue woven of a thousand threads, a cohort of the most varied diseases, with nothing in common but the so-called stigmata, which in fact may accompany any disease;

Gaupp proclaimed:

away with the name and the concept of hysteria: there is no such thing, and what we call hysteria is either an artificial, doctor-made product, or a melange of symptoms which can occur in all sorts of illnesses and are not pathognomonic of anything;

and fifty years later, in 1965, Dr. Eliot Slater says it again:

there is nothing at all consistent in the medical condition of the patients who get diagnosed as 'hysterics' . . . no evidence has yet been offered that the patients diagnosed as suffering from 'hysteria' are in medically significant terms anything more than a random selection.

ILZA VEITH: *Hysteria*. The History of a Disease. 301 pp. The University of Chicago Press. £2 19s. 6d.

Such weighty indictments might be taken as lethal to the concept. But it survives and has powerful defenders. Evidently there is something tough and durable in this condition, whether it is given brevet rank as a syndrome or full commission as a 'morbid entity'. Its colourful history bespeaks the curious changes it has gone through, its tenacity, its abiding link with sexuality, and its excellent prospects of outliving its detractors.

* * *

In Egypt and Greece the uterus was naturally held responsible for many of the diseases of women, including hysteria: knowledge of its anatomy being slender and its power evidently great, it was credited with activities appropriate to an imprisoned, restless demon. Plato was echoing accepted Hippocratic beliefs when he described the uterus as an animal passionately longing for children, and, if unsatisfied for long after puberty, prone to range angrily through the body, blocking the air passages and causing distress and disease.

The migratory tendencies of the womb were more precisely and credulously set out in Hippocratic writings which laid particular stress on the consequences of the womb making its way to the liver and the hypochondrium or mounting still higher to the heart. By the time of Aretaeus the uterus was credited also with appetites: it was believed to delight in fragrant smells and to advance towards them, just as its aversion to foetid smells made it flee from them. Treatment was based on this lively pathology; suppositories of spikenard were given to lure the errant uterus back to its proper seat, evil-smelling fumes and vinegar were squirted into the hysteric's nostrils to drive it down from the upper regions of the body.

* * *

For Galen the uterus was still the affected organ in hysteria, but he thought the trouble lay not in its wanderings but in its incapacity to rid itself of the menses and a feminine counterpart of male semen. In spite of Galen's immense authority over a span of many centuries, his opinions about the nature of hysteria were only partly and somewhat perversely accepted: his repudiation of the migrating uterus as an anatomical absurdity and his contention that men could develop hysteria were little regarded, whereas his theory of retained female sperm was adopted. It fitted in with the frigidity or abstinence from sexual intercourse which Galen and others found to be common in hysterical women. But this clue was not followed up; and indeed it was almost impossible for Galen or anybody else to make sure observations and correct inferences about the pathology of a disease which had 'varia et innumera accidentia'. Nevertheless some efforts were made to confine the supposed effects of uterine vagrancy to certain dramatic seizures. As Rabelais put it in Rondibilis's lecture on cuckoldry to Panurge:

> this terrible animal [the womb] is knit unto, and hath an union with all the chief and most principal parts of the body, as to anatomists is evident. . . . Plato with very good reason did give it the denomination of an animal, for that he perceived and observed in it the proper and self-stirring motions of suffocation, precipitation, corrugation, and of indignation, so extremely violent, that oftentimes by them is taken and removed from the woman all their sense and moving whatsoever, as if she were in a swounding lipothymy, benumbing syncope, epileptic, apoplectic palsy, and true resemblance of a pale-faced death. . . . It is not unknown to me how Cl. Galen striveth with might and main to prove that these are not proper and particular motions proceeding intrinsically from the thing itself, but accidentally and by change.

Personification of the uterus as the instigator of hysterical illness is vehemently expressed in a tenth-century exorcist's formula:

> O womb, womb, cylindrical womb, red womb, white womb, fleshy womb, demoniacal womb: I conjure thee to come back to thy place, and not to occupy this maiden's hands, heart, stomach, spleen . . . but to lie down quietly where God has appointed.

Violent contortions, stupor and abnormally heightened or reduced sensation were phenomena readily displayed by hysterics, and readily attributed to demoniacal possession. Codified in textbook form by Kramer and Sprenger in 1494, the ecclesiastical rules for detecting witches and other traffickers with the devil were so formulated as to entrap hysterics on a grand scale. The *Malleus Maleficarum* linked what we recognize as symptoms of hysteria with a twisted but blatant sexuality, and provided authoritative guidance in detecting witches, extorting their 'confessions', and executing them. Hysterics were not the only victims: senile beldams were equally exposed; and the melancholic and the obsessed too stood in great danger from the inquisitors.

* * *

Towards the end of the sixteenth century courageous and observant physicians, like Johanes Weyer of Cleves, and well-read sceptics like Reginald Scot, published their reasons for disbelieving many of the accepted superstitions about witchcraft, and insisted that mental illness, rather than devilish compacts and incubi and succubi, accounted for the behaviour that brought women before the tribunals. Montaigne put it tersely after he had conversed with notorious witches; he would prescribe them hellebore, not hemlock. As to the tainted men, like Urbain Grandier at Loudun, they were mostly doomed victims of crudely erotic fantasies on the part of hysterical girls and women. The symptoms of hysteria which men developed seem seldom to have brought them under the notice of the inquisitors.

While these enormities were still being perpetrated and denounced, shrewd observers were throwing overboard the long-established pathology of hysteria. The ablest of the innovators, Charles Lepois, physician to the Duke of Lorraine, published his treatise in 1618; he denied the role of the uterus, and argued convincingly against Galen's views regarding retention of menstrual blood or of 'female semen' as the cause of hysteria, and declared that the organ primarily affected is the brain. Edward Jordan, at about the same time, likewise urged that the brain was the true seat and origin of the *passio hysterica*, but thought it consensually affected by the uterus, from which noxious vapours might rise and trouble it. Jordan mingled old and new: he subscribed to the ancient ideas about suppression of the menses and sexual abstinence, but held that perturbations of the mind are often to blame for this disease and that the treatment should be psychological.

* * *

As is inevitable with a disorder so multifarious in its signs and symptoms, the retrospective diagnosis of hysteria from records is full of pitfalls; it is impossible to say with confidence that a particular illness was hysteric since many conditions that must have been so called have been found, by subsequently developed methods of investigation (such as biochemical, electroencephalographic and genetic inquiries) to be essentially physical diseases. Even among the psychiatric disorders that have not been shown to have a somatic pathology, the meaning and application of diagnostic terms have changed. Nowhere is this more evident that in Sydenham's *Epistolary Dissertation*, written in 1681 in response to another physician's request for his observations on 'hysterick diseases which have exercised and fatigued the minds of the ablest physicians of all ages, and often yield not to the methods of cure delivered'. Sydenham opened with an assertion that hysteric disorders made up half of all chronic disorders and that few women 'excepting such as work and fare hardly' are quite free from some form of hysterical illness. Soon after he described it in terms appropriate to depression, as we understand it now: it is the nature of the disease 'to be attended with an incurable despair . . . easily imagining that they are liable to all the miseries that can befall mankind, and presaging the worst evils to themselves'. In another descriptive passage he talks of pain and vomiting 'terminated by an universal jaundice'; and elsewhere of an apoplexy which seizes women frequently after a difficult delivery, attended with much loss of blood. Whatever the conditions thus described may have been, they do not fit into our notion of hysteria. It is hard to echo the enthusiastic references to Sydenham's exposition by medical historians; Dr. Veith, in her new book on *Hysteria*, calls it a landmark in the history of hysteria, and believes that it introduced a fresh approach to the disease and an unequalled understanding of the psyche of its victims. She asks, rhetorically and cryptically, whether his concept of a faulty disposition of the animal spirits 'is any less rational and believable than our modern imputations to the mind?'

Sydenham's contemporary, Thomas Willis, likewise included in the diagnosis hysteria much that we should classify in a neurological category. He supported his contention that hysteria has its origin in the brain by evidence of visible pathological changes he had collected at autopsies, indicating, as he believed, that the fault lay in the 'animal spirits'. Willis took this concept of animal spirits, derived from Galen, and refined it so that if we substitute 'electrical discharge' for 'explosion of animal spirits in the middle of the brain', we have a neurophysiological interpretation of what happens in an epileptic convulsion, which is acceptable to modern knowledge. Hysterical convulsions and discomforts, he thought, originated in certain of the cranial nerves at their origin in the brain, so that the viscera were much perturbed when the animal spirits were discharged along these nerves. It was not a far-fetched idea, and was a notable advance on the uterine theory. Nevertheless when Willis came to deal with the treatment of hysteria, the crudities of his explanation were patent. He advocated tight bandaging of the abdomen because it could restrain and control the animal spirits from 'leaping forth', and he attributed to the animal spirits likes and dislikes akin to those with which the womb had been credited:

sweet odours loosen the animal spirits by pleasing them and too much release them from their wonted tasks . . . but stinking things repress the spirits, drive them back from excursions and exorbitances, and compel from them their explosive force.

After these seventeenth-century physicians, intent on clinical observation and speculative pathology, came the systematists. Fired by the Linnean success in botany, they classified enthusiastically. Believing that hysteria was a physical disorder, they set it, with many indubitably physical diseases, among the neuroses, by which they understood conditions attributable to disturbances of nervous energy: and they organized the time-honoured uterine misconduct of hysteria into a wider genital disorder affecting the ovaries as well. Their emphasis on the sexual accompaniments or apparent causes of hysteria—nymphomania, suppression of the menses, sexual abstinence—was not new, but it gave these phenomena a psychological meaning in place of the older material notions about their origin and effect. A willingness to consider psychological causes of physical disease was generally manifest during the period. It went with a moralizing approach that spoke loudly in the account of hysterical predisposition, which was supposed to be characterized by an over-indulgent upbringing, bad education, selfishness, idleness and boredom, undue sensitiveness, and luxurious habits. This censorious disparagement has been evident ever since. The majority of psychiatrists seem to find hysterics tiresome, if not downright detestable: they have often applied the term 'hysteric' to neurotic patients they disliked, much as the once neutral term 'psychopath' has been made pejorative. The most systematic of writers about psychopathic personality, Professor Kurt Schneider, amassed a catalogue of abusive terms lavished on hysterics and commented that there is scarcely one unpleasant trait that has not been ascribed to the hysterical character; he urged that the term be dropped because of its tone of moral appraisal and its breadth and vagueness.

In the Victorian period the emotional upheavals and unsatisfied sexual needs of hysterical patients were increasingly stressed; psychological treatment, often of a crude kind, was considered the most appropriate—along with isolation—to cope with the 'petty moral deformities' that repression had occasioned. In the latter part of the century Charcot, primarily a neurologist, but fascinated by the extraordinary diversity of hysterical phenomena, gave a strong twist in another direction. His immensely influential teaching was coloured by the dramatic phenomena elicited in many of his women patients when they were hypnotized. In using hypnotism he took great risks, since from the time when Mesmer brought it to life, it had attracted charlatans and simpletons, and got itself a bad name.

* * *

As physician to the Salpêtrière, Charcot had under his care a division reserved for epileptics and hysterics. The hysterics, in these circumstances, developed symptoms remarkably like those of the epileptics whom they had ample opportunity of studying and copying. Charcot, who did not himself hypnotize his subjects but left it to his too compliant assistants, was unaware of the training that went on behind the scenes: he concerned himself with the objective phenomena which he could demonstrate with predictable regularity. Hysteria, he was convinced, had as its prime manifestation the 'grand paroxysm', in which the patient, curved like a bow, was supported only at her head and her heels, with her limbs moving spasmodically; he described four phases in the paroxysm. In hypnosis, induced by his associates, he similarly observed distinct phases—lethargy, catalepsy and somnambulism. He concluded that susceptibility to being hypnotized was the hallmark of potential or actual hysterics: it could be added to the disturbances of feeling and sight which he had described as the stigmata of hysterical constitution. From this time much controversy, especially in France, centred on the relation between hysterical seizures and hypnosis. On the one side were Bernheim and his followers, who rejected Charcot's evidence and construed his 'grand hysterical paroxysms' as artificial products of suggestion and training; on the other side were Babinski and other pupils of Charcot, who entered a half-hearted defence of the Master's teaching. The dispute was aired in the public newspapers, though these were ill-suited to debate an involved issue touching on clinical method, physiological function and psychological interpretation.

For Charcot hysteria and hypnosis were fields for investigation, just as tabes was, or multiple sclerosis; treatment interested him rather less. His adversaries, on the other hand, were little concerned with pathology and physiology, but very much with treatment, especially by suggestion. Towards the end of his life Charcot moved towards their position. In an article shortly before his death he recognized the power of suggestion in hysterics, and indicated that he was recasting his whole conception of the disorder. In a foreword to the monograph on hysteria written by Pierre Janet, one of his most distinguished pupils, he declared his belief that hysteria is largely a mental disorder, and that its treatment must be based on this truth.

Janet divested the condition of much of its mystery. Invited to the Salpêtrière in 1890 to conduct a newly created psychological laboratory, he was closely associated with Charcot for the next three years, during which the fame and activity of the school were at their highest. His studies of the neuroses were masterpieces of exact and penetrating observation; they maintained the prestige of French psychiatry in this field. On hysteria his work served to clear away the spurious glamour that had been attached to multiple personality, the effects of hypnosis, and other such occult behaviour. He developed a coherent theoretical structure, linked closely to the clinical facts and postulating a hierarchy of psychological functions on lines very similar to those of the English neurologist, Hughlings Jackson, though not borrowed from him.

Janet's work did not receive much attention outside France, in spite of the expositions of it by Bernard Hart in this country and Leonhard Schwarz in Switzerland. His fame has been eclipsed by that of his contemporary, Sigmund Freud. Both had sat at Charcot's feet, Janet for a few years, Freud for four months. On both Charcot made a deep impression. Freud wrote to his fiancée soon after he arrived at the Salpêtrière:

> Charcot engrosses me; when I go away from him . . . my brain is sated as after an evening at the theatre. Whether the seed will ever bring forth fruit I do not know, but what I certainly know is that no other human being has ever affected me in such a way.

And in an obituary notice which he wrote in 1893 he said that Charcot had 'for all time the glory of being the first to elucidate hysteria'. Freud's references to Janet were less generous.

Freud's contribution to the understanding and treatment of hysteria, from the joint *Studien über Hysterie* in 1895 onwards, is now more familiar, not only to psychoanalysis but also to the general reader, than most of the other striking developments in psychiatry during the same period, such as the treatment of general paralysis by induced malaria. The development of his views on hysteria, from those early days when he and Breuer hypnotized Anna O. and awaited the catharsis, ran parallel with his increasingly complex metapsychology, but the psychopathology of hysteria remained the least difficult to accept of his major formulations.

* * *

Since Freud the pendulum has swung in the somatic direction. Though not neglecting the psychological motivation of hysterical symptoms, investigators have noted that they occur in association with physical diseases of the nervous system, such as the late effects of encephalitis, and have applied to this suggestive fact our rapidly growing knowledge about the substrate of cerebral and autonomic functions. From one point of view, now widely held, the essence of hysteria is a predilection for using the body to express symbolically feelings and wishes that cannot be consciously acknowledged: and the focus of interest shifts from uncovering the repressed feeling or idea to searching for the factors that determine which organ or bodily function will be chosen as the vehicle of expression. Among the most certain determinants is the expectation of the doctor who examines the hysterical patient:

> c'est pourquoi, des symptômes, nous médecins, nous en aurons, pour peu que nous tombions dans le piège, autant que nous voudrons, et toujours de ceux qui pourront nous intéresser; car l'hystérique a des antennes merveilleusement sensibles pour sentir ce qui nous distraira par dessus tout.

That is why grand paroxysms were the order of the day at the Salpêtrière in Charcot's time, but not afterwards, and why straightforward conversion symptoms are now rare, in contrast to fugues and psychogenic amnesias. It is a long story: much of it is still to be told.

* * *

Dr. Veith was a pupil of Henry Sigerist, to whose memory her book is dedicated. But she falls strangely short of the standard expected of an historian. Her language is exaggerated: she has to yield to an 'irresistible temptation to digress'; banal occurrences are 'astounding'; Freud was subjected to 'torrents of ridicule and abuse'; to pass from general practice, as Brudenell Carter did, to eye surgery is an 'amazing career', 'one can but marvel at his penetration and lucidity and wonder whence this knowledge came'. There are lapses of judgment and fact; the effect of Charcot's theories, she tells us, included the 'publication of voluminous treatises not only by Charcot's disciples but also by such famous authorities as Kraepelin, Moebius and Kretschmer'; Griesinger's writings 'reveal a gross lack of logic and an obtuseness'; Freud's mistaken account from memory of how he came to translate the third volume of the *Leçons* is repeated without any indication of Jones's detailed correction based on contemporary letters. She supposes that in the Greco-Roman world 'the sex act was looked upon as a purely physical phenomenon', 'the pagan concept of sex as a natural function without relation to social stigma or morality'. Most startling of all, she refers quite seriously to the journalist author of *Memoirs of Extraordinary Popular Delusions* as 'the great historian Mackay'. Omissions from her narrative are likewise hard to account for: no reference to Hecker, Morton Prince, Gilles de la Tourette, Binet, Dubois or Buzzard, and only a few words about Briquet and Kretschmer.

* * *

This article was followed by correspondence from D. M. Walmsley and F. Cioffi (22 September) and Rollo Myers (6 October).

7

ANATOMY OF A FASCIST

A LEIDER AND HIS MEN

JORIS VAN SEVEREN was the son of a well-to-do *notaire* Edmond van Severen, from Wakken, West Flanders, where he was born in July, 1894. His mother, a van de Maele, came from Ghent. Both families were *fransquillons*, and Joris and his brothers were given a French education at a Jesuit college in Ghent. While still at school, he became attracted to Flemish nationalism and in the 1900s he had already established close relations with Stijn Streuvels, Modest Huys and other leading members of the Flemish nationalist intelligentsia; the novelist of peasant Flanders visited Wakken on several occasions. By the outbreak of the First World War, van Severen was already committed, much to his father's disapproval, to the more militant manifestations of the nationalist movement. In 1916 he joined the Belgian Army as a volunteer, was promoted to second lieutenant and was near enough to action to write home about it; but having joined a secret, seditious organization, the Frontbeweging, composed of Flemish members of the Army and designed to combat the predominant influence of French as the language of command, he attracted the notice of the Intelligence section of the General Staff, was degraded, and, along with other militants, was sent, as a private soldier, first of all to a special depot at Rouen, then to a disciplinary battalion at Parigné-l'Evêque, in the Sarthe. At the end of the war, he was demobilized as a private.

From 1921 to 1929, he was regularly elected as a deputy of the *frontpartij*—an extremist Flemish group that had grown out of the clandestine wartime Frontbeweging—for West Flanders, already one of the principal strongholds of the various Flemish movements. In 1929, however, as a result of an electoral manoeuvre on the part of his Catholic opponents, he lost his seat. Overnight he became a fierce

---

R. BAES: *Joris van Severen, une Âme*. 288 pp. Zulte: Éditions Oranje.

opponent of parliamentary democracy, denouncing the corruption of parties and the domination of Brussels. In 1931 he formed his own militant armed organization, the Verbond van Dietsche Nationaal-solidaristen (Verdinaso), the senior members of which (*dinasos*) wore uniforms, carried arms, and underwent a paramilitary training; there was also a Youth Section. The Verdinaso, as well as aiming at the destruction of the unitary Belgian state and of all existing political parties, also sought to reunite the Flemish provinces of Belgium with the seven northern provinces to form a large Dutch-speaking state (Dietschland-le Pays Thiois), organized on authoritarian and corporatist lines. In this the programme of the Verdinaso was scarcely distinguishable from that of the Vlaamsch Nationaal Verbond (VNV), though the latter at this time still advocated parliamentary tactics—it was represented in the Chamber; later it was to become completely identified with Collaboration. There were also personal rivalries; van Severen, who described himself as the Leider, was too authoritarian to enter even temporary alliances with an organization over which he did not have complete control.

* * *

In 1934, without any warning, the Leider completely altered the aim of his paramilitary movement. Now it was no longer a matter of destroying the Belgian state, but rather of creating a Grande Belgique composed not only of Holland and Belgian Flanders, but also the Walloon Provinces ('He generously opened his arms', writes R. Baes, 'to take in the Walloon Provinces') and Luxembourg (and even, it seems, the Dutch Empire and South Africa, for these appear on the huge maps displayed at Verdinaso *landdags*). Dietschland became the Dietsche Rijk. At the same time, branches of the Movement were established in Walloon towns and van Severen's bulletin began to appear in (a form of) French. This change of front resulted in a complete break with the VNV, whose leaders denounced van Severen as a traitor to the Flemish cause. From about 1936 onwards the Verdinaso began to affect a demonstrative Belgian nationalism, the tricolor flag appearing alongside the emblems of the movement at the *landdags* held periodically in Antwerp, Ghent, Bruges, Malines and even Brussels; the Leider even laid claim to Egmont and Horn—the occasion for a demonstration in Brussels—and to William the Silent (the present work is dedicated 'à l'ombre de Guillaume le Taciturne, assassiné comme Joris van Severen pour avoir voulu défendre l'intégrité des Pays Bas') and poor de Ligne ('notre cher Prince de Ligne'). At the same time, he professed a deep devotion to the dynasty and to the person of Leopold III.

After 1934 then, the Verdinaso, though undoubtedly Fascist in aims, methods, organization and slogans, could not be described as pro-German. The money seems to have come mainly from Belgian industrialists. In 1939 van Severen publicly adhered to the policy of neutrality, and early in 1940, on the occasion of the first of the invasion scares, he expressed apprehension about German aggressiveness; his followers were told to give their support to the Belgian state, should its existence be threatened. On May 10, 1940, he was arrested at his home in Bruges by the Sûreté Belge, as a result, it seems, of the personal order of the Minister of Justice; in the next few days, several Senators and the leader of the VNV (who had not been arrested) intervened on his behalf with M. Pierlot, the Prime Minister, who gave them reassuring replies. Shortly afterwards, however, with a group of some sixty other suspects—Belgians, Germans, etc.—and on the initiative of a high official of the Belgian Sûreté (the author hints that he was a Freemason) he was transferred, by bus, from Bruges to Dunkirk, where the passengers of the bus were handed over to the French Sûreté. They then followed a zig-zag route across northern France, in conditions of increasing chaos, till on May 19 they reached Abbeville. There the group was imprisoned for the night in a cellar under a bandstand, in a small park, where it was guarded by a French infantry unit. During the night the town was heavily bombarded. In the morning on May 20, 1940, some twenty of the prisoners were taken out and shot; these included van Severen and one of his lieutenants, the *dinaso* Jan Rijkoort. Some of the French officers responsible for their execution were tried in Amiens in 1942; but the trial was *in camera* and its findings were not made known.

During the German occupation of Belgium, a number of adherents of the Verdinaso collaborated with the Germans; some of them fought in the Flemish SS Legions (Vaderland, Flandria, Langemark), other joined the VNV and the various paramilitary formations of Flemish extremism encouraged by the occupant. Some former *dinasos*, however, took an active part in the Resistance, claiming that they were thus best expressing the doctrines of the dead Leider. Since the war several of van Severen's former adherents have been active in the numerous, extreme-right groups that have continued to pullulate in Belgium up to the present time. The O.S.P. (Organisation du Salut Public), extreme-nationalist and royalist and very anti-'European', is (or was very recently) directed by Louis Guening, an ex-*dinaso*; on the other hand, the virulently pan-'European' and Fascist M.A.C. (Mouvement d'Action Civique)—the Belgian branch of Jeune Europe and of the neo-Fascist International—had in 1962 as director of its Flemish section Fred Rassaert, who has written a number of articles defending the memory of van Severen.

The Verdinaso was a movement with a few thousand adherents, mostly drawn from the middle and lower bourgeoisie of the small towns of West Flanders. It also had some support from Ghent and Louvain students. Shunned by the Flemish peasantry, thanks to the influence of the clergy, it had a handful of supporters in Brussels, and virtually none in the Walloon provinces. Taking a long view, it was more effective and better organized than Rex, though van Severen never achieved the spectacular national success of Degrelle. Professor Jean Stengers has described it as the most authentically Fascist and, militarily, the most threatening of the various authoritarian organizations that developed in Belgium, on the model of the French *ligues*, during the anti-parliamentary hysteria of the 1930s. It seems on the other hand to have been the object of some suspicion on the part of the Nazis, and though van Severen frequently expressed his admiration for Mussolini, there is no certain evidence that he received financial help from the OVRA.

Since the war the Belgian Government has never made any effort further to elucidate the circumstances of van Severen's arrest. A number of accounts have been published in Flemish by survivors who were eye-witnesses of what they describe as 'Het Bloed-bad van Abbeville'. An elaborate monument has been erected to van Severen and his companion in Abbeville cemetery.

* * *

It would be sacrilegious to describe this new monument to van Severen as a mere book. A human hand, it is true, has written it; humble workmen have printed it, on the purest Flemish paper; it did not fall from the sky in a shower of golden letters, nor emerge from a black lake, clutched by a beautiful hand. It was printed by Vonksteen S.A., Langemark (Belgium) and published by Éditions Oranje, Zulte (Benelux); it was edited by Staf Vermiere, Rijksbaan 22, Zulte-aan Leie (Benelux). The publisher also has an address in

Wilrijk, in the Province of Antwerp (Benelux). There is no price—how could there be? For this is no ordinary book. R. Baes is reverently aware of the audacity of her undertaking in thus rolling away the stone from the entry to the tomb, to reveal the martyred saint, the bullet holes, the embroidered shirt, soiled after ten days' prison wear, the initialled hat, the scented handkerchief. Her intention, she states in the preface, is, whenever possible, to step aside and allow the Master to speak in his own voice, though in the course of the work she frequently intervenes to draw attention to some particular example of goodness, devotion or heroism. The air trembles with reverence, mysticism and organ music, the complicated harmonies of *carillons*; and we move, soft-footed and hushed, through the stained-glass penumbra, in the best fifteenth-century company—both Breughels are there, van Eyck and Memling too, and noble Flemish knights; at any moment, the Angel of the Annunciation will appear, on the arm of her creator, the Maître de Flémalle. The silence is pregnant; the Master is about to speak. And the Word, whether it comes direct from the Master, or through the recollections of the Disciple—and she must have been a very close one, for there are inventories of his shirts, handkerchiefs, socks, toothbrushes and toothpaste—is wrapped in obscurity, reaching us in a language faintly recognizable as French. It is very hard going.

But it is well worth the effort, for, all unconsciously, the author has assembled the most convincing and complete account of the emergence of a Fascist mentality since Sartre's brilliant short story, *L'Enfance d'un chef*. It is all that the historian could desire—as complete a dossier as has ever been produced of the Fascist mind, the Fascist in action, the Fascist meditating at leisure, the Fascist looking at himself in the glass, the Fascist eating and drinking, the Fascist dressing himself, the Fascist in his garden, among the 'humble flowers' and the 'ancient trees', the Fascist setting his jaws in an authoritarian *rictus*, the Fascist gargling to get rid of the taste of a non-Aryan visitor, the Fascist taking his morning exercises for his physical well-being, placing his arms and head in the position of Christ on the Cross, the Fascist taking his evening dose of Pascal, for his spiritual well-being, the Fascist cleaning his teeth, the Fascist expressing his views on women, the Fascist manicuring his hands, the Fascist acknowledging his debt to the writers of the past, the Fascist putting his people in their place, the Fascist beloved of his men, the Fascist on History, the Fascist on Destiny, the Fascist on

Mother, the Fascist on the Blessed Virgin Mary, the Fascist on Ancestral Roots.

* * *

It is of no less interest because the Fascist in question was markedly unsuccessful as a Fascist, quarrelled with most of the other rival Fascists, was quite remarkably muddle-headed—at times one feels almost sorry for him, he is such an utter ass, such a woolly bore—until one remembers that other highly successful Fascists were utter asses and woolly bores.

There are, of course, many ways to Fascism, and many forms of it once one gets there. Briefly, van Severen was a Flemish *maurrassien*—though, of course, without the great literary and polemical talent and culture of Maurras himself. The influence of Maurras was very considerable in Belgium between the wars, especially among the Walloon sections of the exteme right, but van Severen was the most effective exponent of the Frenchman's particular brand of authoritarian nationalism. And, like Maurras, a clerico-Fascist, he was bitterly denounced by the clergy of West Flanders when, in 1934, he split with the VNV.

But Maurras was not the only influence, far from it; like many of the half-educated van Severen was a receptacle for every type of right-wing thought. He had an unerring flair for the obscure, the bombastic, the violent, the decadent, the studied and the empty. It could happen, too, such was the voracity of his attitude, that works of some value, literature of some quality, might be shoved down, almost accidentally, between two helpings of gobbled, half-digested trivia, so that in his make-up he constitutes a living, hiccoughing, panting encyclopedia of right-wing thought and literature for the whole period 1900–1940. It was amazing what he could take, what he could half-assimilate, chew over.

His favourite sustenance, right up to the end, was a sort of *bouillabaisse* of the French authoritarian right, in literature, the arts and philosophy (*sic*); the clerico-Fascists, those who loved the Princes of the Church, the purple of Cardinals, and who treated their parish priests like servants, the Blood-and-Soilers, the Ancestral Influencists, the pseudo-peasants, the Back-to-the-Landers, the Super-Patriots-who-Volunteer-as-Common-Soldiers (but who somehow miss their way to the recruiting office), the Cruelty-to-Animals right (French hispanophils), the Cruelty-to-Girls right (much the same thing), the des Esseintes right, the pseudo-medical right, the Flying Superman right, the economic crackpot right, the *à bas les métèques* right: they have all been sent down, not one is left on the plate. Barrès and Péguy are, predictably, the favourites; he moans and groans over the pseudo-peasant ('Ah! Péguy!') and, on his only visit to Paris, the rue de la Sorbonne and the Invalides ('Ah! Napoléon; le grand néfaste!') are the two points of a meditatively reverent, *Ah! Ah!*-ing pilgrimage. He wants to be like Barrès and join up as a common soldier (unlike Barrès, as well as talking about it, he actually *does* it). But, equally, meditating in his garden, or on a retreat at 'Swiss Cottage'—a villa in Ostend belonging to an aunt—he fancies himself as a Flemish Saint-Exupéry, above it all, alone with sky, sun, stars and Courage, proving himself in hazard (he has at least in common with the French Superman a total confusion of thought, as well as a violent death). He revels in the violence and indignation of poor Bernanos, and communes in the virility and cruelty of Montherlant, a fellow chevalier and a Warrior like himself. His other French masters are Massis, Maritain, Thierry-Maulnier, Bloy, Claudel, Suarès, Bainville, Georges Valois and Alexis Carrel. But he is closest to Drieu—indeed, in the present book, one is constantly reminded of the effete nastiness of 'Gilles': the same clawing cruelty, the pseudo-aristocratic conceit, the sense of caste, the same physical narcissism. Van Severen, like 'Gilles', scents himself with 'Jicky' (by Guerlain), his shirts, of exquisite cotton, are initialled, his gold cuff-links are initialled too, his suits are dark and cut very severely in a semi-military, semi-monachal line (he is, after all, a twentieth-century Loyola). But in his most extravagant daydreams there are also hints of des Esseintes: here is the Leider, seated on heated tiles, being washed and sponged down and dried by semi-naked, coffee-coloured slave boys, who feed him with exotic fruit (this did not get into the programme of the Verdinaso, being reserved only for those admitted into the intimacy of the Crucje van Bourgonje, the Bruges shrine). Like the hero of *À Rebours*, the Flemish knight sleeps on a black, monklike bed in a white, cell-like room; but the sheets are of best Flemish linen, the cell is centrally heated. There is a studied decadence in the gesture of his tapering fingers.

* * *

But, for a man who frequently refers to a mystic Celtic Union between Flanders, Wales, Cornwall and Brittany, who corresponds with the Breton separatists, who, in the words of his Disciple, possess 'une pulpe Celto-germanolatine' (this is going two better than Maurras: van Severen is God, the Son *and* the Holy Ghost), and who in a flash of light reaching him at 'Swiss Cottage' realizes that it is his destiny (or Destiny) to act as a spiritual bridge between Europe and Asia, west and east (inevitably, he makes a beeline for Tagore), the Latinized French are not enough. Van Severen feels a close affinity to Salazar. He dotes on Kipling, considers 'Land of Hope and Glory' the greatest song in the English language, listens, in reverent communion, to the broadcast of the coronation service of George VI, and likes to show off his English to his followers: 'self-control', 'clean' (meaning Fascist), 'unclean' (meaning a politician, a democrat, a *Bruxellois*, a *métèque*, a Freemason, a Protestant), 'I'm not in the mood' (not on the Swiss Cottage wavelength in personal communication with one of his political or moral advisers, his personal Brains Trust—a very cosmopolitan affair, since it includes the Virgin Mary—'There are two people I will not hear ill-spoken of, my Mother and the Virgin Mary'—Saint Ignatius, Saint Teresa of Avila, Aquinas, Joan of Arc, Pascal, Memling, a certain Guillaume de Juliers, from whom he claims descent and who also has a carnal relationship with Flanders, and van Eyck's Holy Lamb of God). He also, when 'in the mood' has communications from Ibsen, Nietzsche and Kierkegaard. No wonder his Jesuit teachers complained of his inattention (the Chronicler adds that he was a lonely, misunderstood boy who shunned the 'cour de recréation').

There are other, more localized, ingredients, especially Streuvels; van Severen began, quite banally, like any other Flemish nationalist. He was influenced too by the Dutch historian, Pieter Geyl, who, in the 1920s, was advocating an historical version of Dietschland. Where he got the idea of the Dietsche Rijk from it would be more difficult to establish; but van Severen, *le médiéval* (as his Disciple calls him—and she adds that he had a medieval face and looked like Memling) may have had it from an ancestor who was present at the Battle of the Spurs. Each brand of Fascism contains its built-in myth—Breton *menhirs*, Great Treks, Ukrainian tridents, Sviatopolk; van Severen reached his by following the meandering course of the Zwijn, the great tidal inlet that had connected Bruges to the sea, that had become silted up and had eventually disappeared, as a result of a series of great storms, in the fifteenth century. It was just the right combination of half-eaten history, pseudo-medievalism, legend and parochialism to produce a West-Flanders Fascism.

* * *

Van Severen is not interesting as a person; he was a bore and a fool, who had probably been messed up early by a doting mother. But he is interesting as a type, as a *cas témoin*. There is something very satifying about his literary enthusiasms and cultural pretensions for, at each question put to him, the answer comes out pat; he never lets one down. He is the archetypal Fascist, in his arrogance, in his belief in an elite, and in his contempt for the common people, for 90 per cent of humanity. It is all there. Here is the adored and adoring mother who, unlike the reassuring *notaire*, takes the little ass seriously, and, instead of seeing that he gets on with his homework, encourages him in bouts of disorganized and random reading. Here is Tia, 'la servante au grand coeur', the loyal Flemish retainer, in humble admiration for the Young Gentleman, for the booted Leider, eager to welcome him to the Ancestral Home, deeply grateful for a visit to her gleaming kitchen: she is suitably rewarded, the Leider, 'effondré', his noble fifteenth-century face drawn with grief, personally attends her funeral with a *dinaso* bodyguard in full get-up.

Here is the young subaltern, adored by his men who realize in their brutish simple way that he is not as others; when he is sent off to a disciplinary camp, after being stripped of his rank, they follow him to the station—he had ordered them not to—weep noisily (in Flemish) on the platform, and run after the train as it pulls out. The Passion has begun: Rouen, the insults, the persecution, the spittle, Walloon spittle too, or that of vulgar *fransquillons* whose French is not as good as his, Parigné-l'Evêque (Sarthe), the first of many Stations of the Cross. It will never let off. There is the Death of Mother. Vile, vulgar bureaucrats, probably from Brussels, have his poplars cut down to make way for a new road: later, he is driven from his house near Bruges; the owner wants it back as he has recently married and has small children. He is uprooted, has to leave the 'humble flowers' and a garden large enough for revolver practice. In his next place, there is no garden at all. 'Swiss Cottage' is sold. The coat of arms of the Dukes of Burgundy, which he hangs over his front door in Bruges, comes crashing down on New Year's Day, 1940; it is an omen. The Flemish clergy spread vile rumours about him, there are suggestions that the boys of his youth brigades wear shorts that are too short (they certainly are very short and very tight-fitting in the photographs). The VNV fail to understand the grandeur of his vision, the significance of the Revelation—the *nieuwe marsch-righting*—of 1934 (though, in May, 1940, their leader intervenes in his favour). Something terrible happens while he is deputy: it is only hinted at, but it seems that while making a speech in the Chamber, he was *laughed* at. Socialists! While in prison in May, 1940, the vile gaoler laces his soup with spittle (it has all happened *before*!).

* * *

Like the Natural Aristocrat he is, he *vouvoie*'s his Mother and expresses his 'hatred of mediocrity'. The Ideal he pursues is 'invisible aux masses', the world is divided between 'les médiocres et l'élite'; he despises democracy, because it appeals to 'les valeurs basses du peuple'. He holds in horror 'disorder and humanitarianism'. Women are an inferior breed, at best a physical reward for the Returning Warrior. Even then, they had better take care to be properly scrubbed and clean, to keep their traps shut, to be respectful but undemonstrative ('j'ai horreur des femmes qui donnent des baisers en public'). In any case, having carnal relations with Flanders, there would probably not be much left for mere women. There was no female branch of the Movement.

He was a Cold Shower Fascist; his voice was commanding and clipped: once he had spoken, one could only salute and execute a smart about-turn. He wore a uniform, not out of any sense of vanity, but because it was 'la carapace de sa pensée'. He was anti-semitic, speaking of 'le juif Benda'. He thought in Capitals: Order, Discipline, Soul, Tradition, History, Mother (but not Father). He thought in *Gothic* capitals. His programmes—in letters three feet high—are repetitive incantations—*Dietschland en Orde*, *Dietsche Rijk*, *Dietsche Rijk*, *Dietsche Rijk*.

He was a very small man—five foot two or thereabouts. But thanks to all the usual paraphernalia of Fascism—platforms decked in black, covered with emblems, lighting, chin up, the dedicated head, the military stance—thanks to a uniform that included a peaked cap the height of those worn by oyster salesmen on the Paris boulevards—he was able to make himself look taut, severe, brooding and fateful. Thanks to the mirror exercises, he had acquired the full range of Fascist expressions; his smile was reserved for Mother, the Virgin and, so she says, breathlessly—the Author. The photographs of the vast meetings of the Verdinaso are pure Fascist: the dark uniforms, boots, belts, legs wide apart, torches, fanatical, staring eyes, the idiot faces, drums and tasselled trumpets, black and yellow flags, the Leider handing a flagged lance to a thirteen-year-old boy, faces gleaming in the light of torches; this is a Fascism as integral as Rex, as the Flemish SS Legions, and as the yearly gatherings at Dixmude.

* * *

He trained and drilled his gunmen to violence, fed them on hate, persuaded them that they represented an elite, that the rest of the world were *untermenschen*. He sought to crush Belgian democracy by force. The sheer inanity of the present book should not make us lose sight of what it is about, what its purpose is. Van Severen was not very successful; for that we must thank the common sense of the countrymen that he so despised. The Antwerp docker, the Borinage miner, the Brussels tram-driver, the *cheminot*, Flemish or Walloon, of the C.F.B., the student from U.L.B. and Liège were *not* impressed; Bruges should be remembered for Achille van Acker, not for this seedy Knight. That he was ultimately shot by the French was largely accidental. At least it deprived him of the opportunity of giving his full measure as a Fascist. R. Baes is attempting to rehabilitate one of the dark figures of prewar Fascism; she is not very successful either; even so, one hopes that this ridiculous book will be widely read outside Belgium, for it would be difficult to find a record, more representative in its range, of the puerility, the emptiness, the idiocy and the arrogance of the Fascist mind.

* * *

Letters followed from MM. Staf van Velthoven and Guido Eeckels (24 November).

8

NOVELS OF 1966

(*g*) GABRIEL FIELDING

Gentlemen in Their Season

MR. FIELDING'S narratives often appear discursive and leisured, but in some ways he is a restless writer. His new novel is a striking change of direction from *The Birthday King*, that impressive journey of the imagination into Nazi Germany, Catholic Jewry, and concentration camps. *Gentlemen in Their Season* is prevailingly ironic, comic, even farcical.

The gentlemen in question are Randall Coles and Bernard Presage, both middle-aged and married to sensible wives, both unable to stop themselves slithering ungraciously into adultery. Neither of them feels happy about it, even while committing it, but the parallelism of their consciences is modified by the book's most central factor: Presage is a Catholic, Coles a humanist. Coles works in the Religious Broadcasting of the B.B.C.; his uncommittedness gives him that impartiality so valued by the corporation. He does some prison-visiting on the side which gratifies his fantasies while appearing ethically respectable. This involves him with Hotchkiss, who has killed his wife's lover and is nearing the end of his term. Hotchkiss asks Coles to see his wife, and thereafter Betty's coarse attractions lure Coles into a series of situations which not only nearly turn out to be fatal but which also powerfully compromise the introverted, fastidious routine built up by himself and his obsessively neat wife Lettice, whose salad days were clearly of the health-giving variety.

(*g*) *Gentlemen in Their Season*. 287 pp. Hutchinson. 30s.
(*h*) *The Jewel in the Crown*. 451 pp. Heinemann. 30s.
(*i*) *The Soldier's Art*. 228 pp. Heinemann. 21s.
(*j*) *Le Vice-Consul*. 212 pp. Paris: Gallimard. 9.50 fr.
(*k*) *The Sabre Squadron*. 239 pp. Anthony Blond. 25s.
(*l*) *In the Absence of Mrs. Petersen*. 223 pp. Collins. 21s.
(*m*) *Excluded from the Cemetery*. 384 pp. Hutchinson. 35s.

The cool, pretentious, fussy integrity of their menage is ironically but uncorrosively presented.

Presage on the other hand, being as he says 'stuck with religion', can contemplate his sin without losing his balance entirely, even though he has to rely on the charity of others to see him through it. The long suffering of his wife, the appeal of his daughter (preoccupied with her versions of Old Testament love stories), the clairvoyant friendship of Emily Minck, a Catholic lutenist of unremitting sprightliness, are all insufficient to stop him taking Hera Foley, when recovered from the miscarriage of her husband's child for a rather checkered weekend at Calais. (Mr. Fielding's other avocation as a doctor may, incidentally, enable him to deal with the physical in a way that is plain and neutral without becoming too clinical; the fleeting appearance of a foetus is odd, but relevant and unworrying.)

Coles and Presage are thus both strangers and brothers. In this way they oddly recall—despite total differences of context—the brothers of *The Birthday King*: one preserving by his egotism a criminal innocence, the other undone by cravings for the divine. The women mostly share a ferocious desire to dominate and preserve; whether they prey or pray, they are devoted to having or holding. Their gifts are equivocal, their bitterness aggressive; they put up with, rather than forgive. It is the figure of Hotchkiss, the man who has actually committed a crime of passion, that puts all this in perspective, though whether this is the perspective of the whole novel is its chief problem: 'Forgiveness doesn't come from people. It's something they use. It's God's.'

The significance of Hotchkiss (also a Catholic) is difficult to assess. When he breaks out of prison, with only two weeks to go, it seems more out of religious quixotry than anything else. When he catches Coles with his wife, he forces the wretched humanist to kneel and say the Lord's Prayer at gunpoint, and then lets him go. He resurrects himself to forgive, and is betrayed. The general tone of religious farce prevents us from taking him too seriously as a Christ-figure—Mr. Fielding does not go in for that kind of portentousness—and yet the novel has odd, unconsummated leanings towards allegory: why, for instance, is the murdered lover called Paul, and his avenging brother Peter? Because between them they engineer Hotchkiss's break-out from the prison of the self into godliness? Both as a person and as an agent Hotchkiss is uneasily managed and difficult to visualize though it must be added that Mr. Fielding presents his working-class characters with a tolerant briskness of manner appropriate to the surgery of a large practice in a mixed area. Mrs. Hotchkiss at any rate does not share her husband's transcendental shading. Outside her apparently joyless though not infrequent sexual encounters she agrees 'there's nothing'; 'religion's all men', she says sulkily. She shares in her dumb way 'the resentment of modern women' noted by Presage.

'As a Catholic one must be accurate', says Emily Minck, and Mr. Fielding takes the obligation seriously. While the whole novel shows a steady focus on the binding nature of Christian marriage as viewed by Catholic doctrine, he is unlike some Catholic writers in that his writing is not so much dogmatic as exploratory. We are spared apologetic priests and stigmata. However, the approach also forbids any setting-up of alternative myths: we are as far from *A Severed Head* as from *The End of the Affair*.

We are left with a certain heartlessness, appropriate enough to comedy anyway (Mr Fielding, on this occasion, being happy to leave compassion and judgment to God), and also with a certain formal instability. There is much more in the book than the 'metaphysical trap' sprung for Coles and yet this seems in some not fully articulated way to be, as it were, the heart of the matter. As a more general study of how in any marriage 'there might be devils and angels moving about just behind the moods and promises' there is not an extended enough display of that accuracy which is said to be incumbent. Mr. Fielding's empathy with his characters, here as elsewhere, gets switched off by some self-preserving thermostat when it gets too warm. The fluent, witty realism of the presentation gives way sporadically to patches of transcendental burlesque; there have been such outcrops of uncoordinated quasi-fantasy in previous novels. *Gentlemen in Their Season* is a highly absorbing demonstration of Mr. Fielding's versatile and unusual talent, but it looks as if he has not yet succeeded in evolving structural procedures that will adequately take the strain of his various levels of awareness.

(*h*) PAUL SCOTT

The Jewel in the Crown

The place is India, the year 1942. Japanese invasion of the country appears to be imminent, the Congress Party are clamouring for power and Gandhi is asking that the British should quit India, leaving the Indians to prove the effectiveness of non-violent resistance to the Japanese. Within this pattern of major events Mr. Scott shows two minor ones, the multiple rape by Indians of an English girl named Daphne Manners in the Bibighar Gardens at Mayapore, and an attack made on Miss Crane, the elderly supervisor of the district's Protestant mission schools, which ends in the death of her Indian companion. Through these incidents Mr. Scott reveals and infers all sorts of aspects of British-Indian relationships. 'There are the action, the people, and the place; all of which are interrelated but in their totality incommunicable in isolation from the moral continuum of human affairs.'

This attempt to grasp the reality of what Britain did in and to India has been devised with subtlety. A shadowy unnamed narrator is piecing together the story of Daphne Manners. He does so through interviews, conversations, letters and journals. The views of the Brigadier in military command of the district are seen in extracts from his unpublished memoirs and these extracts are then sent to the civilian Deputy Commissioner, who comments on them first by letter and then through a tape recording. The 'distancing' effect is enhanced by the fact that much of the story is seen through the mists of twenty-year-old recollection. Sitting in the Mayapore Club, which was once exclusively British, the elderly Mr. Srinivasan, who was 'reared on briefs and files and nurtured on politics', remarks that all bright young Indians now are business men, budding executives concerned with making money. Mr. Srinivasan is out of date:

> Just look at these young faces that surround us. So many of these boys are telling us that we cannot expect to dine out for ever on stories of how we fought and got rid of the British, that some of us never dine out at all, except with each other, like old soldiers mulling over their long ago battles.

The British who remain are of a lower social class than their predecessors, and their snobbery and rudeness are not natural but painfully acquired.

Mr. Scott is extremely successful at hitting off small but real differences of social attitude, particularly on the British side. Of Miss Crane, the mission supervisor who took down the picture of Gandhi because his attitude to the war had so greatly disappointed her, the Indian Lili Chatterjee says: 'She was an old school English liberal in the sense I grew to understand the term. . . . She loved India and all Indians but no particular Indian.' It is because Miss Crane can never treat Indians as people like herself that her companion Mr. Chaudhurie dies, and only after his death is she able to take his hand and ask forgiveness. Brigadier Reid's memoirs are finely kept just this side of caricature, and his point of view is fairly presented. Why should the Indians, for whom the British have done so much, be so 'determined to hinder our efforts to save [India] from invasion at a time when we could least spare the strength'? The Deputy Commissioner makes his comment on such simplicities, and a variety of Indian opinion is represented, although there is no real exponent of Indian nationalism. Sometimes a single incident is seen from two or three different points of view.

What stops this ambitious and serious book from being a major novel? Partly Mr. Scott's reliance on disquisition rather than demonstration, which gives us pages and pages of all too solid discussion about the condition of India past and present. Certain sections of the book are very much too long. The forty-odd pages of Brigadier Reid's memoirs go into detail about the suppression of the riots that took place at the time of Daphne Manner's rape and do so in a way painfully reminiscent of actual military memoirs, and when the Deputy Commissioner's lengthy controversion of some points is added to Reid's memoirs an effect of petty squabbling is all too realistically achieved. The ingenious devices used to avoid a straightforward chronicle of events also slow down the narrative considerably. But the book's real limitation is that the rape of Daphne Manners is given a symbolic importance, in its contrast with the rape of India by the British, that is never justified.

Daphne, a big awkward English girl, falls in love with Hari Kumar, who has been educated at an English public school. Forced to return to India and find a job when his father takes an overdose of sleeping pills and leaves insufficient money even to pay the servants employed at their house in Berkshire, Hari finds himself distrusted by Indians because of his public school accent, and despised by the British because of his colour. The Superintendent of Police, Ronald Merrick, a product of what is not the top but one of the bottom drawers, dislikes Kumar particularly because Daphne has rejected his own proposal of marriage. When Daphne is raped, Merrick immediately arrests Kumar and several other boys who had nothing to do with the affair. There is a strong suggestion that he planted evidence against Kumar. Daphne dies after bearing a child which she believes to be Kumar's.

The weakness of this affair as a central theme for the book is that it seems such a very special case. Few Indians can have found themselves in the position of Kumar, and to make his persecution depend upon the personal feelings of a police officer is particularly unhappy. The rape and its consequences are of such importance to the book's general theme of British-Indian relationships that the scales appear to have been heavily weighted. The balance might have been adjusted if Daphne had fallen in love with an ardent nationalist rather than with a highly anglicized Indian, and if Merrick had been a would-be liberal in the grip of events rather than a compound of sexual and social frustrations. Solidly powerful as a creation of Mayapore and its shifting society, the book is a little disappointing as a study in depth of Anglo-Indian relationships.

(*i*) ANTHONY POWELL

The Soldier's Art

This eighth instalment in *The Music of Time* opens with one of those scenes that Mr. Powell sometimes provides as a key to the meaning of a single volume. Nicholas Jenkins buys an army greatcoat at a theatrical costumier's near Shaftesbury Avenue where the elderly attendant is under the impression that the coat is needed for a new musical comedy. 'I'll bear the show in mind', he says when told that its name is *The War*. 'I'll wish you a good run.' These two or three broadly farcical pages set the tone. 'The War' is a joke, the fiddles, intrigues and plotting for promotion that go on at the Divisional H.Q. where Nicholas, still with only one pip, is assistant to Major Widmerpool, cannot be taken seriously. France has fallen, the blitz is on, but Widmerpool is concerned with tracing the defalcations of a WO 1 named Diplock, pursuing them through the Sergeants' Mess cellar account and the Commuted Ration Allowance. Nests are being feathered, positions are being established, Colonel Hogbourne-Johnson scores off Colonel Pedlar about the number of bottles in a pipe of port. Yet the things that cannot be taken seriously have appalling implications. Nicholas, on leave in London, meets his sister-in-law Priscilla and then her estranged husband Chips Lovell, and later on the same night learns that both have been killed in air raids on different parts of the city. Such symbolism may sound crude, but in fact the light suggestions of the opening pages remain subsequently unemphasized. The rest is the madness of Div. H.Q.

It is upon the military comedy that Mr. Powell concentrates, with such relentlessness that although the locale is apparently Northern Ireland there is no word about the countryside in which the unit is stationed, nor about nearby towns. We are limited deliberately to the Officers' Mess and exercises, the problem of getting rid of Stringham, who turns up as mess waiter, and of removing an unsuitable officer named Bithel from the mobile laundry. Bithel, General Liddament and other characters appeared in the first war-time volume, *The Valley of Bones*, and on leave Nicholas meets a number of old friends from a prewar life that seems immensely distant, but generally he is confined to camp. There are some wonderful comic passages, including an interview between General Liddament and Nicholas which begins with the General's disgust that anybody should find Trollope difficult to read and ends by his saying in a propitiatory manner, 'You've been very patient with us here', but on the whole this is Widmerpool's volume. Imperturbably complacent and self-centred, he emerges clearly in attitude and language as the model efficient bureaucrat, of a kind and class almost unknown before the war. Widmerpool's dismissal of the idea that Nicholas has any special claim on him after he has learnt of his own ascension to the Cabinet Offices is perfectly done. ('Let me point out that there is nothing startlingly brilliant in your own work to make me press for a good appointment for you. . . . No, Nicholas, if you examine your conscience you will find you have very little to grumble at.') It seems more than ever likely that he will get some kind of job in the 1945 Labour Government.

The style of this book marks decisively the break from the involutions of the first sestet. The writing does not lack Mr. Powell's characteristic elegance but the narrative is plain and straightforward, there is very little of the casting back in time that helped to give the earlier volumes their peculiar flavour, and the section dealing with Nicholas's life on leave is closely integrated with the rest of the book. Any English novelist writing about the Second World War in comic terms was bound to work under the shadow of Evelyn Waugh's fine trilogy. It is part of Mr. Powell's triumph that he has been able to handle what is basically much the same material in quite a different way, to make a wholly original work of art.

(*j*) MARGUERITE DURAS

Le Vice-Consul

Marguerite Duras in India turns out to be as cool and elusive as ever, rather like the live fish which at one point in the book is produced from between the breasts of a mad beggar-girl in Calcutta. All that the girl is capable of communicating is the name of the town where it is presumed she was born, and this is a reticence which Marguerite Duras herself often seems to share. In what she writes the present is usually strange because the past is wholly problematical, and her characters are bound less than emphatically to their environment with hoops of gossamer.

Le Vice-Consul starts, as it happens, with a false attempt to create out of the past an alibi for the present. The early sections of the novel form part of another novel that is being written by one of the characters, who is concerned to assume the sufferings of India and to account for the troubling presence of the beggar-girl. Proceeding from the place of her birth in Cambodia he invents for her a destiny, leading her on a ten-year pilgrimage which ends among the dustbins outside white Calcutta's back door. But the destiny is in fact built from the litter of the novelist's own mind, and from bits and pieces of the collective experience of the group of white people among whom he lives. One point that is well made therefore is that we are more private and separate than words will ever easily express.

The theme of separation and of exclusion seems to be at the heart of *Le Vice-Consul.* It is a novel with plenty of railings and fences to keep people apart, some of them physical, others obscurely emotional. The chief presence which comes to disturb the peace of mind of white India is not in fact the beggar-girl, living under the trees with the lepers, but Jean-Marc de H., newly arrived from Lahore, where he had been the French Vice-Consul. What actually happened in Lahore to bring about his dismissal is as shadowy as what once happened elsewhere in India, in the Marabar Caves, but like that other incident, this one needs to be defined by its effects. Something violent has taken place in the emotional life of Jean-Marc de H., a man supposed to be of an unhealthy chastity, and for the Embassy dwellers of Calcutta he now exists by virtue of what he may have just done rather than by virtue of his simple human presence. In him the wayward individual is opposed to the predictable protocolizing group, a confrontation of which Marguerite Duras has always been fond, and one which reflects a very modern awareness of the freedom of behaviour of the solitary particle compared with the determined behaviour of the mass.

His inhibitions weakened by drink at an Embassy reception, Jean-Marc de H. makes one desperate appeal for help; when he is sober he accepts everything that has happened to him or may happen to him, but on this one awkward occasion he shouts aloud his need for acceptance. Only one of those present is emotionally equipped to hear and understand him, Anne-Marie Stretter, the wife of the Ambassador. She understands him far better than most readers ever will, so oblique does Marguerite Duras make the heavily charged conversation between them. It is hard indeed to be sure what is being said or why, but an affinity is shown before the Vice-Consul is finally rejected. He is told that he does not need Anne-Marie Stretter or anyone else, and he is returned to the death cell of the emotions, while the Ambassador's wife is reabsorbed by her group of young lovers and admirers, softened only to the extent of a few tears.

Le Vice-Consul is a very subtle record of this momentary disorder and its final settlement. It is full of the repetition of names in full, the inversions of word order and the portentous simplicities that give an odd, incantatory weight to Marguerite Duras's novels. *Le Vice-Consul* planes intriguingly somewhere between the world and the mind, hardly stable enough to be recognized as any kind of realism and not easy to identify as philosophy.

(*k*) SIMON RAVEN

The Sabre Squadron

A conventional 'good read' like this needs placing, rather than reviewing. Does Simon Raven more nearly resemble Dorothy L. Sayers or Margery Allingham? The former shared his gentlemanly taste for colleges, clubs, cricket and 'the classics'; the latter was perhaps closer to him in her choice of heroes.

Rugby, Oxford and the shires had produced in Guffy Randall at the age of 28 an almost perfect specimen of the young diehard. He was amiable, well-mannered, snobbish to the point of comedy and, in spite of his faults, a rather delightful person.

Published in 1933, *Sweet Danger* precisely anticipates Mr. Raven's tone. Miss Allingham continued with the background of Jonathan Eager-Wright, 'a member of one of England's oldest families', and the sexiness of Dicky Farquharson with 'his head like the back of a shorn lamb'. Mr. Raven has already rivalled these lovelies with, say, the Hon. Nigel Palairet, 'a notable schoolboy racquets player' (Eton, Christ Church, 'the Carbinier Guards'), and Piers Clarence, 'a very gay nineteen with manly cherub looks, reputed to be highly intelligent . . . very lazy, prone to spend money he has not got . . . all in all, you can see he is an attractive character'.

Thus prepared, we are ready to be seduced by the heroes of *The Sabre Squadron*—Major Giles Glastonbury, 'who looked like an overnourished version of Douglas Fairbanks Junior' and Captain Fielding Gray, 'a bright, nervous youth in his mid-twenties who had a girlish but ravaged face and dazzling auburn hair'. In the customary Raven manner, additional background material is supplied in a letter from a gossipy Cambridge don: 'Your new gang seems entirely *comme il faut*. Giles Glastonbury is well worth attention. He's a second cousin of John Dorsetshire's.' When Glastonbury half-kills a Kraut in a sabre duel, an American remarks: 'He had a bad streak. They often do in these old families of yours.' Like the prewar who-dunit writers, Mr. Raven likes his more class-conscious information to be mediated through knowing outsiders, as who might say: 'Well, sir, he wasn't exactly wot I call a gentleman.'

According to his autobiographical study, *The English Gentleman*, Mr. Raven served most of his time in a county infantry regiment; but his impression of post-war life in the cavalry is not too inaccurate. True, the average cavalry officer would scarcely have the nerve (or hypocrisy) to criticize a county infantry regiment for teaching rankers to 'bang and shout'. Nor would he be able, without stammering, to say: 'The oath I have just sworn to you was sworn on what I live by—the honour of an officer'. But then, this desperate attempt to vivify the bookish concept of 'honour' is Mr. Raven's principal concern. There is verisimilitude, at least, in his young officers' eccentric affectations of aristocracy and their patronizing fondness for their men—though he assumes too readily that troopers reciprocate this affection.

The function of the gentlemen in this novel is to protect a British

Jew from bullies. He is a young scholar called Daniel Mond, soft-hearted and left-wing. Working in occupied Germany of the 1950s on the uncompleted papers of a dead mathematician, he discovers a method of disintegrating the universe; naturally he does not wish to disclose this to any political authority, 'the low men, the grinning and the greasy and the cunning'. An Anglo-American anti-communist organization is determined to wrest his secret from him and mounts a series of Ravenian charades of persecution—concentrating on his Jewishness—to frighten him. Rescued by the knightly cavalrymen, Daniel is finally nobbled by the anti-comintern, half-suffocated in a radiation suit (appropriate emblem of hateful modernity), but only brought to the point of suicide-or-surrender by a simple, primitive manipulation of his sense of loyalty; he must betray either his secret or his cavalry friends—to whom he has sworn an oath 'on his honour as a Jew'.

The romantic-reactionary school of novelists has always been perplexed by Jews, increasingly so since the war. Currently the watchword is: 'Treat 'em like gentlemen'. Constantine FitzGibbon's political fantasy, *When the Kissing Had to Stop*, offers a good example. (If he, or Kingsley Amis, had written this novel, we may suspect that the cavalry officers would have been less attractive, the anti-comintern less despicable.) Mr. Raven accepts that a gentlemanly Jew is more equal than other Jews or Goyim—but insists that he needs special protection by upstanding Britons. Thus he leads us back to the world of Richard Cumberland and Charles Reade:

> Young George Fielding had luckily a stout pig-whip in his hand, and by one adroit turn of his muscular wrist he parried a blow that would have stopped the old Jew's eloquence for ever. . . . He held out his hand like the king of all Asia; George gripped it like an Englishman. 'Isaac Levi is your friend', and the expression of the man's whole face and body showed these words carried with them a meaning unknown in good society.

This is from Reade's *It is Never Too Late to Mend*, another anticipation of Mr. Raven's tone—but 110 years old and written by a reformist. (It is dedicated, Raven-wise, to Magdalen College 'by a grateful son of that ancient, learned and most charitable house'.) Generally—in Cumberland, Reade and Mr. Raven—the protected Jew is supposedly to be girlishly tearful, tremendously grateful and rather ugly. Mond, though, is better looking than Mr. Raven's other

Jews (in *The English Gentleman* and *Doctors Wear Scarlet*), both of whom are called Stein, and hideous to boot.

(*l*) NIGEL BALCHIN

In the Absence of Mrs. Petersen

Mr. Balchin's new novel has the Amblerian theme of a cat's-paw prevailed upon to journey to foreign parts. The dupe here, however, is no innocent, but an English writer of Hollywood film scripts whose accidie after his wife's death in an air crash makes him a half-willing victim of the heroine's wiles. The story moves from Beverly Hills to Paris, to Venice, and thence for the dénouement to Yugoslavia, and all is clear and readable, as Mr. Balchin ever is. But perhaps he himself would not count it among those fictions of his where real difficulties are grasped and overcome: the heroine's character has substance and attractiveness, and the crude abstraction inherent in treating life behind the Iron Curtain is resourcefully stepped over, but the essential lightness of the thing is pointed by our sense of how Mr. Ambler himself has come in his post-war novels to do such a *tour de force* with far greater subtlety and power.

In other words, nothing here relieves our disappointment, in general, with Mr. Balchin's career as a novelist over the past twenty years. Of course his work has never competed in the senior league of contemporary fiction. At the core of it is a simplifying cosiness or sentimentality which militates against disturbing us or conveying real truth about the life of its times. The character of the schizophrenic's wife in *Mine Own Executioner* springs to mind: she is just brave, loving and gamin-like to the backbone. Yet her creator rises imaginatively to the demands of his crises: when she has been shot he describes her as no longer looking 'like a child but like a dwarf woman'. It is the action of these early novels that gives them their power to sweep away our objections to such things as conventional characterization and pat rewards and punishments. The shooting in *Mine Own Executioner* is a case in point: that it takes place at the moment the psychiatrist-hero is at an adulterous assignment is worked for with great skill and thus accepted by the reader as completely plausible. And the three strands of *The Small Back*

Room—the love relationship, the investigation of the German booby traps, and power politics among the boffins (and, incidentally, Mr. Balchin's power struggles make Lord Snow's seem woolly)—are woven so perfectly that the story unfolds freshly and absorbingly at repeated readings. This book is a masterpiece of its kind, and if the kind is not awfully profound it can be said that, as with Rachmaninov's Second Piano Concerto, it is a work we can sit through again and again with greater pleasure than we can through very many works nominally more exalted.

One other factor has contributed to Mr. Balchin's falling away since those earlier books (among which must be included *Darkness Falls from the Air*) and that is his less excited relationship with know-how. The technicalities of *The Small Back Room* could scarcely have been better done, and the alienists in *Mine Own Executioner*, though allowing an occasional pang of doubt, are delineated and placed in their individual professional settings with enviable aplomb. It might have been expected that the business background of a later novel, *Sundry Creditors*, would have permitted similar triumphs, for Mr. Balchin is no stranger to that world. However, by then a slackening had already occurred, and the machinery—too crude, really—of the company's constitution at the heart of the book does not stand up to the strains it has to bear. It is symptomatic that the hero's trade in *In the Absence of Mrs. Petersen* is not only script-writing, but script-writing talked about in a way a hundred other novelists never within 2,000 miles of Hollywood could have fudged up.

Without the reflected richness of a specialized background, the nagging tension of personal relationships, another Balchin hallmark, fails to make a proper effect. The notion of the 'games' played by women, so effective in the case of the over-solicitous Susan in *The Small Back Room* and the eager but sexually inhibited Patricia in *Mine Own Executioner*, seems wasted in the present novel, lavished as it is on a heroine whose milieu is a mere contrivance. Besides, the early Balchin heroes were—satisfactorily, to our modern taste—all disabled in some way. Jim Petersen is altogether too successful—too many dollars, too knowing about food and drink and travel, and by no means the slave of his feelings. It seems a pity to be knocking a thoroughly gripping yarn in this way, but it is Mr. Balchin's fault for having formerly convinced us that he is one of a very few English novelists capable of writing about a wide area of English life.

(*m*) PETER MARSHALL

Excluded from the Cemetery

Excluded from the Cemetery has an eye-riveting opening. A woman suddenly expires in an archaic provincial slum. A shabby old man shoves his way through a crowd of scandalized onlookers, apparently embarks on some awful necrophiliac act—and then delivers from the corpse a wailing infant. 'And to the dead woman he said, "Congratulations".' Although nothing in the remaining pages quite lives up to the grotesque brilliance of that start, Mr. Marshall's opening teaser does not cheat because the rest of the book bristles with an excitement and fecundity which make it almost freakish in the bland company of most current British novels.

In one (unsympathetic) light *Excluded from the Cemetery* is a treatise on the Meaning of Life, since the writing is heavily laced with symbolic punning names, microcosmic acts and places, and occasionally over-broad hints that the individual experiences are meant to be generalized and 'stand for' those of whole peoples or civilizations. But this side of Mr. Marshall's aims is best left alone by the reviewer since the strength of his work is not in its concepts but its concreteness, its detail and worth as *story* rather than idea.

The baby born so spectacularly grows into Joseph, adopted child of the local Minister and leader of the strange community, the flavour of which is somewhere between an early puritan sect and a residents' association in the Pinner of today—dogmatism, warmth, and formidably efficient collective self-interest. The boy's unofficial and frowned-on mentor is Uncle (or is it really Father?) Tony, the ad hoc midwife of the opening—a reluctantly licensed fool. When Joseph is apparently framed for the rape of a precocious schoolgirl, Uncle Tony appears at the trial as a kind of accessory. In the second part of the book, the whole of this convincing and moving tale is revealed as the paranoid delusion of the boy, now called Joe, a young man under prolonged treatment in a psychiatric ward. Sessions with an analyst and visits from a girl more or less identifiable as the one he did or did not rape alternate with his own continuing schizoid conflicts, between Joe and 'Mad Joe'. There also goes on the nastier struggle to come to terms with the horrors of the hospital itself. In these pages Mr. Marshall seems committed to a litany, sometimes incoherent and intolerable, on the elusive junction where notions of madness, decency, betrayal, personal freedom and conformist tyrannies all come together. This difficult debate is accompanied by another theme embodying an image which often clarifies the main drift, but sometimes obscures it. Since the patient has a dangerous cataract condition, his physical 'sight' and his 'visions', encroaching blindness and psychotic delusions, are part of a single isolative predicament. His partial release is found through an operation and through the well-intentioned treachery of the girl on whom he comes to depend. In the last section of the book he is Uncle Joey, old, decrepit and living in a version of his mythical childhood village, a place at once more nightmarish but more fully, if more painfully, human.

It would be a disgrace if the maverick quality of Mr. Marshall's talent meant that he was less read than his more ordinary and more acceptable colleagues. The intellectual defects and longueurs are occasionally tiresome but there is more genuine realization, more coming alive of experience here than is to be found in many writers twice his age and reputation.

9
BACK TO THE SOURCES

ONCE HISTORIANS wrote to instruct men in right examples and warn against evil ones. Now wiser in their generation they write to instruct other historians in true methodology and to warn against false ones. Traditionally academic historians have been trained in disciplines derived from textual scholarship. Exact analysis of diplomatic, palaeographic and linguistic evidence and the rigorous editing of texts have been essential for the full understanding of many more sources in medieval than in modern history. To many this seemed to make medieval history the more scholarly discipline. Increasingly historians now feel called upon to be amateur economists, demographers, sociologists and above all statisticians. There are examples to show that such callings can be gainfully pursued, when evidence is almost totally wanting. As historians still have strong prejudices against pure theory, the feeling grows that such demands can be more readily met in modern history which is richer in evidence capable of being analysed statistically. Thus the historian is liable to turn from the sifting of evidence, according to rules related to jurisprudence and philology, to margins of error, communication theory, the insights of social anthropology and the calculation of cycles.

* * *

Though dedicated to new approaches and radical reappraisals, Professor Lawrence Stone remains an old-fashioned individualist who works on sources himself without needing a team of research assistants or graduate students. This is the more remarkable since he has used an astonishing range of sources in public and private custody. Professor Stone's industry and enthusiasm command admiration and, unlike some labourers in archives, his appetite for other sources remains unimpaired. He cites an enviable variety of

---

LAWRENCE STONE: *The Crisis of the Aristocracy, 1558–1641.* 841 pp. Clarendon Press: Oxford University Press. £5 5s.

printed sources both literary and non-literary and uses his knowledge of architecture and iconography. He shows historical imagination and he is anxious not only to instruct, but also to explain. These are important virtues, so perhaps it is churlish to complain that sometimes instruction seems to involve a heightening of language, as if he were addressing a somewhat backward class who would be capable of grasping only the most extreme and emphatic contrasts, or that he is so persuaded by his own insights that he sometimes sweeps away possible objections with debating points rather than considered argument. This is part of a price which may be worth paying for creative originality, that boldness in fruitful error which befits the former pupil of Professor Trevor-Roper.

First Professor Stone's purpose is:

> . . . to describe the total environment of an elite, material and economic, ideological and cultural, educational and moral; and secondly to demonstrate, to explain . . . the course of a crisis in the affairs of this elite that was to have a profound effect upon the evolution of English political institutions. It is therefore at once a static description and a dynamic analysis . . . designed to serve as the prolegomenon to, and an explanation of, political history.

However, he does not concern himself with political history as such and so omits considering the role of the House of Lords. Nevertheless he wishes to explain why

> The Commons emerged as a far more important political assembly than the Lords, and peers were unable to exercise that influence over parliamentary elections which they had wielded under Elizabeth and were to wield again under the Hanoverians . . . the middle of the seventeenth century saw the eclipse of the monarchy . . . of the peerage . . . and of the Anglican Church . . . all this did not last, and by the end of the seventeenth century the peers, like the Anglican clergy and the King, were firmly back in the saddle. But it should be noted that the bit and the curb . . . were now of a different design.

There were three main causes of the breakdown of 1640–42. The first was 'a long-term decline in respect for and obedience to the Monarchy' which began in the last years of Elizabeth and accelerated thereafter. The second was the failure of the established church to be genuinely comprehensive. 'These two factors could not alone have caused the prolonged upheaval of the 1640s if it had not been for a third, the crisis in . . . the aristocracy.' It declined in power, capital resources, in land and prestige. By 1602 its wealth had fallen sharply; although its numbers had doubled and its average income had recovered by 1641, this had been done at the price of breaking old ties of personal allegiance and acquiring the odium of 'association with a corrupt, licentious, and in the end tyrannical Court . . .'. 'The rise of the gentry is to some extent . . . an optical illusion, resulting from the temporary weakness of the aristocracy.'

* * *

The general pattern of Professor Stone's explanation seems to involve either himself in some confusion over definitions or his readers in some uncertainty about his meaning. This arises from tensions caused by his belief that there was both long-term continuity and a decisive short-term crisis. Thus the first page of the book tells us that the period saw 'fundamental changes in politics, society, thought and religion', the fifth that

> the political and social crisis of the seventeenth century has been largely misconceived . . . since it has been interpreted as a product of a changing social structure. In fact relatively little structural change took place in English society between the fourteenth and the nineteenth centuries: what altered was the role of the various social classes within a fairly static framework.

If this is a rather abstract way of saying that peers and parliament are important in both the fourteenth and the nineteenth centuries, no one will dispute it, or the English liking for preserving the names of institutions, however much their functions may change. But to infer a static social structure from this seems to be carrying nominalism to either absurd or uninteresting lengths. However, Professor Stone assures us there were 'seismic shifts in English life' leading to the civil war, one of which was the loss of power, prestige and land by the peerage. This eclipse was only temporary, because of the comparatively open nature of English society and because the main challenge came from men who were members of the land-owning class and shared its general ethos, but also because the aristocracy itself was ultimately able to achieve 'a major readaptation in almost every field of thought and action in order to fit into a rapidly changing environment'. For between 1580 and 1620 lies 'the real watershed between medieval and modern England . . .'; then the British Isles 'were first effectively united', the nonconformist conscience became established, 'political objectives began to be stated in terms of abstract liberty', the exchequer developed 'as the most important administrative department', inflation undermined old methods of estate management. This is only a selection from a page-long list of such propositions, culminating with the transformation of literature by Shakespeare, Sydney, Spenser and Donne and of historical research by Selden and Spelman.

Thus Professor Stone's explanation invokes structural continuity, cultural and psychological transformations, seismic and fundamental changes in environment, all with equal enthusiasm. There is certainly something in it for everyone, especially for those who want to have their total cake and eat it, and for those who find historical explanations the sounder the more factors they attempt to embrace. Professor Stone does not go as far as Mr. Peter Laslett, who asserts that revolutionary reshaping of society was impossible in pre-industrial times, but he uses a definition which drastically restricts the possibilities of structural change. For in this period, although social mobility 'was occurring at an unprecedented rate', class structure was not breaking down or being significantly changed, because of 'the extraordinary stability of class character, resulting from the chameleon-like adaptability of new families'. Only 'a major revolution and the confiscation and redistribution of land and capital' can produce major changes. This appears to be a general proposition, though arising from an English context. In the seventeenth century only the English conquest of Ireland and perhaps the Habsburg reconquest of Bohemia would satisfy this criterion. This is a sociological version of Marxist propositions which at their simplest state that true revolutions must change the distribution of property; as almost everyone in the seventeenth century, except the Diggers and more awkwardly Hobbes, believed that property rights were absolute, only the Diggers were revolutionaries. Such exclusive definitions are not very useful tools for historical analysis.

However, this is not Professor Stone's view; although suspicious of 'the clumsy old Marxist bulldozer', he has happily hitched his wagon to the stars of Freud, Malinowski, Weber and Veblen. Thus, though still convinced that the aristocracy experienced a 'grave financial crisis at the end of the sixteenth century', he no longer believes 'that this was the sole, or even necessarily the prime, cause of their troubles'. This conversion may explain why the reader is given so little analysis of peers' finances based directly on the surviving evidence. This may seem scarcely possible in a volume of 841 pages, replete with thirty-seven statistical appendixes and references to hundreds of financial documents. What is provided is a series of estimates of the total income of the peerage and of their gross rentals, putting each peer into one of eight sub-divisions, without giving individual rentals, for 1559, 1602 and 1641. Professor Stone defines the terms used in these estimates carefully and sensibly, but there is virtually no information about how the estimates themselves were constructed, how much rests on good evidence and how much on interpolation and guesses. In the one instance (the debts of the peerage in 1641) when the full evidence for part of an estimate is given, Professor Stone's reading of it does not inspire confidence. This reluctance to offer detailed evidence is in marked contrast to other parts of the book, where the reader may sometimes feel that every instance and anecdote in Professor Stone's card index has been included. The chapter on the inflation of honours originally had its important findings accommodated quite adequately in an article occupying less than half the space now needed, mainly because of an inflation of instances. Whatever the trend of Professor Stone's recent interests, most historians will look for the meat of his book in its economic investigations and can only regret the thinness of some of the slices.

* * *

Professor Stone believes that social and economic mobility was higher than 'at any time before the nineteenth and twentieth centuries' and that direct evidence of this can be found in the number of transactions recorded in the Close Rolls and in the Feet of Fines for three counties. These roughly doubled between 1560 and 1620, remained just below this level until 1640, and fell sharply after about 1670. The transactions include mortgages, trusts and recoveries as well as sales, but Professor Stone denies that changes in conveyancing practices can have significantly influenced the results, except perhaps at the end of the seventeenth century. Yet in fact we are largely ignorant of conveyancing usages, so it is difficult to see how we can be sure that they do not influence the earlier statistics. Moreover if, as Professor Stone believes, the number of gentry landowners increased substantially, this ought to have produced an increase in the number of settlements and trusts. While it may remain a plausible guess that more land was on the market before 1640 than in the eighteenth century, it does not follow from the figures that 'this mountainous rise and fall must represent a tremendous upheaval in the mobility of land . . .'.

These figures are not essential for Professor Stone's thesis, but those concerning the incomes and manors of the peerage are. As some of the estimates of income derive from the manorial data, these will be considered first. Professor Stone argues that 'a major change in the number of manors held must reflect a real shift in landownership', provided that the comparisons use large numbers of statistically unbiased samples of manors. By calculating standard deviations for two large samples of whole manors taken from the *Valor Ecclesiasticus* and the Close Rolls for 1597–1608, he shows that the dispersion of manor values relative to the mean was much the same in 1535 and 1600 and that the margin of error in a random sample of 400 manors would be about 16 per cent. It is assumed that the dispersion of values in 1641 is much the same as earlier, though it has just been stated that the number of manors with very low values grew in the seventeenth century and they are already numerous in the two samples. The counts of peers' manors include an unknown number of fractions of manors; if this number was appreciable, it might raise the question of how far values derived from samples consisting exclusively of whole manors would be applicable. Professor Stone's estimate of the total manorial holdings of the peerage is subject to a margin of error of 20 per cent, though we are not told why this should be so large or how it was calculated. In 1559 sixty-three families held 3,390 manors, an average of fifty-four each; in 1602 fifty-seven families held 2,220 manors, an average of thirty-nine; in 1641 121 families held 3,080 manors, an average of twenty-five. Thus by 1641 the peerage had almost doubled its numbers, but owned slightly fewer manors than in 1559; the average held by each family had more than halved; the number of families owning forty manors or more fell from thirty-nine to twenty-three. If manors are a measure of wealth, there had been striking changes which had not been reversed by 1641.

* * *

The force of these figures would be considerably weakened if it could be shown either that some sales of manors were in order to consolidate estates in other areas, or that peers tended to sell off their small manors and keep their big ones. Professor Stone denies that consolidation was enough to affect the result, though for once he forbears to offer an estimate of the amount involved. As to the second problem, he gives the mean value of ninety-one manors sold by peers between 1595 and 1610 as £2,180 compared with the mean of the Close Rolls sample of £1,730. These ninety-one represent about a quarter, possibly much less, of the total sold by peers in these years, so it is important to know how adequate a sample this is. Unfortunately, Professor Stone has no space to offer even a distribution table to reassure us. Any information about the distribution by value of peers' manors would be valuable in case their holdings differed from the samples used. On the present showing there is a distinct possibility of this.

A more important point is whether the counts of manors are consistent with the estimates of the peers' income. Professor Stone regards them as less speculative than his estimates of income, and so presumably a better means of measuring wealth. This may seem somewhat surprising in view of the fact that the great majority of the estimates for 1559 and 1641 are apparently founded upon contemporary financial documents. If we divide the total landed income of the peerage in 1559 by the total of manors then held, the average value of a manor is £42·8. The same operation shows little change for 1602 giving £44 at 1559 prices. However, the incomes of one-fifth of the peerage were estimated by an undisclosed process which converted their manorial holdings into income so that the two estimates for 1602 are not really independent ones. Those for 1559 and 1641 are 'virtually independent' and by 1641 the average value of a manor had more than doubled to £93·6 at 1559 prices, an increase of well over four times at nominal prices. Even if adjustments are made to meet the possibility that Professor Stone may have included Irish estates in his landed income for 1641, it would seem that the same number of manors conferred at least twice as much purchasing power in 1641 as in 1559. Now Professor Stone does point out that the mean value of manors 1602–41 rose in real terms and that any fall in the number held 'will tend to exaggerate the fall in real income', but he nowhere hints at a rise on this scale, which is greater than any of the examples of movement of landed income in Appendix XVI.

These confrontations raise serious doubts about whether both sets of figures can be true. Alternatively, if both are true, Professor Stone's account and conclusions will need modification. As things are, when he wants to demonstrate the decline in the peerage's power between 1559 and 1641 he points to the manorial figures, when he wishes to stress the economic recovery of the peerage between 1602 and 1641 he invokes the figures for income. The law of large numbers may persuade us that manors have some meaning as a measure of current value, but if we are also to be persuaded that they are units for the measurement of power and unrealized capital assets, much more evidence will be required.

Professor Stone's estimates of income at his three chosen dates include not only figures for landed income but also for the fruits of office. From the sum of these he deducts interest payments on estimated totals of debt to give totals for net income. These totals are divided by the number of peers to give figures for mean net income. The last stage of the operation is to compare these at 1559 prices; comparing 1559 with 1602, this shows a fall of 26 per cent, and with 1641 a rise of 4 per cent. Although the estimates of landed income are more reliable than the others, they are not a sure basis for comparisons. As we have already seen, the 1602 estimate is based for one-fifth of the families on manorial counts. That for 1641 is based to an unrevealed, but probably considerable, extent on particulars for compounding submitted by the defeated royalists. After quoting five examples where the particulars considerably understated the true income, Professor Stone asserts without further proof that these were exceptional cases. Yet Professor H. J. Habakkuk, who has studied this problem more thoroughly, has arrived at the opposite conclusion. Thus the 1641 estimate is evidently too low by some unknown amount.

The estimates of debts and interest for 1559 and 1602 may seem questionable on very general grounds, but little evidence is provided. For *circa* 1641 the evidence is in Appendix XXII showing that fifty-seven families had debts amounting to £1,500,000 on which interest of £120,000 a year is assumed. This would be over one-fifth of the total landed income of the peerage and approached what Professor Stone considers a dangerously high proportion. £183,538 of the total consists of 'family debts', apparently provision for payment of annuities and portions. Yet it was exceptional for such provision to involve long-term borrowing. The £35,000 attributed to the Petre family was to be raised from lands assigned to trustees, whose responsibilities were reduced by £10,000 by the death of two younger sons in infancy; the first payment had been of £3,000 in 1646. This information is all in the documents cited by Professor Stone. Further evidence shows that no interest had been paid on the £40,000 owed by the first earl of Carlisle in 1663, twenty-seven years after his death, when the creditors agreed to abate a third of their principal.

The £46,000 owed by the second earl of Devonshire had been paid by 1638, mostly by sales of land which ought to affect Professor Stone's estimates of income; the third earl claimed that his mother owed him £50,000.

* * *

Even when dealing with debts left at death Professor Stone seems to find it unnecessary to make any deductions for a man's personal assets or debts owing to him. While it would be unreasonable to insist upon too restrictive a definition of debts *circa* 1641, Professor Stone seems altogether too liberal in including, as he does on several occasions, debts which had been wholly or partially repaid by 1641 and debts which wholly or partially arose from the civil war. A check on thirty out of the fifty-seven items suggests that the total is too great by some £375,000. This alone would suffice to increase the mean net income at 1559 prices by £120 and thus make the increase over 1559 9·5 instead of 4 per cent.

Professor Stone does point out that one factor which made 1602 a financial nadir for the peerage was the failure of Elizabeth to create a sufficient number of new peers, especially after the deaths of Leicester and Warwick. However, it would have helped in measuring the importance of this factor if he had provided estimates for 1597 and 1604. Even in 1597 the income from fruits of office should have been appreciably greater than in 1602. Another factor which affects comparison between 1559 and 1602 is the way in which Professor Stone has constructed his index of 1559 prices.

Here the choice of base is important. The years 1558–62 are used; Professor Stone carefully points out that grain prices were too high in 1557 for it to be used, but he does not point out that the recoinage of 1560 is generally thought to have had a short-term deflationary effect so that his base years may be too low. Such problems can be overcome by using a decennial base, either 1558–69 or 1560–69; compared with 1600–09 these show a rise of 70 per cent instead of Professor Stone's 79. This would produce a fall in mean net income in 1602 of 21 instead of 26 per cent at 1559 prices. The index may still be unnecessarily low in the 1560s since it uses Thorold Rogers's wheat prices which are then appreciably lower than the series collected by Beveridge. Professor Stone has inadvertently chosen a base which exaggerates the increase until 1602, though it does not affect comparisons with 1641.

The comparison with 1641 demands some consideration of the nature of the index used. Professor Stone points out that this was 'compiled by Professor Phelps Brown in order to measure changes in the price of goods—mostly food—consumed by the labouring classes'. He does not claim it is 'an accurate cost-of-living index for the peerage . . . however the degree of error is not large', because aristocratic expenditure on 'marriage portions, cost of living at Court, cost of embassies and other forms of royal service . . . increased faster than the index'. The first of these items is the only one for which a body of evidence covering the whole period is offered.

* * *

But it can also be shown that the rise in marriage portions is exaggerated mainly because Professor Stone has underestimated their size before 1550. Professor Stone elsewhere tells us that embassies had ceased to be a general burden on the peerage by the 1620s and that most peers 'were receiving foodstuffs to the value of between 5 and 10 per cent of their gross cash income from land . . .'. He does not tell us that Professor Phelps Brown has also constructed an index of industrial prices, consisting mainly of building materials, which rose by 50 per cent by 1641 instead of the 119 per cent of the other index. There is at least fragmentary evidence that the price of luxurious textiles, such as velvet, behaved like the industrial index. A compromise figure of 85 per cent would give an increase in mean net income of 22 per cent since 1559.

Thus, even after allowing that the fruits of office may be put too low for 1559, there are several grounds for thinking that Professor Stone seriously underestimates the peerage's real income in 1641 and exaggerates its decline between 1559 and 1602. He has disarmed criticism in advance by proclaiming the conjectural character of his estimates and suggesting that only acidulated antiquaries would reject the attempt to make them. He would have disarmed it more effectively by providing more evidence and by providing alternative estimates to feed our speculations rather than by entitling his own 'the facts of economic change'.

However, Professor Stone thinks it a vulgar error to consider his crisis solely an economic one; it was also social and moral, resulting in the peerage's loss of power. The chapter on power is one of the most original and rewarding and has many illuminating things to say about the part played by personal violence and the ability to command a following in Tudor times. He believes that the peerage's military power and their authority over the gentry declined together and that this process is demonstrated by the decline of peers' armouries. These reached a peak under Elizabeth, declining thereafter, until by 1641 equipment was widely distributed among the propertied classes. If the argument assumes that arms held by commoners were negligible under the Tudors, the musters under Henry VIII disprove this. The unprecedentedly great military efforts of the 1540s involved both peers and greater gentry in direct service or preparations. The crown's demands lessened and changed; especially after the 1580s the habits and expectations of both peers and gentry changed with them. This may have lessened the burdens on the peerage, but no evidence is offered that their relationships with the gentry or their share of private armouries were transformed, except the opinion of Sir Walter Raleigh.

Even when military considerations were more dominant, Professor Stone exaggerates the peers' political domination of the gentry. What we know of fifteenth-century parliaments and elections and the behaviour of indentured retainers and greater gentry does not suggest that they were simply the deferential pawns of magnates, even in times of civil war. If peers were more powerful in the mid-sixteenth century, this needs demonstrating. Professor Stone's preconception about the distribution of power is so strong that it seems to distort his recollection of a significant episode. He twice says that the peers opposed the first draft of the Statute of Uses which made their lands inalienable. Professors T. F. T. Plucknett (the only source cited) and Holdsworth both believed that the peers supported the 1529 bill and that it was the Commons' resistance to what had been agreed by king and peers that wrecked it. If in 1532 the Commons could successfully resist the wishes of the king and lords on an important issue, this undermines Professor Stone's assumption that such an event was unthinkable until the end of the century.

It is a curious feature of this total portrait of a ruling elite that there is little direct description of their activities as rulers or analysis of their political behaviour except as rebels. Professor Stone might profitably have heeded ex-President Nkrumah's favourite slogan; one of his aims was to explain why the peerage lost the electoral influence it had enjoyed under Elizabeth, yet it is doubtful whether this ever happened. He offers some individual instances of loss of patronage after 1614, but such vicissitudes had also happened under

Elizabeth. He continues, 'the final *débâcle* came in 1640 when the high tide of political passion broke the dykes of clientage and temporarily engulfed the ancient traditions of aristocratic control and influence'. Five instances are given, four of which illustrate the unpopularity of the Court rather than the loss of long-standing local influence by the peerage. Wiltshire was one of the most heavily represented counties and the only one which has been fully studied. Aristocratic influence there in the 1620s was as strong as or stronger than at any time under Elizabeth, and was certainly stronger in 1640. A rough, but more general, indication is the number of peers' sons sitting in the Commons: twenty-four in 1584 and 1614, thirty-nine elected to the Long Parliament, forty-one in 1701 and fifty in 1734. By 1640 the peerage had not increased its electoral power in proportion to its increased numbers, but its influence had not been destroyed.

* * *

Whatever the phenomena to be explained, Professor Stone also has a more structural explanation to offer. For most of the period 'the hierarchy of ranks corresponded very roughly to categories of income . . .'; if this were not so 'the system of stratification will sooner or later be discredited and overthrown'; 'social stratification was very rigid indeed' in the seventeenth century. Social mobility into the upper ranks which had been so common around 1600 became 'increasingly difficult by 1640'; 'legal status remained a reasonably close indicator of financial means'. 'The gentry *élite*', of thirty to forty families in 1641, and the titular peerage form a single class; normally the peerage embraced 'about two-thirds of the total families in this economic class'. This is difficult to reconcile with an earlier statement that there were 500 upper gentry families 'similar in attitudes and way of life to the lower reaches of the peerage'; later there is a 'fairly stout barrier' between the peerage and the gentry which suffered 'striking if temporary erosion' under the early Stuarts. This in turn was due to the failure of the peerage to maintain its position of 1559 as a reasonable majority grouping or 'an exclusive club' of the major landowners.

In 1559 to ensure stability there should have been no more than about thirty families of greater landowners outside the peerage, according to the two-thirds rule. In 1436 there were 183 greater gentry with an average income of £208 (over £500 at 1559 prices, when according to Professor Stone the average rental of the twenty-five poorest peers was £640). It is difficult to believe that the numbers of such gentry were fewer in 1559. If there was more than one to each county, this would be too many for the rule; in 1597 Professor Stone reckons there were 280 principal gentry in the country.

* * *

Although Professor Stone's definitions are somewhat confusing, it seems likely that the discrepancies between social and economic ranking which are supposed to be part of the crisis around 1600 were already critically great in 1559. They may have grown greater by 1600, but the extent and significance of this needs to be demonstrated.

Although in Chapter II it is emphasized that there were great discrepancies of wealth within the peerage, it is also stated that their incomes 'tended to bunch about a mean'. This and the use of figures for mean income of the whole peerage lead to certain semantic difficulties. When Professor Stone speaks of the power and prestige of the early Elizabethan peerage, he seems to be identifying it with the magnates; when he speaks of the difficulties of the late Elizabethan peerage, many, but not all, of the illustrations come from poor peers, such as Lord Vaux. We hear of 'the massive fortunes required to maintain the dignity of a baron', or that Elizabethan peers lived 'in semi-royal state surrounded by swarms of attendants'. We may wonder how the nineteen peers with an average gross rental of £736 and the six with an average of £333 in 1559, comprising 39 per cent of the peers, managed to meet these requirements.

If we consider the figures for gross rental more particularly, the most important changes are at the top. In 1602 the average rentals of the bottom 29 peers had slightly improved at 1559 prices. The intermediate levels showed little change, but the average of the four highest at 1559 prices (£3,500) had fallen compared with the then five highest (£4,900). Comparing 1559 with 1641, there were two peers with rentals over £4,999 (average £5,750) and in 1641 ten with over £10,400 (average £13,500). This may exaggerate, since, if we take the five highest in 1559, their average was £4,900, while above a comparable level in 1641 there were ten averaging £12,900; the total rental of the group had increased about 2·3 times at 1559 prices. The number of the poorest peers also increased disproportionately from six to 22. If the greatest changes were at the top, to think too much in terms of average incomes of the whole peerage may mislead. Where numbers were so small and on heights where the winds of favour and political change blew so strongly, there had been considerable fluctuations since at least the thirteenth century. Tudor infertility had prevented recruitment of magnates by the endowment of royal cadets. The culmination came with Elizabeth's reluctance to create peers and failure to replace her favourites, while ensuring that Leicester left no legitimate son. Even if Professor Stone's estimates for 1602 can be accepted, is such an all-embracing crisis necessary to explain the situation?

There are a number of other sweeping statements about aristocratic marriages, the management of estates, social status and other matters which are either not supported by a careful examination of Professor Stone's evidence, or are contradicted by it, or by other evidence. These arresting conclusions and beguiling and often unfathomable statistics are what will be repeated. They are already circulating in paperback anthologies, divorced from the complexities and contradictions which Professor Stone's sometimes repetitious analysis provides here. For this is a book which anyone seriously concerned with Tudor and Stuart history must read and ponder. It cannot fail to stimulate thought and to introduce even the most learned and sophisticated readers to new perspectives and new sources. The accounts of the varied corruptions of the Jacobean court, the description of the peers' business activities and the suggestions about the changing patterns of family life are all particularly rewarding.

* * *

The Clarendon Press has not helped scholarship by producing footnotes, often containing a dozen references each and sometimes several times more, referring back to as much as a page of text. To discover the source for any particular statement often involves much laborious counting, sometimes without any sure result. Unpublished documents are normally only given call numbers so that the character of the source remains concealed, unless the reader has prior knowledge.

The needs of scholarship are suspect and unfashionable in today's academic powerhouses. They consume time and may not attract benefactions. Scholarship may pursue truth and aspire to certainty, but seldom achieves either. Like science it must be content with probabilities, yet scholars are usually less content with them than scientists are. To attain even probabilities, hypotheses, guesses, inspiration and imagination cannot be despised. But they should be controlled and the reader must be told precisely how much is based on evidence and how much on conjecture, however plausible. Scholars should welcome statistics, but they must explain fully how estimates and series are constructed and the nature of their limitations as evidence. All this is tedious and may be abused as a means of evading the duty of attempting meaningful conclusions, however provisional. But such duties are not discharged by calculating standard deviations and calling in a professional statistician as adviser.

* * *

Sir,—The numbers game being played by your reviewer (April 7) would be easier to follow if he would get his figures right in the first place, if he took account of my repeated warnings of the roughness of the estimates he is questioning, and if he made up his mind what he wants to prove. I cannot accept all the calculations he deduces from my book, and I have no difficulty in understanding how total income from land, urban rents, business and Ireland could have risen by a factor of 4 between 1558 and 1641, relative to manors held. My modest conclusion (p. 144) was that 'most noblemen must have been quite comfortably off on the eve of the Civil War'. Columns of the review were devoted to indicating that they were *better* off than I suggested. But this particular line of argument, if valid, would show that they were *worse* off. Which does the reviewer want to prove? Or is he merely insinuating that there *must* be something fishy about my methods of counting manors—methods on which, it is interesting to note, he avoids serious comment, except a parting sneer about 'calculating standard deviations and calling in a professional statistician as adviser'. The problem of mean manorial values in 1641 admittedly needs cleaning up. I scanned two miles of Close Rolls to establish values for 1602, and then got tired. Would your reviewer care to demonstrate his devotion to scholarship by doing the same chore for 1641?

LAWRENCE STONE.

Department of History, Princeton University,
Princeton, New Jersey 08540.

***Our reviewer writes:—If Professor Stone chooses to express himself so civilly about an arithmetical error which was in his favour, did not seriously affect the argument and which he had not detected, that is his concern. However, it is of more general concern that after declaring in his introduction that his statistics are '. . . the bony skeleton of this book

. . . as necessary as the bone structure to a vertebrate . . .', he now dismisses any attempt at assessing the consistency and comparability of his estimates for the movements of the manorial holdings, landed income and rents as playing a 'numbers game'. The rougher the estimates, the more important it is to tell readers how exactly they were made and to provide sufficient detail to enable others not merely to check their consistency, but to use them for other purposes, instead of continually repeating that they are rough. Rather than let anyone else join in what is now called a game, Professor Stone shuts his statistical skeleton in an opaque cupboard of his own making. He should not complain if others hear it rattling.

In my review I did suggest reasons for thinking that his estimates of net and gross income in 1641 might be too low. If this were so, it would of course increase the discrepancy between the estimates of manors and those of income and rent, already present in Professor Stone's figures. The issue is not whether most peers were 'comfortably off' in 1641. For if the mean real income of the peerage in 1641 was underestimated so that it was appreciably higher than in 1559, this, according to Professor Stone's own method of argument, would call in question his conclusion that 'their position both among the land-owning classes and in society was much inferior to what it had been . . .' (p. 162, cf. p. 748).

The comparison between manors and income in 1641 is a crucial test, because then, unlike 1602, the estimates are said to be 'virtually independent'. Thus Professor Stone's failure to carry his own statistical methods to a proper conclusion was the more unfortunate and his present expectation that his reviewers should do his work for him the more unreasonable.

IO

THE NOBLE KNIGHT

PRINZ EUGEN IN WAR AND PEACE

On August 17, 1717, at Belgrade, an Imperial army under the command of Prince Eugene of Savoy decisively defeated an Ottoman army commanded by the Grand Vizier Chalil Pasha. After the battle one of Eugene's soldiers—his name is unknown—wrote a narrative poem realistically describing the fierce hand-to-hand fighting in which Eugene, 'though a General and Field Marshal', 'fought like a lion' and showed himself a modern exemplar of 'the noble knight' ('der edle Ritter') of the minnesinger's lays. His verses set to the stirring music of a traditional Bavarian folk-dance became widely known and sung throughout the Holy Roman Empire. As the 'Prinz Eugen Lied' they made Eugene a legendary hero.

* * *

Twenty years before this song was written Eugene was the most famous commander in Europe whose victories over the Turks and over the French afford convincing proof of his military genius: at Zenta (September 11, 1697), Peterwardein (August 5, 1716) and Belgrade (August 17, 1717) over the Turks; over the French in Italy at Chiari (September 1, 1701), Luzzara (August 16, 1702), Cassano (August 16, 1705), Turin (September 7, 1706) and in the Low Countries with Marlborough at Oudenarde (July 11, 1708) and Malplaquet (September 11, 1709); and perhaps above all the others his and Marlborough's great victory at Blenheim on August 13, 1704. But Belgrade was the summit of Eugene's military achievement as it was also its end. A former comrade-in-arms, the Swedish General Count Sparre, wrote to congratulate him on this victory and told him that whenever he was asked about him he always replied:

Max Braubach: *Prinz Eugen von Savoyen*. Band I: *Aufstieg*. 473 pp. DM. 30. Band II: *Der Feldherr*. 500 pp. DM. 35. Band III: *Zum Gipfel des Ruhmes*. 464 pp. DM. 33. Band IV: *Der Staatsmann*. 497 pp. DM. 36. Band V: *Mensch und Schicksal*. 576 pp. DM. 44. Munich: R. Oldenbourg Verlag. DM. 165 the set.

I know the workman and he knows his job. Believe me—he will watch for the right moment in conformity with the rules of war in which to strike a decisive blow at the enemy. Now—thanks be to God!—he has finally done so and by the stroke of this mighty hammer everyone is freed from anxiety and feels secure from an impending disaster which would have been fatal.

Christendom owes Eugene the tribute of lasting remembrance for his liberation of central and western Europe from the Islamic menace.

The impression Eugene made upon his contemporaries of a man of extraordinary personality was so indelible that it persisted into the nineteenth century to inspire Grillparzer to poetical admiration and even into the present century to prompt Hugo von Hofmannsthal to write a perceptive characterization of Eugene in whom he found wisdom excelling all his other qualities. A wisdom shown by the fact that Eugene regarded his campaigns and victories not as opportunities for self-glorification but as means to the fulfilment of political aims in the spirit of Clausewitz's celebrated saying that war is nothing more than politics pursued by other means. Yet Eugene had long to wait for a biographer worthy of a subject so formidable and enigmatic. A century and a quarter after Eugene's death on April 21, 1736, Alfred Arneth wrote the first authoritative biography, described by Professor Braubach as 'a wonderful achievement'. Arneth's three volumes remained without a rival for a century but have now been largely superseded by Professor Braubach's massively informative and scholarly but immensely readable life of Eugene. It will undoubtedly take its place beside the great historical biographies.

* * *

Professor Braubach as a former Hussar became early in life interested in the personality and career of the young Colonel of Dragoons who lived to become the most famous soldier in Europe, and he has devoted many years to the study of Eugene's multifarious activities by research in national and private archives throughout Europe—France, Switzerland, Holland, Spain, England, Italy, Germany and, most important of all, Austria—as well as by reading the many books listed in his valuable bibliography. Despite the paucity of information coming from Eugene himself about his thoughts and intentions, hopes, fears and ambitions in comparison with the overwhelming documentation for his career, Professor Braubach has nevertheless been more successful than was Arneth in restoring the spectral figure of Eugene to life as a man of flesh and blood with human faults as well as virtues. He has also succeeded in making the secret and involved politics of Eugene's day understandable and—what is infinitely more difficult of achievement—engrossingly interesting. Eugene is chiefly remembered today as a brilliant strategist and commander whose military career spanned thirty-four years (1683–1717) of nearly continuous fighting in which he was wounded no fewer than ten times. Hence Professor Braubach fills the first three of his five volumes with an admirably clear narrative free from impeding minutiae of that career after giving in his first chapter an account of Eugene's family antecedents and upbringing and explaining the reason that compelled him in 1683 to flee from his native France to seek service in the Emperor Leopold's army as a volunteer.

* * *

Eugene of Savoy was born in the Hôtel de Soissons in Paris on October 18, 1663, as the fifth son of Eugene Moritz, Comte de Soissons, and Olympia Mancini, who was Cardinal Mazarin's niece. His father was a distinguished soldier whose sudden death at the age of thirty-eight in 1673 cut short what promised to be an exceptionally brilliant military career and deprived his son of a mentor whose example he was to emulate and surpass in later life. From his father, Eugene inherited his love of soldiering, military ability and personal bravery. His inheritance from his mother is more difficult to estimate. Professor Braubach draws a revealing pen-portrait of this woman who though not the most beautiful of the five Mancini sisters—the 'Mazarinetti'—was the cleverest and the most ambitious. Witty and unguarded in her conversation, dissolute and recklessly extravagant, dangerous to her rivals yet her own worst enemy, Olympia was a gambler who played for high stakes in politics as at the card-table. Her magnificent eyes look out from her portrait in the Prince de Ligne's possession with an intent and calculating gaze, concealing the thoughts passing through her mind. Eugene inherited her fine eyes with the veiled look which vanished only when his interest was aroused, and then they sparkled with intelligence. Otherwise Olympia passed on nothing of her beauty to her famous son, who was portrayed by Liselette, Duchess of Orleans, in a letter written in April, 1708, to the Electress Sophie of Hanover as having a short upturned nose, rather long chin and such a short upper lip that his mouth is always open a little to show two broad yet white teeth; he is not tall, small-waisted and when he was here in my time had smooth black hair.

Her memory of the child whom she used to tease in Paris was of 'a dirty and debauched scamp whose conduct offered no hopes for his future'. She openly accused him of homosexuality, which was widespread among the aristocratic youths of his day; and indeed when his neglect by his mother and his upbringing among the servants of the Hôtel de Soissons is taken into account, the marvel is not that he was immoral but rather that he grew up to be a man famed for his sense of honour and his irreproachable conduct. Professor Braubach considers that an unknown writer in 1718 fairly explained the development of Eugene's character in these words:

C'est en passant par tous les vices imaginables qu'il est parvenu à se donner le caractère d'un honnête homme; ainsi il est plus honnête homme qu'un autre qui ne l'est que par tempérament, puisqu'il l'est par connaissance de cause.

The year 1680 opened disastrously for Olympia with the signature by her former lover Louis XIV of an order for her arrest on charges of being implicated in the deaths of members of Parisian society from poisoning. Louis sent her brother-in-law the Duc de Bouillon to her on January 24 to give her the choice between leaving the country immediately or going to the Bastille. Olympia chose flight and by the following morning was on her way to Brussels into an exile from which Louis XIV implacably refused to let her return. Eugene was left behind in the Hôtel de Soissons in charge of his redoubtable paternal grandmother, Marie de Bourbon, Princess de Carignan, and only saw his mother again briefly on two occasions before her death in Brussels in 1708 at the age of sixty-eight. It is not known what effect his mother's disgrace had upon her not yet seventeen-year-old son, but it seems reasonable to suppose that if he believed her to be innocent it aroused in him that fierce personal enmity towards Louis XIV that inspired him through the War of the Spanish Succession.

* * *

Eugene had at first been destined for an ecclesiastical career and had received the tonsure from the Papal Nuncio in Turin in 1678 with the title Abbé de Savoye and the promise from the Duchess-Regent of Savoy of benefices to come. Eugene had other ideas about his future and, soon after his mother's flight, he threw away his clerical garb and petitioned Louis XIV to give him a commission in the French Army—a request that met with scornful refusal. The French Army being thus closed to him, Eugene resolved to seek his fortune elsewhere, and in 1683 fled from France to Austria, where he found the Emperor Leopold I at Linz and Vienna besieged by an Ottoman Army. His petition to serve with the Imperial Army was granted by Leopold I and shortly afterwards he received his baptism of fire in the battle that ended in the defeat of the Turks and the relief of Vienna. His reward for his gallantry was the colonelcy of a regiment of dragoons known thereafter as the Prince of Savoy Dragoons, which won glory on many battlefields up to the end of the First World War, when it disappeared with the Habsburg Monarchy which it had served for more than two centuries. At this moment in Eugene's life Professor Braubach begins the story of his military career.

The author has been mindful of Frederick the Great's admonitory words:

> Whoever studies the campaigns of Prince Eugene must not be content merely to fill his memory with military facts. He must instead seek to grasp the broad principles and to think in that way.

Military historians reading these volumes will find little to criticize and will agree with Frederick the Great's opinion that what specially characterized Eugene above other contemporary generals was that he united keen strategical insight to a superior ability, not only to recognize and make full use of the opportunities offered to him, but also to make good the mistakes committed by the greatest generals. Two years before his death Eugene in the summer of 1734 gave the young Frederick the Great some advice on the art and conduct of war:

> When you are making plans for a campaign always think in large terms, envisage them to the utmost possible limits since one never wholly fulfils them, turn over in your mind unceasingly the work you have in hand, your military actions and those of the generals who have shown themselves capable. This thinking over things is the sole means of acquiring that mental dexterity which apprehends everything and recognizes what is of advantage in the particular circumstances.

As in every great commander so in Eugene—Professor Braubach

observes—'something was at work which did not depend upon thought and reflection and therefore could not be comprised in theories or rules'. Nevertheless he attempts a description of this 'something' which serves to convey the essential quality of Eugene's generalship:

It was the observant look, the lightning reaction to every change in the situation no matter how unexpected, the assurance with which new orders were given that under certain circumstances reversed previous dispositions. It was also the fearless personal intervention in the fighting which filled his soldiers with unhesitating trust in him, carried them on to unexpected feats of arms and notwithstanding all the sacrifices and sufferings demanded of them aroused in them that same emotion which had been given unforgettable expression in the song about Prince Eugene the noble knight.

* * *

Promotion in the seventeenth and eighteenth centuries was rapid, and within a decade of his arrival in Austria in 1683 Eugene had risen to be a Field Marshal in command of an army in Italy fighting against the French. The War of the Spanish Succession gave him the opportunity of displaying his military genius, and he made brilliant use of it. It also, like other wars, gave rise to acrimonious controversy in which Eugene was involved over war aims and the conduct of campaigns of which the echoes may be heard in these pages as in those of Churchill's biography of Marlborough. Eugene was more fortunate than Marlborough in not being dependent upon a parliament for financial support for his campaigns and moreover, as President of the War Council in Vienna from 1703, and from 1709 as a member of the small Secret Council presided over by the Emperor which determined policy, he gradually came to unite the political and military direction of the war in his own hands.

Professor Braubach has not only accompanied Eugene throughout his campaigns in these three volumes but has also observed his gradual evolution into a statesman through his concomitant diplomatic negotiations with Italian states (most notably with Savoy of which his kinsman Victor Amadeus II was the reigning Duke); his political discussions with German Electoral Princes, and in 1708 with the Grand Pensionary of Holland, Anton Heinsius; his mission in January–March, 1712, to London where he failed to persuade Harley and Bolingbroke to resuscitate the Grand Alliance; his brilliantly conducted negotiations in February–March, 1714, at

Rastadt with Marshal the Duc de Villars which resulted in peace between France and the Holy Roman Empire and out of which Eugene emerged as renowned and formidable a figure on the international political scene as he already was on the battlefields of Europe; and, finally, four years later, his conclusion on July 21, 1718, as victor at Belgrade of the Treaty of Passarowitz with the Sublime Porte which ended hostilities between the Holy Roman and Ottoman Empires. These Treaties of Rastadt and Passarowitz were the twin summits of Eugene's diplomatic achievement. Professor Braubach in his fourth volume, sub-titled 'The Statesman', follows the conduct and makes clear the aims of Eugene's foreign and domestic policy in the years 1717–1732 in which he was in all but name the 'Prime Minister of Austria', as Frederick the Great styled him. He also makes an interesting and critical study of Eugene's administration of occupied foreign territories, first from 1706 to 1716 as Governor-General of the Stato di Milano and then from 1716 to 1724 as General-Statthalter of the Netherlands, in both of which offices he failed to achieve the success that had been his on the battlefield.

Absenteeism was the fundamental reason for this lack of success. After 1707 Eugene was never again in Milan and during the eight years in which he was Statthalter he did not once visit Belgium. If the continued prosecution of the war furnished him with a valid reason for not returning to Milan his oft-repeated excuse for not visiting the Netherlands was tenuous—'the importance of political affairs' was the reason he invariably alleged for remaining in Vienna. Contemporary observers blamed his intimate friend, Countess Eleonore Batthŷany, who feared lest in his absence she might lose her political influence and power over appointments. It is also not impossible that Eugene may have feared for his own political power. Moreover, Eugene was guilty of a serious error of judgment in appointing as his deputy in Brussels an Italian—Marchese de Prié—who soon showed he was insufficiently strong-willed to govern a country resentful and weary of foreign domination, religiously divided by Jansenism, politically torn and embroiled by an aristocratic Fronde. Eugene was alive to his administration's weaknesses. 'I cannot too often tell you', he wrote to de Prié in March, 1721, 'how sensitive I am to complaints of *non administranda justitia* since these touch upon the honour and conscience of those in power.' His well-intentioned efforts to improve Belgium's economic situation, reform its legal system, promote education and religious toleration deserve recognition, as does the political farsightedness shown in his disapproval of Charles VI's encouragement of the Ostende Company, which he foresaw would lead to conflicts with the maritime powers. There is certainly no reason to doubt the truth of what he said to a Belgian friend, Comte Baillet, in 1724, after he had resigned from the Statthaltership:

> I have always had before my eyes in all my actions only what was best for the administration and for the assurance to everyone of his proper rights and indeed for the good of the country which His Majesty entrusted to me.

But good intentions were no substitute for efficient administration by Eugene in person.

* * *

What light does Eugene's administrative work in Austria, Italy and the Netherlands throw upon his political beliefs? Professor Braubach says that these were restricted in practice to the maintenance of law and order within a still largely feudal ordering of society and to the economic development of the country for the benefit both of its inhabitants and their ruler. And he goes on to say:

> In this as in all his political opinions he followed in the path of an absolutism progressing from fiscalism to the fulfilment of progressive demands and the realization of social well-being. An absolutism moreover which subordinated the clergy and the nobility as estates of the realm and imposed burdens upon them without at the same time taking from them their rights and pretensions or their advisory functions.

Moreover, Eugene held that the monarch in the exercise of his sovereign power of decision and command must not be allowed to become the object of public criticism or restraint. He poured contempt on the press in a letter in 1732 to Duke Ferdinand Albrecht of Brunswick-Bevern because it was well known 'how little attention such newspapers deserve since they are almost invariably filled with untruths'. Eugene was neither a political philosopher nor a political reformer. He was content to let the day-to-day tasks of government be carried out by men whom he probably regarded as far more competent at them than himself—the civil servants. He showed little interest in, and certainly no desire to solve, great internal political problems such as the bringing together of the disparate Habsburg dominions in a unified political entity. Moreover, Professor Braubach declares that it is:

> an anachronism and at the same time a complete misunderstanding of the nature and work of this true child of Fortune when it is sought to ascribe to him German nationalist feelings and aims . . . for even as he remained in cultural matters a product of Romance civilization so his attachment to Germany and the Germans was solely determined by his recognition of the fact that they supplied the foundations and the constructive forces for the Habsburg Monarchy and for Austria.

And he adds: 'The shaping of Austria and Europe in accordance with the notions of the *ratio status* and of the *aequilibrium* was Prince Eugene's aim.'

International politics and Austria's relations with other European Powers were Eugene's greatest interest and with the years his almost exclusive preoccupation. Professor Braubach believes that if Eugene had died not in 1736 but in 1732 he would have gone down in history 'not only as one of the greatest soldiers but also as one of the most successful statesmen'. It is a bold claim that invites challenges. But Professor Braubach with his vast knowledge substantiates it in his summary review of Eugene's achievements as a statesman:

> He was a most resourceful diplomatist who knew how to handle skilfully, make use of and combat the other players in the game of European politics. His glance surveyed and penetrated into the heart of great political combinations and he clearly realized that politics is the art of the possible. As in his military campaigns so in his diplomatic moves he displayed courage and audacity but also caution and moderation. He never even after his greatest triumphs dreamt of the extension of the Empire's sphere of influence to Constantinople or of the establishment of Austrian hegemony in Europe; nor did such phantasies ever influence his diplomacy. . . . The summits of his statesmanship were the peace treaties of Rastadt and Passarowitz and then once more in the years 1725 to 1732 when his secret direction of the Empire's diplomacy in which he made use of the subterranean warfare, deceit and cunning he had employed as a commander-in-chief brought him astonishing successes. As opposed to the Western Powers, who had allied themselves in a reversal of the fronts in the War of the Spanish Succession, and who appeared to be striving for the 'Arbitrium' over Europe, the Prince had allied Austria's strength to that of the rising States in the North and East—Prussia and Russia—to restore the balance of power and then finally had sought by an understanding with England to break up the Western coalition and to assure peace by this restoration of the 'Old System'. The Empire seems then to have taken on a role similar to that which it was to fill a century later under Metternich.

The test of statesmanship must be the duration of its achievements. If this be accepted as the criterion Eugene's place in the hierarchy of European statesmen becomes difficult to determine, since Professor Braubach admits that political and military reverses for Austria followed in the wake of his diplomatic successes. Nevertheless Professor Braubach also says with truth that what Eugene began in attempting to establish a European state system based on a balance of power was subsequently continued by Maria Theresa, Kaunitz and Metternich as well as by Frederick the Great and Bismarck.

* * *

A final question calls for an answer. What manner of man was Eugene of Savoy, whom his close friend and admirer the Prince Bishop of Würzburg, Count von Schönborn, in his letters to him addressed as 'sire des honnêtes gens' and Jean Baptiste Rousseau called the 'philosophe guerrier'? The fifth and final volume, subtitled 'The Man and his Destiny', contains Professor Braubach's reply to this question in the form of a full-length portrait of Eugene set against the background of his palaces in and outside Vienna and at Ráckeve on an island in the Danube near Budapest; his great library now housed in the Austrian National Library; his priceless collection of engravings, drawings, miniatures and illuminated manuscripts now in the Albertina in Vienna; his menagerie, aviary and zoological garden; his orangery and, dearest to his heart, the lovely gardens where he pursued his favourite hobby of what he called 'pleasurable gardening'. He never married, but in these surroundings he entertained his friends and acquaintances—Leibniz, Rousseau, Lady Mary Wortley Montagu, Cardinal Passionei, Montesquieu among others—though the circle of his intimates was very small. Rousseau wished to write Eugene's biography, from which he was only dissuaded by Eugene's warning that history is much more dangerous to write than poetry. Of this brilliant and intellectually stimulating background to Eugene's life Professor Braubach draws a realistic picture with an informed pen, and never more so than in describing the architectural marvel that is the Belvedere in Vienna. In its superbly chosen and designed setting this forms an unsurpassed memorial to the penniless French émigré who not only became one of the greatest soldiers in history but also a statesman who restored to Austria her former renown and her rightful place in the councils of Europe.

Eighty and more portraits embellish these finely printed and attractively bound volumes, forming a portrait gallery of Eugene and his English, French, Italian, German and Austrian contemporaries. Among them is a pencil sketch dated 1706 by an unknown artist of Eugene's head at the age of forty-three, which stands out from his other portraits by its striking revelation of character. The narrow, finely shaped head with the thin nose and arching nostrils like those of a thoroughbred horse, the superciliously curving eyebrows, the quizzically penetrating glance of the fine eyes alight with intelligence, the pointed and faintly cleft chin betokening resolution and will power; and, perhaps most noticeable of all, the slightly upturned, disdainful poise suggestive of his inborn aristocratic hauteur and reserve—these traits considered together go far to explain why the 'dirty and debauched scamp' in the Hôtel de Soissons could discipline himself to become the 'noble knight' of the 'Prinz Eugen Lied', the kind of man of whom he himself once wrote: 'Les jalousies ne doivent faire aucune peine à un homme d'honneur, et il est au-dessus de tout ce que l'envie fait dire et marche son chemin.'

II

ROSA LUXEMBURG

THE REALITIES OF REVOLUTION

ROSA LUXEMBURG is a proper subject for a full-length biography. In the 1890s she was a key figure in the development of Polish socialism; for twenty years before her assassination in January, 1919, she was a focus of every issue and every controversy in the ranks of German Social-Democracy; she consorted on equal terms with Lenin on the platform of the Second International; she wrote one of the very few (half-a-dozen at most) critiques of Marxist economic doctrine which still have to be taken into account; hers was the most eloquent and influential voice raised from the Left in Germany against the First World War; she played a leading, though ultimately ineffectual, role in the founding of the German Communist Party; and her murder by military thugs, with the tacit encouragement or complicity of higher authorities, was symbolical not only of the defeat of the German revolutionary movement but also of the forces which were to gain absolute control in Germany fourteen years later.

* * *

Mr. Nettl's two volumes are the first thorough and scholarly attempt to do justice to this amazing and dramatic career. He is perhaps a little hard on his one serious predecessor, Paul Frölich, who was a personal friend of Rosa's and produced a sympathetic and knowledgeable, though selective, biography a quarter of a century ago. But Frölich, as a former communist, had his commitments and his prejudices; and, above all, he did not have access to many of the sources now available to Mr. Nettl. No one biographer can indeed possess all the qualifications. Mr. Nettl's strength, apart from his industry and devotion, is a wide understanding of the German political scene and of the German Left; and this was the main forum

---

J. P. NETTL: *Rosa Luxemburg*. Vol. I, 450 pp. Vol. II, 451–984 pp. Oxford University Press. £6 6s. the set.

for Rosa Luxemburg's activities. He is evidently less at home in Polish affairs, and seems to have relied on translation for Polish material; and his relatively few references to the Russian scene betray no more than a cursory acquaintance.

In Poland Rosa's importance consisted in her role in splitting the Polish socialist movement between Pilsudski's strongly nationalistic party (the P.P.S.) and the internationalist S.D.K.P., which rejected nationalism as irrelevant to socialism and refused to regard Polish independence as a goal of the slightest interest to sincere and consistent socialists. Resistance to nationalism (and later to Lenin's endorsement of the slogan of national self-determination) was one of the guiding threads in Rosa's career. Her university thesis had been concerned with the industrialization of Poland, and had demonstrated the close integration of the Polish with the Russian economy; and politically she was prescient in foreseeing that Pilsudski's preoccupation with Polish national ambitions would frustrate and cancel out his socialism. In all her Polish work Rosa Luxemburg was in intimate partnership with Leo Jogiches, her husband in all but name (she later contracted a legal marriage with a nonentity in the German party in order to secure German citizenship); and, when she moved to Germany, Jogiches continued to direct the S.D.K.P. Mr. Nettl, with many unpublished letters at his disposal, has thrown more light than any previous writer on this intimate friendship, and on its breakdown in 1907. But much remains obscure; nor is there any reason, given Rosa's own reticence on the subject, to expect or even to desire that much more about it will ever be known.

* * *

Rosa's arrival in Germany coincided with the great controversy about 'revisionism' provoked by Bernstein's attempt to promote a pragmatic, and non-doctrinal, version of Marxism. She threw herself with passion into the defence of orthodoxy, and from this time moved more and more over to the Left, or revolutionary, wing of the party. Her pamphlet of 1899 *Social Reform or Revolution* already put the issue quite unequivocally. Bernstein's motive was to:

> change the ocean of capitalist bitterness into a sweet socialist sea by pouring in individual bottles full of social reformist lemonade.

She was equally hostile to the conciliatory tactics of Jaurès in France, and *a fortiori* to the participation of French socialists in bourgeois governments. Later she told the German trade-union leader Legien that he was 'childish, and had no idea of the real circumstances of revolution', and denounced 'the old arthritic English conception that trade unions can prosper only through peaceful growth and development'. There was plenty in her record, even before the anti-war agitation of the war years, to justify the sobriquet 'Red Rosa'.

* * *

The characteristic which has given Rosa Luxemburg her special place in the socialist pantheon was a fundamentally humanitarian and idealistic outlook which shrank from the violence which she in theory advocated and justified. She bridged this gap—to her own satisfaction—by a fanatical but Utopian, almost anarchist, faith in the masses. The 'mass strike' became on her lips a political panacea. Action was more important than organization. Mass action, as the expression of the will of the majority, was the antithesis of dictatorship, though it had equally little to do with liberal or bourgeois democracy.

Rosa was never obliged formally to take a stand as between Russian Bolsheviks and Mensheviks, whose differences were little understood outside Russia. Temperamentally she certainly leaned towards the Bolsheviks and the doctrine of revolutionary action. But it is easy to see how quickly her idealism was bound to clash with Lenin's hard-headed demands for strict party discipline and an elite of trained revolutionary leaders. The difference arose, as Mr. Nettl says, 'out of the totally different circumstances absorbing their attention'. But, since both Lenin and Rosa generalized their ideas, and invested them with a claim to universal validity, the contest was none the less obstinate. Rosa, in an article of 1904, declared her preference for 'the collective ego of the working class' over 'the infallibility of the cleverest central committee'. The opposition was a trifle forced as well as harshly phrased; and Mr. Nettl convicts her of 'deviousness' and 'sophistry', pointing out that she never protested against the firm discipline which Jogiches (and she too in her day) had imposed on the Polish S.P.K.P. in conditions far closer to the Russian than to the German. Lenin's rejoinders were comparatively mild. He and Rosa collaborated amicably enough on the anti-war resolution of the Stuttgart congress of the Second International in 1908; and Lenin's sharpest attacks on Rosa came only with the war on the issue of national self-determination. Even so he never ceased to treat her with respect as a revolutionary leader.

The dispute with Lenin played only a subsidiary role in Rosa's life, and was more significant of her ambivalent attitude to revolution in action than of anything else. But it had an unfortunate sequel. In 1918 Rosa, immured in a German prison, began to analyse the victorious Russian revolution. The divergence between ideal and reality, between dream and fact, emerged all too clearly. The Brest-Litovsk treaty administered a traumatic shock; Rosa would have been a passionate adherent—at any rate in theory—of the 'ultra-left' platform of the revolutionary war. The civil war, the rising of the Social-Revolutionaries, and the beginnings of the terror filled her with horror. She proposed to publish a critical analysis of the revolution; and, when her German friends dissuaded her (this was no time for carping at those engaged in the heat of the struggle), she none the less wrote a long essay on the subject and handed it to Paul Levi for his personal perusal. There it remained for three years. But in 1921, when Rosa had been dead for more than two years, Levi broke with Moscow on the issue of revolutionary tactics, was expelled from the German party and published the essay in a slightly abbreviated form by way of reprisal.

* * *

It was, like all Rosa Luxemburg's writings, vivid and impassioned, a plaint inspired by the glaring contrast between glorious vision and sordid reality. She hails the revolution as the culmination of 'a century of European development', criticizes the Mensheviks for their 'reactionary tactics', and congratulates the Bolsheviks on having 'solved the famous problem of "winning a majority of the people" '. This, then, was the 'mass' revolution of which Rosa had dreamed. But this dubious premise (after all, the essay was written in prison with limited access to information about what was going on) led to a paradoxical conclusion. If this was really a revolution of the masses, then why all these compromises—on the land question, on the national question, with imperial Germany at Brest-Litovsk? Why the curtailment of the freedom of the press? Why dictatorship and the terror? All these things are passed in review, and Lenin's policies found wanting.

What Rosa Luxemburg was doing was clearly enough (and the circumstances in which she wrote should again be stressed) to judge the practice of the revolution in the light of the revolutionary ideal. This was a salutary exercise for those committed to the revolutionary cause, but of little relevance to those opposed to the revolution as such. As Mr. Nettl justly observes, 'those who are made joyful by criticism of the fundamentals of the Bolshevik revolution would do better to turn elsewhere'. But this would be asking too much of the propagandists. Today this fragmentary essay, which its author never completed or prepared for publication, is far better known, at any rate in the English-speaking world, than any of her finished writings. Yet another edition of the English translation has recently been issued for propagandist purposes, with a polemical introduction, by an American university press.

This sort of thing has, of course, been matched, and to some extent provoked, from the other side. For some years after her death Rosa Luxemburg continued to be honoured in the Soviet Union as a revolutionary leader and a martyr to the cause, an adversary of Lenin, but a respected though misguided adversary, on certain specific questions. But, as the blight of Stalinism settled down on the U.S.S.R., and as her writings came to be freely used by hostile propagandists, Rosa came more and more to be identified as one of the great heretics, and her views were assimilated to Trotskyism and Menshevism. The economic analysis of *The Accumulation of Capital*, pointing to the inevitability of the collapse of capitalism when it no longer had 'colonial' areas of the world to exploit, was denounced not only as a derogation from true Marxism but as an endorsement of the 'determinist' aspects of Menshevism. With the collapse of the extremer forms of Stalinism, vituperation of Rosa Luxemburg is no longer in order; and her memory is honoured, though not without mention of her errors, in eastern Germany and in Poland. It would be pleasant to be able to look forward to a propaganda truce on both sides. There is something indecent in the use of Rosa's name and writings as a cold war missile.

* * *

Mr. Nettl's biography is so well balanced, and makes so valuable a contribution to our knowledge, that it may seem carping to dwell on its defects. If it is too long, this is partly because Mr. Nettl has devoted a good deal of space to the German background; and, since he is extremely well versed and informative on this subject, this need not be regretted, even if it sometimes holds up the narrative unduly. More dubious are the frequent excursions into elementary sociology. It is well to be at home in current sociological literature, and insights may sometimes be derived from it. But it is not necessary to display all this scaffolding, even in footnotes; and some of the parallels which Mr. Nettl draws are either so banal or so far-fetched as to irritate the reader. It does not, for instance, throw much light on the personal struggles within socialist parties (only marginally interesting for Rosa Luxemburg's career) to invoke

> the difference until recently between the public air of good fellowship in the Conservative Party, where leaders traditionally emerged, and the personal back-biting in the more highly structural and democratic Labour Party, where leaders are elected.

In spite, however, of a tendency to wordiness, and some unlovely stylistic exuberances ('Parvus's radical but rusty pen was dipped into fighting ink once more'), Mr. Nettl's book remains thoroughly readable. And, if the heroine sometimes seems in danger of being submerged in a sea of detail, this is partly because Rosa, though her political profile is extremely clear-cut, remains to some extent, and is likely to remain, an enigmatic figure as a human being. But it would be difficult to think of another work of this magnitude in this difficult and controversial field which has so brilliantly justified itself or preserved so fair and even a balance between sympathy and criticism.

12

OUR SACRED COWBOY

MR. MUGGERIDGE'S THIRTY-NINE ARTICLES

MR. MALCOLM MUGGERIDGE'S best work is in his reviews and occasional essays, and wonderfully stimulating it is. Yet if he sometimes has a cosmetic impact, a distinguished yet routine astringency like a superior brand of after-shave lotion, the cause is to be found in an obstinate disability he has imposed upon himself.

It emerges in the collection of pieces he has assembled under the symptomatic title *Tread Softly for you Tread on my Jokes*. Deep down, Mr. Muggeridge is as serious a man as anybody so intelligent and sensitive can scarcely avoid being, unless he struggles. He does struggle, hard. He has such a horror of pompousness in others that he goes to crippling lengths to avoid even sustained seriousness in himself. The result is that he is constantly hitting out with bladders when he ought to be using brickbats or pamphlets or curses, or at least earnest persuasion. Apparently he was badly frightened by social do-gooders and journalistic preachers as a young man, people like C. P. Scott and the Webbs. Although naturally addicted to the pulpit himself, he has long been determined that his own sermons shall be free from any taint of piety or intent to convert. This can be misleading, for though Mr. Muggeridge is highly amusing he is not by nature frivolous.

Also it makes for the overdone sort of disenchantment that is his particular form of vulgarity. (Thus, in the piece impishly headed 'The Queen and I', he ruins his perfectly reasonable complaint at the sycophantic nonsense talked and written about royalty by implying that all disinterested behaviour, every attitude not based on the expectation of benefit or reward, is somehow derisory.)

Worst of all, this attitude is absurdly limiting. Pointed and coura-

---

MALCOLM MUGGERIDGE: *Tread Softly for you Tread on my Jokes*. 320 pp. Collins. 30s.

geous Mr. Muggeridge certainly can be. Yet he seems to avoid ultimate responsibility by constantly undermining his own platform. It is all very well to point a mocking finger at old Liberal leader-writers who thought they were helping to shape tomorrow's world, instead of merely providing (as Mr. Muggeridge prefers to believe) tomorrow's firelighters and fish wrappings. The fact is that those old pundits did make their mark on the world whether Mr. Muggeridge likes it or not, and they are hardly diminished by his scorn. 'O God, as Thou wilt have read in the *Manchester Guardian* this morning. . . .' So a northern parson is reputed to have begun an impromptu prayer, about the time Mr. Muggeridge was himself writing leaders in Cross Street. It would be a fine irony if he wrote the one that set off the invocation.

But evidently God thought more of the *Guardian* than Mr. Muggeridge did. Soon he was following more worldly paths that led to *The Daily Telegraph*, the editorship of *Punch* (though Bouverie Street, in its different way, seems to have proved as disenchanting as Cross Street), and finally to the freelance public personality we now enjoy. Let us never underrate his usefulness. A Public Chastiser, however limited or self-limiting his powers, is at least as valuable as an Ombudsman. Not until the recent satirical wave subsided as quickly as it had arisen did we realize the rarity in Britain of the truly sceptical mind. We are a conformist society, and the brief activity of the knocking critics turned out to be nothing more alarming than an old domestic dog complacently scratching its fleas.

Mr. Muggeridge belonged to a different order of critics. He was capable of attack where it really hurt and, still more to the point, *when* it really hurt—nor did one expect to see his victims among the audience, enjoying every minute. Yet apart from a belief in ridicule as a cleanser and sterilizer, he remains an obstinate non-reformer. He is too ludicrously outnumbered for there to be any hope or fear of that. He is the only one in step, the single sober man in a ravingly besotted world. How, he demands, could *Punch* be expected to compete with *The Times*, in which everything is funny except the fourth leader? This is charmingly traditional of him, Gilbertian and Carrollian rolled into one and spiced with a touch of Firbank. It does not manage to disguise the fact that laughing at everything except jokes is itself a form of escapism. He would hurt us more, but probably do us more good in the end, by being more selective.

Still, it makes a wonderfully readable book, an elegant pot-pourri of sense and fun (Mr. Muggeridge makes an exception of his own jokes, which are funny) and professional cosmopolitanism lightly carried. The globetrotting is never oppressive, though at any moment he can throw off a line like 'I remember when I was living in Moscow' or make it clear that he has actually *talked* to de Gaulle. But where does the reality end and the jesting start? For Mr. Muggeridge the frontier scarcely exists. He is bitterly funny on the subject of espionage, making it sound rather like the more confused kind of self-service store where agents, counter-agents and double agents jostle each other in the utmost bewilderment, wondering about the origin of the secrets they are helping themselves to. He can make the reader laugh out loud, as in his account of how he defended P. G. Wodehouse to Duff Cooper, then Minister of Information, at the end of the war:

> I was able to produce to him one instance of an authentic contribution by Wodehouse to the war effort. The Germans, in their literal way, took his works as a guide to English manners, and actually dropped an agent in the Fen country wearing spats. This unaccustomed article of attire led to his speedy apprehension.

Or in his belief that the B.B.C. has superseded the Church of England and that its departmental heads should sign themselves episcopally—'George Light, Raymond Home, Archibald Third, etc.'.

His edged but easy style deserves to be the despair of everyone else in the business. He can set off a whole social trend in a phrase ('our professors have a restless taste for television, semantics and sociology'). He can beat the cartoonists and parliamentary sketch writers at their own game, as when he sees Harold Macmillan and Selwyn Lloyd as 'Don Quixote, Knight of the Woeful Countenance, and Sancho Panza, his squire'. His most formidable gift of all scarcely emerges in a round-up like this—the ability, and the nerve, to attack our more dangerous and absurd self-delusions when they are at their height, like the nonsense written in adulation of the late President Kennedy. It was understandable nonsense. All the more reason for a corrective. Now and again, as when he dared to criticize the monarchy, the anonymous letter-writers in a thousand seaside bedsitters sharpened their poisoned pens. It is when these deep nerves start wincing that the British know they have been injured.

Most of the time, however, the atmosphere is nothing like as tense as this. You might even call it relaxed, watching Mr. Muggeridge, with many a mock-fierce cry and many a hearty thwack, driving before him the sacred cows of the British. Nothing escapes—Winston Churchill, the sex cult, the Liberal conscience, even the judges who 'know better than most of us which side their bread is buttered'. The crassness of our rulers is matched only by the credulity of their victims. A certain degree of overstatement is forgiven; it is the Muggeridge method, and few are likely to be seriously put off the Athenaeum by seeing it described as a place where 'seedy clerics and atrocious dons desperately wash down bad food with bad wine'. But there are limits. Not even Mr. Muggeridge should be allowed to get away with such nonsense as his statement that:

> in our time man has not written one word, thought one thought, put two notes or two bricks together, splashed colour on to canvas or concrete into space in a manner which will be of any conceivable *imaginative* interest to posterity.

Whatever gloss he may choose to put on that 'imaginative', the fact remains that some of his most confident pronouncements would be put down to ignorance or stupidity if they were perpetrated by anyone else. Coming from him, we must presumably attribute them to perversity.

Yet in the end it is not exaggeration or even nonsense that is Mr. Muggeridge's chief danger, so much as a deadly predictability. The hates we feel we know in advance. We long for the things he approves of, the people he likes, even if they can be numbered on the fingers of one hand. Randolph Churchill, Evelyn Waugh, Hugh Kingsmill, Claud Cockburn, Dwight Macdonald? It is a pleasantly off-beat list, even though Waugh showed little sign of returning the interest and Macdonald persists in the absurdity of working for the American equivalent of *Punch*. Macdonald's well-known apprehensions about Masscult and Midcult may possibly extend to Muggcult when he reads, in the chapter doing him qualified honour, what Mr. Muggeridge thinks of the 'grisly quartet' of Joyce, Eliot, Picasso and Stravinsky and their effect on our culture.

But at this point we must remember the warning expressed in the title and watch our step. Mr. Muggeridge is artfully insured by the risk that to attack him for excess or vulgarity or a lack of discrimination may be to class oneself with the lowing herd. 'The fellow doesn't know where to draw the line' is precisely what the retired majors say at Bournemouth or Frinton-on-Sea, and the moment they say it the joke is on them. The famous English sense of humour is itself one of the most vulnerable of the sacred cows. Still more cunningly, Mr. Muggeridge is prepared to mock himself with the rest. He is not vain. He is not motivated by spleen or frustration or any sense of neglect. To many a mixed-up loyalist, as to many a genuine rebel, his serenity must in itself be an affront. For all his fulminations he is not obviously unhappy—not unhappy enough. Anger he deprecates because he sees it as 'a product of a hurt ego rather than of others' wrongs or sufferings'. It seems too easy an alibi.

And though it may seem ungrateful, after the pleasure and stimulation his writing provides, one is driven to the suspicion that after all Mr. Muggeridge really belongs to the acceptance world. When he tells us that his aim was to make *Punch* 'the gargoyle grinning beneath the steeple' we remind ourselves that a gargoyle is a built-in piece of structure, a part of the establishment. There was a difference between gargoyles and dissenters. Perhaps he is implying that *Punch* was the one and he is the other. One doubts it. He is the royal jester, the licensed grimacer, rather than an architect of change. His sardonic face, with cap and bells, might well be on the reverse of Her Majesty's coins. And this makes him, in a sense, a figure of equal absurdity with any he mocks. A virtually powerless monarch who commands obsequious devotion is not more illogical than a scoffer at mass media who uses them so avidly. They are the better for it, but Mr. Muggeridge would hardly claim that as a justification. The obvious fact has to be faced that no demon whips his reluctant fingers to the typewriter keys, or drags him kicking and screaming in front of the tyrannous arc-lamps.

So is he nothing more than just a talented performer? He is something more. He was not frightened by those devout men in his youth for nothing. He is an anti-preacher, an ardent non-believer. He enjoys quoting the scriptures he condemns. For instance, the religious excesses of the sex cult are flogged so mercilessly by Mr. Muggeridge that he devotes a large part of his book to them, complete with some of the most outrageous quotes from Frank Harris and the healthier confessions of Fanny Hill. (He even discovers a new fantasy symbol, 'aural contraceptives'.) And he has this to say of D. H. Lawrence, about whom he is more perceptive and sympathetic than he can bring himself to be about other important writers of our time:

The sense of a civilization dropping to pieces dwelt with him, as with all of us, but he had nothing really to suggest except flight and imagined ecstasies of the flesh.

What has Mr. Muggeridge to suggest? This is where he needs to be more than the royal jester. Even Lear's fool, whom he so much admires, tried to make the silly old man change course before it was too late. But Mr. Muggeridge is not going to waste his breath in arguing to the incorrigible. Not that he is himself resourceless. He has his own answer, and it may come as a surprise to many. If there is an overriding theme in these essays it is that what he calls the age's 'grisly buffooneries' are due to the lust for power, disguised by various cloaks and masks of pretence.

Human life, I have come to feel, in all its public or collective manifestations is only theatre, and mostly cheap melodrama at that. There is nothing serious under the sun except love; of fellow-mortals and of God. Everything is ridiculous save ecstasy.

So it's love, including ecstasy though not of the flesh, that makes the world go round. Well, it could be (to invert one of his own remarks) that only extreme sceptics have it in them to be mystical. Yet one can well imagine testy protests from less publicized and far from melodramatic quarters where people are busy trying, according to their lights and in the teeth of endless frustration, to make the world a bit safer and saner. They may well withhold a cheer at the discovery that hiding behind the disenchanted mask of Mr. Malcolm Muggeridge is an authentic Man of Feeling studying to take the mystical veil. Unable to rid themselves of the boring idea that he ought to put his vitality and intelligence to more constructive use, they will consider him to be opting out too easily. It is hardly enough for him to end his recital by putting his hand on his heart and announcing, like some Victorian drawing-room baritone, that love is all.

13

THE LAST OF EVELYN WAUGH

As PART of the revised edition of his novels Mr. Waugh has edited the trilogy of *Men at Arms*, *Officers and Gentlemen* and *Unconditional Surrender* to make a single book. Nothing now indicates the breaks between the original volumes; the two or three 'books' into which each was divided have (roughly speaking) been demoted to the status of Chapter; the original chapters have become numbered sections within them; a good few of the lesser divisions—spaces between paragraphs—have been eliminated. The result is above all a change of pace, suitably adjusted to the longer distance. At the end of 800 pages the reader feels that he has read a large and very fine novel, whose scale and seriousness are offset by a remarkable lightness of texture.

The trilogy has its flaws, and these have not been set right. The hiatus before the start of *Unconditional Surrender* becomes less conspicuous now that the synopsis ('The story so far . . .') has been dropped; but those two years remain puzzling, and the explicit suggestions that Ludovic murdered both Major Hound and the sapper captain have gone with the synopsis. Ludovic himself remains far-fetched in his subsequent appearances; these and the quite unnecessary air crash in Yugoslavia still stick out as the weak points of the last third of the book. The one thread of the whole intricate web that led absolutely nowhere still does so, though the end has been tied with a fresh knot, the fizzling out of the security authorities' interest in Guy being feebly excused by a dozen interpolated lines consigning Colonel Grace-Groundling-Marchpole to insignificance and confusion. There has only been a single major change, and that is effected by a tiny amendment on the last page of the book. In *Unconditional Surrender* Guy and his new (Catholic) wife had 'two boys of their own' as well as the cuckoo planted by Trimmer. This has been cut, and now Box-Bender says 'Pity they haven't any children of their own'. The happy, lucky ending is for some reason

---

EVELYN WAUGH: *Sword of Honour*. 796 pp. Chapman and Hall. £2 10s.

no longer acceptable. Mr. Waugh's picture of divine providence has been seriously altered.

A number of small episodes or descriptions have been cut, running to between one and four pages each, and this, so the preface suggests, is because they struck the author as tedious. In one or two cases he may be right; thus it is not unreasonable to curtail the account of the trip out to the Middle East and the hospitality of Cape Town, while the fishy Haw-Haw-type lieutenant-colonel encountered in Crete seemed improbable and led nowhere. But in the main the excisions seem a great pity. We have now lost the delightful account of Mr. Crouchback's reactions to the auctioning of his own furniture; we have lost Guy's memories of the house after his death; Brigadier Ritchie-Hook's descent into the jollities of Bingo has gone; so has the description of Sergeant Soames and the penetrating account of relations between officers and N.C.O.s; so has everything to do with the flight of the Greek General Miltiades; so has the lunatic but all-too-true incident of the bathers and the Bren gun towards the end of *Men at Arms*. None of these was at all tedious to the reader. If the real idea (as one must suspect after the admitted disingenuity of other of Mr. Waugh's prefatory notes) was to keep the book to 800 pages and fifty shillings it was a short-sighted piece of economy.

What is more interesting to connoisseurs is the many much smaller cuts and changes, sometimes two or three to a page, right through the book. These are very seldom designed to reduce 'repetitions and discrepancies' (the other pretext given by the preface); indeed, fresh discrepancies have arisen as a result; the proof-reading has also been less successful than before. In a number of cases the amendments are obviously meant to thin out the minor characters, or at least to expunge those characters' surnames; thus Roots, Slimbridge and Smiley of Hookforce H.Q. are all disidentified; the mad commando colonel Prentice is more or less eliminated (which seems a pity), and the otiose Welsh conductor from the Yugoslav episode is rightly thrown out, except for one quite unnecessary and now doubly puzzling appearance on page 762. There is a considerable reduction in the use of the overworked phrase 'in the picture', but otherwise it hardly seems that Mr. Waugh is doing what he claims.

For the effect of the great majority of such alterations is slightly to tilt characters, opinions or apparent judgments. With Guy, for instance, the references to his having been at Downside and at university are removed; so is more than one mention of his relative poverty (which was always hard to believe); so is the solicitor's computation that his father's estate will bring in an income of some £7,000 a year. Four separate mentions of his romantic, almost schoolboyish attitude to war have gone; so has a good part of Mr. Goodall's disquisitions on Catholic genealogy, together with the author's implied ridicule. Ian Kilbannock's former job turns out to have been gossip-writer, not sporting journalist as before; the phrase is cut in which he admits to having been 'pretty red ever since the Spanish Civil War'. The air-marshal's vulgar rhyme about Elinor Glyn is omitted; so is the mention of 'some nonsense of Brendan's' and the reference to Churchill's 'sham-Augustan prose'.

The most important of these retouchings affects Ivor Claire, the gentleman rider who to Guy represented quintessential England but disobeyed orders and abandoned his men in Crete. Though he is still the pivot on which the whole story swings, the shock originally represented by his action has been toned down; it is no longer said that he 'behaved abominably', or that Tommy Blackhouse would bar him from any responsible job and might even be less friendly to him at the Club. On the contrary it is suggested that Guy, now, resigned 'an immeasurable piece of his manhood' on the same 'fatal morning', and although it is far from clear what this means—Blackhouse has no such criticisms of Guy as he originally had of Claire—profound significance is presumably intended by the fact that Guy now loses his brother's Lourdes medal during his escape. It is much simpler with the Yugoslav incidents, where three or four minor changes ('betrayal' for 'intrigue' as a term for our break with Mihailovic) indicate the author's stiffening disapproval, and the communist Frank de Souza is no longer allowed an M.C.

Nothing is too trivial for amendment. The allocation of capital letters, for instance, now favours the church rather than the military, so that instead of 'mass at the Castle' we have 'Mass at the castle'. The members of the Auxiliary Fire Service operating outside Bellamy's are no longer 'progressive novelists' but 'experimental novelists'. Mr. Crouchback brushes up his classics from a pale blue *Xenophon* only; the North and Hillard's Latin Prose he was previously also holding has now for some baffling reason been cut. Whether such decisions in any way improve the novel is a moot point, but no doubt they will make it more interesting to academic students.

The book remains what it set out to be; 'a description of the

Second World War as it was seen and experienced by a single uncharacteristic Englishman', and the view remains less uncharacteristic than Mr. Waugh thinks, for the aspects covered—the initial stagnation, the raising (and publicizing) of the Commandos, the defeat in Crete and the irregular campaign in Yugoslavia—are all fairly representative of the war we waged, so that a surprisingly wide swath of history is illuminated, as well as the individuals on all levels who made it. Perhaps Guy is not quite so uncharacteristic as his author, for certainly the view of the book which Mr. Waugh himself now takes is one that would hardly occur to anybody else:

On reading the book I realised that I had done something quite outside my original intention. I had written an obituary of the Roman Catholic Church in England as it had existed for many centuries. . . . When I wrote *Brideshead Revisited* I was consciously writing an obituary of the doomed English upper class. It never occurred to me, writing *Sword of Honour*, that the Church was susceptible to change. . . .

It would hardly be more far-fetched to call it a study of the servant question. After all, we start with a hotel kept by former Crouchback servants, where the staff's failure to fetch Guy's luggage is remedied by the servant of a Halberdier major. Guy joins the Halberdiers, and the service in barracks (the wine butler, the 'toiling old Halberdiers' who stoke the fires) is part of his initial love affair with that regiment. Then comes the disillusionment of Kut-al-Imara House ('it won't kill you to hump your own gear for once'), where all men are equal and 'the whole hierarchic structure of army life was offended'; it becomes a symbol of 'that new world' which Guy had enlisted to fight. Worse still, the barracks themselves are undermined; 'they've taken my servant away', the embittered Adjutant tells Guy on his return from Crete, while in the officer's mess—ichabod—'an A.T. came in from the serving door whistling . . .'. Yet here as in so many other respects the experience of Crete seems to transform all values. The lady who, at one of the crucial points of *Unconditional Surrender*, is cited as believing that the 'normality' to be restored by peace will include a full staff of a dozen servants is plainly being ridiculed. At the beginning of the book a household of twenty sees Guy off from Italy; at the end he is in The Lesser House.

And the name of this study? *Active Service*? *Divine Service*? Never mind. For it is not the book that Mr. Waugh has in fact written, any more than is the 'document of Catholic usage of my youth' which he now feels that he has produced. All the same, the test of a first-rate work of fiction (or drama, for that matter) is that each re-reading should reveal fresh aspects, undetected threads, new implications. This the trilogy fulfils, in both the original and the revised versions. It says more than it was consciously meant to say; more than any single reading can reveal it as saying. Admittedly the author's amendments are often to be mildly regretted. But if they encourage more people to read it as a whole then they will have added both to our literature and to our knowledge of what we were really up to between 1939 and 1945.

14
HENRY TREECE
LAMENT FOR A MAKER

HENRY TREECE was a prolific and regular writer, though until 1959 a full-time teacher. As well as his nine deeply-imagined historical novels, much poetry, some plays and criticism, he produced more than thirty stories for the young. In one field in particular he was making himself a master, in his Viking stories. Perhaps his ability to get inside the Viking skin, to produce an utterly convincing extension of the saga tone of voice, is due to his own evident delight in fast, suspenseful, surprising action: and also, surely, to an imaginative sympathy with their way of meeting life.

The picaresque, take-what-comes kind of action arising from the Northmen's voyages of discovery, plunder or revenge, is almost bound to make a rapid episodic story, and suited Treece. He first uses the voyaging pattern in *Viking's Dawn*, which begins the story of one Harald Sigurdson, who goes with a Northman, Thorkell Fairhair, and his sinister Danish blood-brother, Ragnar Raven, in a ship the Nameless. The modern writer for the young is hard put to it to make plunder and treachery part of his story without seeming to extol them. Treece manages this problem well, using the Dane Ragnar as scapegoat. Sworn brother though he is, Ragnar has left a longship of his own lying in wait to take Thorkell's. But it is wrecked by the storm-raising powers of a brilliantly drawn character, Horic the Laplander. The incident is told with the starkness of a ballad and shows how Treece's often over-colourful writing gains in pungency and strength when he willingly submits to the saga style, an objective, allusive economy. When they pass the wreck, Thorkell changes course to pick up a survivor, but Ragnar reaches for his seal-spike and silences this last witness to his treachery:

> Horic whispered to himself, but every man near him heard, 'Look, there is blood upon the point of Ragnar's sealspike'.

So we know what Ragnar is, who later treacherously robs hospitable

Picts, and steals treasure from a boatload of unarmed Christian monks. Convincingly he gets his deserts when he loses his treasure and his life to some wreckers. Ragnar's tortuous character, as discussed by the others, is real enough. The book explores, too, the Viking character in general, their love of ridiculous, exaggerated tales and jokes (like Horic's about bears); their interest in philosophical talk, their courage, fatalism and humour in disaster. There is a man called Smörke, convinced, though all laughed at him, that this voyage would be his last:

As he was swept overboard, Gnorre swore that he heard the man yell out, 'There, I told you so!'

More important still is the seafarers' love for and faith in their leader, movingly shown when Thorkell goes blind. Wolf comforts him:

'I will be your eyes, Thorkell Fairhair,' he said. 'You have lost nothing.'
'I will be your right arm, Thorkell Fairhair,' said Aun, 'you have gained something.'
'I will be your spell-master, Thorkell Fairhair,' said Horic, crying a little as he said it. 'You will gain everything.'

* * *

The Road to Miklagard, a second book about this Harald, is not a complete success. The richness of Constantinople tempts Treece into lush writing and melodramatic action. Also, a comical fairy-tale quality enters with the giant Grummoch, alien to the saga kind of supernatural, omen, dream and vision, which Treece later uses so well. Yet there is grim comedy in Radbard drowning their treasure (with some of themselves) rather than letting it fall to the enemy. Treasure is often elusive in these stories: Prince Nial reburies the lot when he rifles a barrow too clumsily in *Splintered Sword*: and the Vikings who raid the howe in *Horned Helmet* pay for the treasure with Gauk's death. Both these stories, written rather later, are different in having their emphasis upon a young hero, rather than upon a whole crew; and are of vintage quality while slighter in scope. Set late in the Viking period they show, subtly, its drawbacks as a way of life.

The last tale of Harald, *Viking's Sunset*, is splendid. The taut, ironical tone and the shipmen's conversation are better than ever.

Harald and Grummoch (now perfectly convincing and endearing, as Harald's blood-brother) chase Haakon Redeye in the Long Snake, in revenge for his burning their village. From Greenland, where there is a humorous Eskimo interlude, they finally reach Vinland, and their story becomes intertwined with the red men with whom they settle. The fusion is as happy as this image of it:

> The longship sailed among them . . . like a mother goose among her many goslings, for in truth the canoes of the Beothuk floated as thick as seeds upon the broad waters.

But the jealousy of the red chief's maimed son brings Harald and his own brother down with him: and Long Snake is sent burning over the lake with the three bodies upon her, an ending superb in its epic restraint and sadness. (A longship prow *was* found, Treece tells us, in one of the Lakes.) Grummoch and Thorgeif turn away from the ship-burial, comforting each other with a Jomsborg ditty, but are soon silent again:

> For a while there would be nothing worth the saying. They knew that well enough.

* * *

Now although the Northmen's 'joy in doing' (including the frenzied action of the berserk or 'baresark' which Treece often describes) is the mainspring of these stories, there is no doubt of the importance of 'the saying'. Henry Treece has forged and used a pointed weapon of conversation between his Northmen which has a flash and twist and bite peculiar to itself. Inspired by the old sagas, yet individual and more expansive, the flavour of this talk is as recognizable as a favourite wine. Maturing with time, it has perhaps reached perfection in *Swords from the North* (coming from Faber and Faber in 1967). Irony is its basic ingredient: 'the men of the North were not given to self-pity', as Treece remarks: and the ironical, stoical attitude is part of their very nature. But its shifts and variations are like the glitter of sword-play. It ranges from plain irony—'A man would not know unless he was told . . .' replies Summerbird to Harald Hardrada's protest that he is a Christian—to the euphemism that brings a shiver: 'And I speak for my brothers, who do not wish to talk . . .' says a warrior in his death-verse, his brothers being dead. It includes a constant grim or comic use of understatement—'Something must have kept them awake . . .' remarks a Varangian escaped from a Byzantine 'death-cell' and hearing his agonized ship-mates loudly planning revenge—and a balancing use of gloriously exaggerated bombast. It explodes into that kind of banter heard among schoolboys or service men (the sound of it still, no doubt, in Treece's ears) as when Hardrada protests that

'we will be drinking out of our cupped hands like dogs before long.'
Wulf laughed and said, 'When you next see a dog drinking out of his cupped hands, call to me. . . .'

and so on, for a page of uproarious absurdity. It includes much brusquer teasing—'No one wants your front teeth, friend . . .', remarks Gyric to Haldor, who has wagered these—and a gentler kind, as is Hardrada's solemn reply to young Helge, who says he dreamed of flying, tried it, and fell in the fjord:

'So you cannot fly eh? I should have thought that a brisk young fellow like you could fly, Helge. . . .'

For Treece's great achievement in individual characterization in these tales is this re-creation of the Norway giant King Harald Hardrada, into so awesome yet lovable a figure: audacious, joyous, poetical, warm-hearted, immensely brave, yet also hard, calculating, savage and proud. In *The Last of the Vikings*, a haunting and shapely book (perhaps artistically the best of these), the author draws all Harald's young life into the compass of his thoughts on the battlefield of Stamford Bridge, where he is to die. *Swords from the North* tells of Harald as head of the Varangian guard in Byzantium, and remains episodic—but what episodes, and changes of mood! Scenes of violence, mystery, stark drama, controlled pathos and wild comedy follow one another with unflagging gusto, related with crisp, ironic invention. When the not young Empress Zoe proposes marriage to Harald (a hint the author has taken from the *Heimskringla Saga*, which he uses skilfully and imaginatively), the Varangian sits on the mosaic floor and laughs like a maniac. When the two boatloads of Vikings rush the harbour-chain to escape from Byzantium and Harald's boat rides over while the other breaks her back, drowning two of his dear friends, grief gets Harald in its grip like ice. When he ruthlessly sends ashore the stolen Princess Maria for whom he has a passion (beautifully indicated in more than one scene) because she keeps reminding him that he owes her his life, he retires to his cabin and does not watch her go. Saint Olaf, Harald's dead brother, is a familiar and convincing visitor throughout Harald's life, and it is he who has come to Maria the last night in Byzantium and said:

> 'Be about it and send a ladder to my brother.'
> 'Northern Saints [remarks Harald] are brisk fellows and stand on no ceremony. But they get things done.'

Treece always describes Harald's faith—genuine, calculating and virile—with perfect insight, and uses Olaf's interventions with great dramatic effect.

* * *

Closely connected with these two books in conception and period is *Man with a Sword*, a life of Hereward the Wake. Little is known for fact of Hereward and the author has imagined an episode when Hereward is Hardrada's man, so that we see the middle-aged King of hard counsel in Norway. Hereward has suffered a loss of memory after a cowardly attack by the English Godwines, and his moods, his foolish wisdom and uncalculated wit (delighting Hardrada, the good conversationalist) are partly due to this. Coming with Hardrada to England in the fateful year 1066, Hereward leaves behind his wife and son, who are taken into his court by the wily Sweyn of Denmark. It is the promise of their return to him which Treece uses as Hereward's main motive in leading the fen men to help King Sweyn in the sack of Peterborough. The Isle of Ely episode is hauntingly done and includes an encounter between Hereward and a strange Norman—the Conqueror himself: a long and stormy friendship develops between them. Hereward emerges as individualist and outlaw, but also as a peace-loving family man, driven mad when William removes his wife and son to his court. Sometimes immensely pathetic, this picture of Hereward is a high achievement, and remains unaffected by an overwrought last few chapters.

The Godwines, naturally enough, are ill-thought-of in this book. In a much earlier story, *Hounds of the King*, Treece dealt interestingly with the making of Harold's housecarles, conditioned into dog-like loyalty at Wallingford. But Harold Godwinson's magnetism is described rather than felt and we remain looking at events as well-told history rather than rapt by the tragedy of Hastings at the end. The book deals also, for the first time, with the battle of Stamford Bridge.

Treece's three versions of this famous battle in this famous year are a fascinating study in imaginative and emotional concentration. He has not made us care much about Godwinson, and the house-carles Beornoth and Finn are slight figures, so their battle moves us least. We care considerably about Hereward, through whose eyes we have a fine sense of the shield-ring and the fall of Hardrada. But in *The Last of the Vikings* Treece seemed to gain the freedom of that battlefield through the eyes of Hardrada himself: and the glow of reality spreads outwards, lighting up English Harold and all the figures around, with that kind of passionate sympathy which is creative love.

In what appears to be his last story of all, *The Dream-Time* (coming from Brockhampton Press in 1967), Treece, touchingly enough, has written a lucid poetical fable, set back in the dawn of time, about a 'maker' among warriors. In it there are some statements of simple profundity about the artist among ordinary men. There is a time when Twilight, the boy who can draw and work in metal, tries to make the likeness of his girl who is lost:

> At first he was afraid that he could not make the right shape . . . but his hand caught his dream and he drew her so rightly that he felt she might speak . . .

Treece's hand often 'caught his dream' among the men of the North, and when it did they speak most splendidly. His choice of material is skilful, his treatment of it increasingly 'adult'.

Treece's other earlier historical stories are ambitious in theme, sometimes uncritically bold in scope, giving an impression of impatience to reach the end. This may be because they have a recurring tendency to compress too much material into too short a book, with a consequent sacrifice of depth to breadth, both in plot and characterization. This is in turn partly due to his fascination with themes from cross-roads in history and the desire to hitch his young heroes on to those historical characters of huge stature who are so often centred there. In doing so he sets his sights very high, gives himself two major (but differing) imaginative tasks. Treece loved British history and myth and in his use of the Arthurian material in *The Eagles have Flown* he discarded Malory and Tennyson (and did T. H. White's brilliant conception of the boy Arthur go too?) and presented Artos, Count of Britain, only half-willingly Romanized, leading the three kings of the west against Aella and Cissa, the

Saxon invaders. Merlin is the spirit of paganism, the round table is the great round shield Artos throws down to teach his men equality. But the young hero Festus and his slave-friend remain thin. The interested young reader had best go straight to *The Great Captains*, the novel for which this story seems a blue-print. Despite doubtful things, like equating Camelot with Camulodunum, the book is fully imagined, and powerful.

Other unsettled periods Treece chose as themes were the Claudian invasion in *Legions of the Eagle*, and the new waves of herdsmen-invaders in the bronze-age story *Men of the Hills*. Caught up in the vast movements of history, Treece failed to create flesh and blood people within small pockets of convincingly woven circumstances, against these panoramic backgrounds: so that the books somehow do not move us. We feel little for Lalo, but we weep with Drem of Rosemary Sutcliff's *Warrior Scarlet*.

A new story, *The Queen's Brooch* (Faber and Faber, 18s.), tells of Boudicca's uprising through the eyes of a young tribune of the Ninth Legion at Lincoln. The liberal-minded young tribune's attempts to keep good relations with the tribesmen of the Coritani (whom he has grown up among and loves) and the edgy uneasiness of Cynwas, their chieftain; the insolence of a tactless decurion, the army-bound mind of the faithful old centurion Tigidius: these are described from inside with tremendous conviction. But once among the hordes of the Iceni, Treece loses the concentrated vision and the story becomes broad instead of deep, panoramic rather than moving. The Marcus of the beginning, loyal to the Legion yet brother to the Britons, would not so easily have thrown in his hand.

There is needed a fusion of the personal and the historical vision, and this is more easily achieved in private than public events. *The Bombard*, for instance, really comes alive when a youth and his friends, returned from Crecy, make their own bombard and fire it at the crack in their enemy's castle wall (a magnificent piece of description). The young man's love of the bombard they have so arduously made, the horror of the priest whose skill has helped them, and his death when the bombard is blown to pieces at his order, are entirely convincing and moving.

* * *

An author of immense creative verve, Treece wrote six suspense stories with contemporary settings, which show that same pleasure in (almost *need* for) fast, dangerous opportunist action as his Viking tales, and are compulsively readable. The author makes skilful use of all the devices of the thriller from double-chase to hidden identity. In *Ask for King Billy*, for instance (the first story to deal with Gordon Stewart, private detective, who later works for government intelligence), we do not know until the end which side the sinister large man in black is on. The pace in these stories never flags, the suspense mounts, there is a reckless uninterest in minor, inexplicable details and a certain repetition of situations. Only rarely is Treece's considerable ingenuity misplaced. There is a most enjoyable use of place, London, the Humber, the Welsh borders, Spain, Gibraltar, Sark; and a detailed knowledge of boxing and of firearms. The characters that lodge in the mind are the pointed miniatures (a West Indian boxer, an old Boer War shepherd) rather than the main characters, caught up in a game which moves too fast for us to see their features. A slighter story for younger children, *The Jet Beads*, has, on the other hand, a very live picture of an eleven-plus boy, and such humorous school scenes as to make one wish he had done more in this line.

In a letter in 1965 Henry Treece confirmed his belief in that wholeness of intention in writing for the young which must be the guide of all serious writers for them: the expression of something important to the writer himself, within 'that common territory shared by human beings of all ages'. He saw the gap between books for children and books plain and simple narrowing, and it is sad that he should not have had longer in helping to bridge it.

15

AUDEN, US AND THEM

THE ORATORS NOW

THE ORATORS, W. H. Auden once said, was one of 'the good ideas which [his] incompetence or impatience prevented from coming to much'. Since he now considers poems like 'Sir, no man's enemy' and '1 September, 1939' (for many years among the most frequently invoked by admirers, critics and explicators) to be little more than 'trash', the verdict on *The Orators* which once seemed likely to force it into early retirement (fragments creamed off into the *Collected Poetry*, and the whole out of print since 1959) now has something of the air of praise. He has allowed two facsimile editions of *Poems* (1928), and such comparative rarities as 'Letter to Lord Byron' have reappeared, so that one learnt of this revised edition less with surprise than with an impatient curiosity to see how much of it might be allowed to survive intact.

First published in 1932 and revised in 1934 (the tinkering habit came early), this was the work which set the seal on Auden's initial reputation. Subtitled 'An English Study', it forms among other things a surrealist anatomy of a country in crisis, and much of its power lies in its pictorial or aphoristic incidentals, the lists from Whitman or Perse, the definitions and classifications (always the imaginative backbone of Auden's thought), the whole cinematic range of images. Auden was not concerned to purify the dialect of the tribe, but to restore its flavour, and it is precisely here that he was able triumphantly to transcend his debt to Eliot. The book was everywhere received with impressed attention, and the ultimate accolade came almost from the throne-room itself when John Hayward wrote in the *Criterion*: 'I have no doubt that it is the most valuable contribution to English poetry since *The Waste Land*'.

Since this new edition is more than 340 verse lines shorter than the version Hayward praised, one must first describe the latest omissions

---

W. H. AUDEN: *The Orators*. An English Study. 102 pp. Faber and Faber. 21s.

and changes. A claim like that can only be considered if one is sure one is talking about more or less the same work. There is some correction of misprints and wrong spellings, a very little rewriting of not much importance, and the names of friends in the first Ode are replaced by invented ones (as they have been since the poem's separate appearance in the 1945 *Collected Poetry*). One regrets most of the omissions. The Ode to the rugger fifteen has gone, as have most of the references to Gabriel (its dedicatee) in 'Journal of an Airman'. 'Beethameer, Beethameer, bully of Britain' has disappeared, and so has 'Attractions for the coming week/Are Masters Wet, Dim, Drip and Bleak'. The fine Envoi to the fourth Ode has been removed, along with 'Last day but ten', 'After the death of their proud master' and 'To return to the interest' from the 'Journal'. So also has the invocation to Ferrers Locke for delivery from 'the death-will of the Jews', which must have seemed (*pace* Miss Arendt) a little tasteless now.

* * *

It may be argued that these omissions do not make a great deal of difference to the work, and it is clear that Auden this time has not gone out of his way to reslant its original message, but though the Enemy was not helpfully epitomized by the Beaverbrook/Rothermere victim, his absence erases some of the period flavour. Auden was once in a quiet sort of way quite enthusiastic about this kind of satire ('A modern satirist in search of a subject', he suggested in January, 1932, 'would be far more likely to select a Criterion dinner than a Newspaper peer'). The smokescreen drawn in front of the autobiographical elements (Gabriel, Uncle Wiz, 'Derek my chum', the Essay Club and so on) will merely make the biographers look harder in the future: it was never very clear what was going on anyway, though there are some clues in a notebook of the period (see John Whitehead, *London Magazine*, May 1965, page 91). The rugger Ode was delightful Hopkins parody:

> Defeats on them like lavas
> Have fallen, fell, kept falling, fell
> On them, poor lovies . . .

And it was more than just this, for it brought the half-mystical Lawrence/*Wandervögel* sentiments directly into line with public school hero-worship.

The training of the ruling class provided an ambience of homoerotic *kameradschaft* which itself, it appears, could be felt to be spiritually regenerating. The Ciceronian political ideal, mirrored in the British educational and diplomatic system, provided an ironical structure for the work, one would guess, with parallels to be found in the three-part form between *De Oratore*, on the orator's training, and Book One ('The Initiates'); between *Brutus* and Book Two ('Journal of an Airman'); and between *Orator*, partly autobiographical and concerned with the ideal orator, and Book Three ('Six Odes'). Auden shows that he is as much concerned with rhetoric as with politics by a virtuoso range of parody and stylistic allusion; and of course the whole work shows a powerful interest in education. The title has puzzled many critics; it might be more profitable to consider Cicero than soap-boxes in Hyde Park.

* * *

But critics have had more important worries about this work. Auden now supplies a preface which directly confronts the frequent charges of unconscious fascism: 'My name on the title-page', he says, 'seems a pseudonym for someone else, someone talented but near the border of sanity who might well, in a year or two, become a Nazi.' In the 1930s he said he opposed fascism because he knew what a fascist state was from his preparatory school. As a schoolmaster at the time of writing *The Orators* his opposition thus assumed the status of espionage, a prominent factor in the work. But the spy is shown to be an introvert and a failure ('Which Side Am I Supposed To Be On?'), incapable of serious political action. The book is certainly about the need for revolution in 'this country of ours where nobody is well', but it is concerned with revolution according to Blake, Baudelaire or Homer Lane, not to Marx, whose insistence on its proletarian character is effectively denied both by Auden's messianic mythologizing and his direct Skeltonic sneers at the working class:

Poofs and ponces,
All of them dunces.
Those over thirty,
Ugly and dirty,
. . .
Content for the year
With foods out of tins and very small beer.

If an American poet were to say this today about families in Harlem it would be hard for him to get a reputation for being 'pink liberal', let alone left-wing. And surely Edgell Rickword was right to see implications of Nazi 'degradation of women and regimentation of the Strength through Joy variety' in the following lines?

Living in one place with a satisfied face
All of the women and most of the men
Shall work with their hands and not think again.

But we have to remember the period in which this was written. Hitler was still a 'false-alarm' (he did not come to power until January, 1933) and Mosley was only recently thought of as a future socialist Prime Minister. A poem like 'Get there if you can' is fairly unequivocal in its fear of proletarian revolution: it is the 'invalids' ' fault, and they had better do something about it. Mosley's answer (the Corporate State) did not seem immediately fascist. In June, 1931, Harold Nicolson had dreams of gaining the Foreign Office through the New Party, and in December Christopher Isherwood was singing the praises of the New German Youth Movement in Mosley's *Action.* ('They are sombre, a trifle ascetic and absolutely sincere. They will live to become brave and worthy citizens of their country'.) It is clear that Isherwood's 'Test' complex, ingenuously and sympathetically elaborated in *Lions and Shadows* (see especially pages 77–78) as being overtly about the missed 1914 war and covertly about sex, had its lasting effect upon others of his generation. *The Orators* underlines its programme of youth and spontaneity with half-serious metaphors of world war, derived from General Ludendorff's doom-laden account of the probable mobilization against Germany of the French-Italian alliance, in his *The Coming War* (which also provided Eliot with sources for 'Coriolan', a contemporary poem instructive to compare with Auden's). Hair-raising enough in Ludendorff, with its allusions to a Jewish-Jesuit-Freemason conspiracy, this mobilization is given a Bosch-like apocalyptic turn in 'Journal of an Airman' directly reminiscent of Isherwood's and Upward's Mortmere stories, which they themselves recognized as a 'special brand of medieval surrealism' and an indulgent escape from reality. Ending the 'Journal' with a snatch from one of Wilfred Owen's letters to his mother ('Nerves in perfect order') only throws this guilty fantasy into sharper relief.

* * *

In fact, the political dicta can usually be shown to be products of the influence of the Lawrence of *Fantasia of the Unconscious*. The passage Rickword attacked can be paralleled by others stressing the mistrust of conventional education: it is 'thought' that perverts the power of the deeper sensual centres, just as the love-sympathy between parent and child arouses these centres but provides no outlet for them:

Self-regard, in origin a mere accident of over-crowding, like haemophilia is a sex-linked disease. Man is the sufferer, woman the carrier. 'What a wonderful woman she is!' Not so fast: wait till you see her son.

All the witty social and psychological definitions of the Enemy centre on this. Auden gets as much fun out of his Them/Us distinctions as Apollinaire did with merde/rose, or Wyndham Lewis with Blasting and Blessing, but these antagonisms are very private, e.g.: 'Three kinds of enemy clothing—fisherman's pockets—Dickens' waistcoats—adhesive trousers'. No, the real Enemy quite clearly has his HQ in the mother. Lawrence said that spiritual mothering was responsible for introversion and masturbation: these 'enemy' traits are sublimated in the Airman as spying and as kleptomania, the subconscious cry for help ('They stole to force a hearing') which seems to be his eventual undoing. The comfortable conventionalized world of the mother stifles not because it is bourgeois ('our homes and duty') but because it is the mother's. It is the black-sheep Uncle who becomes the Airman's hero ('my real ancestor' according to the Germanic heroic code, and some spoof diagrams of Mendelian biology) and his hinted homosexuality is heavily overlaid by quasi-divinity ('Uncle, save them all, make me worthy'). The Airman learns that:

1. The power of the enemy is a function of our resistance therefore
2. The only efficient way to destroy it—self-destruction . . .

This really only makes sense if we see it as the Airman's resistance to his mother: his exploits cannot lift him beyond his emotional crippling ('The giantess shuffles nearer, cries "Deceiver" '). The Airman finds parallels in other early heroes like John Nower in *Paid on Both Sides* or Ransom in *The Ascent of F6*, where Feud or Quest is similarly motivated by the mother. To pretend that the enemy is capitalism, or even the bourgeoisie, is part of the same evasive and adolescent heroics which yield the increasingly sinister practical jokes, whereby 'Derek's seduction of Mrs. Solomon by pretending to have been blessed by the Pope' soon becomes 'Secret catalysts introduced into the city reservoirs convert the entire drinking supply into tepid urine'. The account of a quest for psychological health inevitably draws on all the grisly resources of the illness: a whole society is indicted by the quality of the response, the vindictiveness and sexual aggressiveness of a little boy. Far from evading the issue by tackling the problem in psychological terms, as Edgell Rickword concluded, Auden blended the psychological and social terms in perhaps the most satisfactory way of all his early work.

And what a brilliant performance it is! Without the threads of fiction which the central section directs forcefully into our reading of the whole work, it might arguably be seen to be more of a 'notebook' conglomeration than it has thereby succeeded in being. But it is also true that the discrete prose and verse items of the first and third sections have the most individual impact: the parodies of the Anglican responses, the Prize-day speech, the sentimental novel; the fastidious prosody of the third, the satiric vigour of the fourth or the absurd hymn syntax of the fifth Odes; these are the remembered successes of the book, and they indicate a widening of range in Auden's career at this point of vital importance to his stature.

Critics who tended to scold the author of *About the House* for using rare words might consider the following (and their *use*) in *The Orators*: mawmet, gletcher, concha, oxter, barratry, darkmans, quarrons, pooty, blips, bambling, gonsil, and so on (the last four not in the *O.E.D.*). Far from being an indulgence in his later period, the concern for surprising diction has been there from the beginning: the way these words achieve authority in context is a lesson in how to use language:

> Falcon is poised over fell in the cool.
> Salmon draws
> Its lovely quarrons through the pool.

The abbreviations intensify nature: without the article, these creatures cease to be mere species and impress their tangible qualities (we use the same process to talk of them as food). And that 'lovely' is so daring that there are many who will think it does not come off. Surely attached to 'quarrons' it does: the cliché and the obsolete thieves' slang justify each other, and the lines typify the work's continual leaning towards the observed lyrical moment.

The comparison with *The Waste Land* seems appropriate. Indeed, it is possible to feel that Auden with more ease and directness and energetic invention involved himself in the world he created. Today, as his preface shows, he looks upon the work with amused toleration: actually, it preserves its power well, and is still surely the most disturbing long poem of its era.

16

POETS TODAY

(*a*) DENISE LEVERTOV

The Jacob's Ladder

EDWARD DORN

Geography

JAMES DICKEY

Buckdancer's Choice

HOWARD MOSS

Finding Them Lost

THE ENGLISH READER with nobler things in the mind to suffer may soon be reaching for his gun at the mention of Black Mountain poetry or projective verse. The products of this latest American orthodoxy come to us swathed in theories about the Syllable and the Breath and bristling with all the aggressive-defensive machinery of American cultural chauvinism: 'no ideas but in things', 'an aesthetic based on energies', pragmatism, muscularity and Walt Whitman. Over here, we are often told, we don't speak the same language.

Projective verse, while repudiating ideas not in things, also opposes the kind of haphazard static perception that made up the typical Imagist poem. It seeks, through an openness of rhythm and syntax, to reassert the poet's control of his material and to restore him to his

---

(*a*) *The Jacob's Ladder*. 83 pp. Cape. 18s. *Geography*. 74 pp. Fulcrum Press. 25s. *Buckdancer's Choice*. 79 pp. Connecticut: Wesleyan University Press. $1.85. *Finding Them Lost*. And other Poems. 121 pp. Macmillan. 25s.

(*b*) *Poems 1950–1965*. 227 pp. Calder and Boyars. 35s.

(*c*) *The North Ship*. 48 pp. Faber and Faber. 15s.

(*d*) *The Far Field*. 95 pp. Faber and Faber. 18s.

rightful place in his own poem. So far so good. But a true poem belongs to its author not by technical *force majeure*, but because the perception itself, static or otherwise, is an expression of his subjectivity and an imaginative bodying forth of it into the world. This is the method, if such we can call it, of Shakespeare and Keats. It is also the method of Eliot, Hart Crane and Robert Lowell; but Black Mountain aesthetics ditch such models in favour of the more technical and anti-symbolist eccentricities of Pound and William Carlos Williams. In the projective poet's bid for dynamic syntax and what he thinks of as American speech rhythms, not only the stasis gets left behind but the perception too. In the quintessential Black Mountain poem, vision has given way entirely to talk. And not always interesting talk either: the trailing syntax and the line-breaks shorn of gestural significance can be as insulting to the intelligence as the poems themselves, gobbety, off-hand, and trickling in thin rivers down the page, are offensive to the eye and ear.

Mercifully there is no quintessential Black Mountain poet. Denise Levertov, though very much of the school, has a sharper eye and a plainer syntax than many of its practitioners, and there are moments in *The Jacob's Ladder* when her flat description gathers itself up into an actual image, as when she sees:

Red tulips
living into their death
flushed with a wild blue

But the moments are rare, and more often, if she uses words 'poetically' it is with a self-consciousness and imprecision that seems deliberately designed as a kind of alienation-effect against the entrancements of poetry:

Last night
as if death had lit a pale light
in your flesh, your flesh
was cold to my touch, or not cold
but cool, cooling, as if the last traces
of warmth were still fading in you.

The influence of Williams is strong in these poems and their conversational tone is probably meant to be anti-traditional and anti-academic. But with the threat of philistinism always present the result is just as likely to be anti-poetry and anti-mind.

The authentic! It rolls
just out of reach

Miss Levertov writes. Mostly it does; but she would stand a better chance if she would reach after it less and learn to trust her imagination.

Likewise, Edward Dorn might do better to publish his fulminations against America—

> this Theocracy where the *Structure* has rolled—

as prose. They are justified enough, but they take on life only when the ideas they contain really do get rooted in things. This happens in a long poem called 'Idaho out', where the poet drives through America as well as talking about it and renders its sadness into a series of personal experiences. Mr. Dorn's adherence to Black Mountain principles is never slavish, but it is there, and his prosy manner and chopped-up lines work against his deeper feelings even in his love poems. Somewhere in the background there is real humanity and strength, but the poems in *Geography* go down too easily; the arresting perception and the memorable line are always missing. Perhaps he should try looking around for some new models.

James Dickey, who has himself severely criticized projective theory, writes a free verse that is nearly always unmannered and businesslike. He gives his images a chance—if never a chance to take over entirely—and in *Buckdancer's Choice* there are some interesting tensions set up between fantasy and everyday life. But Mr. Dickey seems tired of his 'Twenty years in the suburbs', and inside the domestic man there is a wild man signalling to be let out. The signals are there in the violence of his war memories, but they are strongest in a fine piece of Prufrock-voyeurism called 'The Fiend' and in the suppressed sexual frenzy of a poem called 'Slave Quarters'. There are fellow suburbans who would be grateful to Mr. Dickey for more of this kind of thing.

Something of what projectivism was up against can be seen in Howard Moss's *Finding Them Lost*, where the rhyme-schemes and pentameters carry all before them and a Christmas tree becomes 'The season's casualty of squandered green'. When he leaves off his worried frown Mr. Moss can be wry and pleasing, but for the most part he is a stern devotee of the shapely and the passionless. Not unfittingly his book includes a translation of Valéry's *Le Cimetière* (always misspelt *Cimitière*) *Marin*.

There was a time when such academicism was widespread and a legitimate target for attack. But that time is past, and the theory of projective verse has now become an academicism in its turn. If American poets are really as interested in poetry as they are in America they should forget the poetics of Olson, Zukofsky, Duncan *et al.* and give the shaping spirit a chance.

(*b*) ROBERT CREELEY

Poems 1950–1965

There is perhaps no longer much point in dividing new American poetry into those once convenient camps called paleface and redskin, cooked and raw. American poets in general today seem to be in a mildly experimental mood, whether they take as their model Williams, Zukofsky, Olson, Ginsberg, or Lowell. These models are not mutually exclusive, of course, but the result is often parboiled or rehashed; and the wild unlettered brave often seems to have had a dose of Rimbaud or *haiku*, while the bookish academic has learnt a thing or two from the 'long Hebraic breath' of *Howl* and the theorizings about so-called projective and open-field verse.

Robert Creeley's collected volume and James Merrill's new book suggest that what perhaps divides American poets now is an attitude to imagery. Mr. Creeley, who has been an influential figure in the whole nexus surrounding the *Black Mountain Review*, is a poet who does without imagery in any usual sense. In his poems much cogitation goes on, about perception, about relationships, about language, but though these poems exist in a peopled landscape neither people nor landscape has much substance. The whole tone is so interrogative that it is a little surprising that Mr. Creeley generally dispenses with question-marks: perhaps in these insubstantial contexts they would look too coarse and demonstrative, since there are so many unanswered or unanswerable questions:

> Stepping
>
> Out of
> the car with these
> endless people,
> where are
> you, am I happy,
> is this car
> mine.

Mr. Creeley seems to trust in a kind of magic conjured up by the numb repetition of colourless words, as if casting some non-denominational spell:

What do you
want, love. To be
loved. What,

what wanted,
love, wanted
so much as love . . .

Yet the effect is that of wading interminably through some unfamiliar shorthand or of listening to a glazed monotone, as of some drear party guest one has to watch because his boringness is hypnotic and girls are apt to fall under his greyly malign influence. Mr. Creeley goes on about love a great deal, but without much warmth, and what warmth there is seems the product of sentimental bathos:

The huge dog, Broderick, and
the smile of the quick eyes
of Allen light a kind world.

(Allen, we learn from the dedication to this poem, is predictably Allen Ginsberg.) Sometimes the poems are *simpliste* to the point of idiocy, as in 'The Bird', where the rhymes—unusual in Mr. Creeley—suggest an odd echo of Humbert Wolfe:

What did he say to me
  that I had not heard.
She said she saw
  a small bird.

Where was it.
  In a trcc.
Ah, he said, I thought
  you spoke to me.

But Mr. Creeley is not a *naïf*. He has read Whitman ('Out of the table endlessly rocking'), Byron ('She walks in beauty like a lake'), and even has a shot at a poem 'After Mallarmé'. For 'I Know a Man', probably his best-known poem, he deserves some praise. Here his shorthand seems proper to what he is saying, it mimes well: here is a situation, a mood, a response. And in 'The Rhythm' there is a more compelling movement, suited to the title, which shows that Mr. Creeley does not need to shatter himself to fragments before he can make an utterance. But in general this fifteen-year bundle of almost 200 poems makes crushingly dull reading.

(*c*) PHILIP LARKIN

The North Ship

One sometimes has the feeling that poets used to emerge early and nowadays emerge late. There were, for example, several poets in the 1930s who produced their first volumes when barely out of their teens: Auden (twenty-three), Spender (twenty-one), Day Lewis (twenty-one), MacNeice (twenty-two), Dylan Thomas (twenty), George Barker (twenty), David Gascoyne (sixteen). The post-Second World War poets seem a tardier crew, first publishing in their late twenties or early thirties. To most readers, Philip Larkin would appear to be such a case: *The Less Deceived*, which immediately made his reputation, was published when the poet was thirty-three.

But Faber and Faber remind us that Mr. Larkin in fact made a much earlier start: *The North Ship*, now reissued, appeared in 1945, when he was twenty-three. In a characteristically funny and self-deprecating introduction to the new edition Mr. Larkin writes of the circumstances surrounding the book's original publication by the Fortune Press. He is diffident about the merits of the poems, putting much of the blame on his infatuation at the time with Yeats's 'music': 'in fairness to myself it must be admitted that it is a particularly potent music, pervasive as garlic and has ruined many a better talent'.

In fact there are fewer traces of Yeats than Mr. Larkin leads one to suppose. The influence can be seen at its strongest in the poem beginning 'I see a girl dragged by the wrists', where both the stanza-form and the imagery echo 'A Prayer for my Daughter' and 'Among School Children' ('A sack of meal upon two sticks', 'All that's content to wear a worn-out coat'). And there are signs of the potent music being particularly unhelpful in some of the 'pure' lyrics, which are among the weakest in the volume. There is the occasional touch of Auden, to which Mr. Larkin draws attention, such as 'Conscript'. It might have been an idea, by the way, to have included an uncollected piece that one takes to be earlier than any of these: the equally

Audenesque but extremely assured poem he published in *The Listener* in November, 1940, when he was only eighteen. This, on the poet's own authority—see his autobiographical essay of some years ago in the Coventry arts magazine, *Umbrella*—was his first publication. There seems to be no evidence at all of Dylan Thomas, the third influence whom Mr. Larkin mentions.

What is chiefly interesting now about these poems is, rather, how they foreshadow the mature and authoritative Larkin of *The Less Deceived* and *The Whitsun Weddings*. One supposes that the poems in *The North Ship* were written between the ages of twenty and twenty-two. How astonishing it is that so young a man, in the stiflingly 'literary' atmosphere of wartime Oxford (Mr. Larkin is amusing about his early confrontations with the dominant Oxford poets of the time, John Heath-Stubbs and Sidney Keyes), was capable of such lines as:

> To show you pausing at a picture's edge
> To puzzle out the name, or with a hand
> Resting a second on a random page . . .
>
> Only a name
> That chimes occasionally, as a belief
> Long since embedded in the static past . . .
> This is your last, meticulous hour.
> Cut, gummed; pastime of a provincial winter . . .

It is true that these lines are a little softer, a good deal more open to sentimentality, than the lines they remind one of in the later books. But they are clearly by the same man.

Sometimes it is no more than a cadence, or such pieces of phrasing as 'wind-mastered', 'No gale-driven bird / Nor frost-encircled root', that suggest the future. Occasionally there is an image that seems to have been resurrected later and with greater power, as

> I am wakened each dawn
> Increasingly to fear
> Sail-stiffening air,
> The birdless sea . . .

which points one forward to 'Next, Please' in *The Less Deceived.*

Mr. Larkin marks the fresh impetus in his work as coming from his reading of Hardy's poems in early 1946, and he has included one poem, slightly later than the others in *The North Ship* and hitherto uncollected, which shows the confidence won from this new master.

This poem, 'Waiting for breakfast', also shows a clear link stylistically with the earliest poem in *The Less Deceived*, 'Wedding-Wind'. Altogether, though, there is no gainsaying the fact that intrinsically *The North Ship* was not, and is not, a particularly fine collection. But Philip Larkin is now of sufficient stature for it to be a positively welcome addition to the record: the juvenilia of the best poets are always worth reading.

(*d*) THEODORE ROETHKE

The Far Field

In America, as elsewhere, the twentieth century has been a period of doubt and self-consciousness, and the American poet, looking around him for order and support, has found little to rely on in a world that seems farther gone each day in chaos and inhumanity. For all the high hopes of the 1920s, he has not found it easy to think of poetry as something pure and self-justifying, as having its own authority and speaking with the voice of it.

Theodore Roethke was very much a poet of our age. The difficulty of being human became the very substance of his poetry, and in almost everything that he wrote the note of self-awareness is to be heard. Like other poets profoundly at odds with their world—Lawrence comes particularly to mind, but so does Blake—he devoted some of his best poems to plants and animals, and in all these, working away behind the minute and sensitive description, there is a deep subjectivity, a powerful reference back to the poet and his own condition. At other times the self-consciousness breaks out explicitly, and the poet talks about himself in the first person. Always there is a conflict present between some vision of the natural life and the actual circumstances of the adult human world. Roethke wrote movingly of the innocence of childhood and, more frequently as the years passed, of sensual love haunted by age and death. If the philosophizing tone of his earlier work is Lawrentian, it yields gradually to something more like the defiance of Yeats, and eventually, as this too gives way, to a conscious groping after spiritual grace—though not at first without a trace of embarrassment:

> O sweet field far ahead, I hear your birds,
> They sing, they sing, but still in minor thirds.

In *The Far Field*, arranged by Roethke himself shortly before his death in 1963, the resignation is more nearly complete. The vivid perception remains, but it has been gathered up into a backward-looking reflectiveness, and the prevailing tone is that of Eliot:

I am renewed by death, thought of my death,
The dry scent of a dying garden in September,
The wind fanning the ash of a low fire
What I love is near at hand,
Always, in earth and air.

The poet has come to accept death, and nature, which was once a living challenge, has now become the source of images of serenity. The power of these final poems lies in the fact that Roethke's hold on life was always too full-blooded for him to renounce it easily, and even at the end the desire survives, not for death or *nirvana*, but for the natural life that Roethke had always dreamed of. Perhaps the heart of his poetry is to be found in a line from 'The Manifestation':

What does what it should do needs nothing more.

In the far field the dance of life goes on.

But what *should* the human creature do? How should we live? Perhaps it is here, at its heart, that the weakness of Roethke's poetry also lies. For nature alone is not enough: the problems of human existence lie with the mind, and in whether the mind can cope. Unlike Blake, Roethke had no strongly personal philosophy, and without such machinery to help us we must create order from chaos with our bare hands. This Roethke could not do. His poetry could not really deal with the modern world, but only with himself as a victim of it. And so inevitably the end was renunciation. For the animal, life ends with the individual. Only the human being, and above all the human poet, can grasp and believe in the living future in the very moment of his own death. We miss such a belief in Roethke's poetry, even while we admire its stoic power.

What's madness but nobility of soul
At odds with circumstance?

Roethke asks. But we could as well turn the question round. The nobility of Roethke's work is there for all to see, in his awe of nature, his love for defenceless things, his rejection of timidity and drabness. But it remains at odds with circumstances, rarely transcending them in poetry. And the madness was never far away. His very best poems are perhaps the few where Roethke gets outside himself entirely—in this book there is the fine 'Elegy' for his Aunt Tilly:

> I recall how she harried the children away all the late summer
> From the one beautiful thing in her yard, the peachtree;
> How she kept the wizened, the fallen, the misshapen for herself,
> And picked and pickled the best to be left on rickety doorsteps.
> And yet she died in agony,
> Her tongue, at the last, thick, black as an ox's.

Roethke's nobility, in fact, is of the man, not of the imagination. What we miss, in the end, is the unique perception, the hard tip of the poetic iceberg coming clear of the personal depths. For the most part the authority of these last poems, like those of Eliot, is the authority of religion, not the truly human authority of poetry itself. But his voice, like Eliot's, is one of the true voices of the twentieth century.

17

G.B.S. ON THE LARGE SCREEN

MR. COSTELLO'S PURPOSE is to tell how His Verbosity, the 'Sweet Irish Pope' Shavian I, and his Legate, Pascal, set out to convert the film-philistines, how they first broke box-office records and finally well-nigh broke the burgeoning British film industry. It is a tale told by a scholar signifying abundant research but failing to discover the cause and effects of a nine years' wonder so auspiciously begun, and ended in spectacular fiasco. For the degeneration of this enterprise was to be traced, not in Shaw's pronouncements or in the industrious comparison of his texts, but by studying the personalities and inviting the recollections of those who, for better or worse, ministered to this strange coalition of Celtic genius and Hungarian rhapsody.

In a foreword Mr. Cecil Lewis pays an affectionate tribute to G.B.S., but the evidence he cites of their collaboration convicts him of being accessory before the fact of his benefactor's suicide as a film scenarist. Evidently having had no experience as a film maker he persuaded Shaw to let him direct a film of *How He Lied To Her Husband* and so fostered the dramatist's delusion that moving pictures of a stage performance could entertain film-goers. The failure of this static reproduction of a comparatively trivial comedy did not diminish G.B.S.'s self-esteem as a screen-writer, nor did it encourage him to believe that the medium could extend his preachments to millions, to their great delight and intellectual profit, if his plays could be translated to the screen by skilled and subtle adaptation. An itinerant film entrepreneur, Gabriel Pascal, was the first to discern these possibilities. His ardent faith and protestations of devoted loyalty prevailed on his venerated Master to let him prove himself by filming *Pygmalion*. What *The Serpent's Eye* sadly lacks is another foreword conveying the character and gifts of Shaw's *farouche*, and in many ways naive, disciple.

DONALD P. COSTELLO: *The Serpent's Eye*. Shaw and the Cinema. Foreword by Cecil Lewis. 209 pp. University of Notre Dame Press (American University Publishers Group). £2 10s.

Mr. Costello does not seem to appreciate the unusual consortium of talents that went to the making of *Pygmalion* or the extent of the influence this team exerted upon Pascal and Shaw. It was Pascal who, unlike Korda and most of the movie mandarins of that time, had an aesthetic flair that led him to enlist the services of three forward-looking young film technicians—Anthony Asquith, a director with an intellectual grasp of the medium and with the *savoir-faire* that would preserve the wit and elegance implicit in the play, David Lean, an editor of genius on his way to becoming the foremost director of his time, and Laurence Irving, a graphic artist who had learnt in Hollywood from the great production designer, William Cameron Menzies, that the pictorial as well as the literary preparation of a script could ensure engrossing continuity by the precise and imaginative preplanning of camera set-ups. Added to them were sensitive and reflective leading players who, while respecting Shaw's text, would interpret his characters with perception and style that outdated the dramatist's conception of ideal performance. Those sufficiently interested to discover the epitome of the unique quality of Pascal's *Pygmalion* will find it in the montage accompanied by Honegger's score of Eliza's oral education—the wittiest harmony of sound and abstract forms. Unhappily few prints of this film remain (three are in the possession of the British Film Institute). Most of the rest were destroyed by unregenerate philistines in order to secure the copyright of the extra sequence Shaw had written after seeing sketches depicting Eliza's triumph at a diplomatic reception.

The success of *Pygmalion* was immediate and joyous. For the first time movie audiences the world over, having been entertained by sparkling and sophisticated dialogue, left cinemas with something to think about other than self-identification with romantic routines. Shaw's film future depended on the successful exploitation of this success. The reasons for Pascal's (and, indeed, Shaw's) failure to profit by it are not wholly understood by Mr. Costello. They agreed on *The Doctor's Dilemma* as their next venture—possibly the most filmable of all the plays. At the height of *Pygmalion's* popularity in America Pascal arrived with his production designer in Hollywood. Their twin purpose was to prepare the script in collaboration with a reputable American screen-writer and to rescue an actress (acknowledged by all to be the perfect Mrs. Dubedat) from the giant Metrogoldwynmayer in whose castle she was chained, if not languishing, by fetters of contract. What proved to be a tactical error was their presentation to their American colleague of a library edition of Shaw's plays signed by the Master which promoted in him a stultifying veneration for Shavian writ. Though the fantastic receipts from *Pygmalion* caused movie magnates, who previously had scarcely heard of G.B.S., to speak of him in tones usually reserved for the illustrious dead, those who held the coveted actress in fee would not release her to encourage further British poaching on their box-office preserves. Moreover exhaustive tests did not discover a presentable Dubedat among the younger generation of film actors.

So, although a faithful but lively script had been completed, *The Doctor's Dilemma* was abandoned in favour of *Major Barbara*. When Pascal and his designer returned to England with a scenario that liberated the play from the bonds of stage-craft, Shaw declared that Irving must have been drunk when he conceived such a treatment—principally because the nocturnal temptation of Cousins by Undershaft was conducted in the sybaritic setting of the latter's club and in an elegant night-club such as the mephistophelian Maundy Gregory might have operated. At that point war on Hitler was declared. The services of Pascal's team were needed in other spheres. All its members had an affection for their producer that, being reciprocated, held him in restraint, for prompted by their suggestions based on sound technical principles he was able to convince Shaw (always amenable to professional logic) of the need for compromise. Left to himself, and perhaps in desperation, Pascal assumed the role of director—a role for which he was quite unsuited, lacking the mastery of film technique or of the English language necessary for handling his subordinates with authority in the exacting conditions of wartime filming.

Soon Pascal succumbed to *folie de grandeur*, not from personal vanity but from his belief that his Master deserved the best that talent and money could provide. So, having decided upon *Caesar and Cleopatra*, Shaw took a mischievous delight in fanning Pascal's passion for meaningless pomp in circumstances that led to both of them being condemned, not only for their artistic folly, but also for the almost treasonable squandering of money and material syphoned from the nation's economy in its hour of war-time need. Rightly no such accusations were levelled at the same time against the producers of *Henry V*—unlike *Caesar and Cleopatra* the end justified the means.

Mr. Costello faithfully records the ruinous progress of this pair of missionary rakes, but he does not stress the consequences of the debacle on the British film industry. Mr. Arthur Rank, now Lord Rank, had done all in his power to encourage native talents to improve the quality of the films he was financing, to this end seeking the advice of distinguished artists in every field. His calamitous loss on *Caesar and Cleopatra* lent force to the arguments of those determined to bring him to commercial reason, to debar Pascal from his studio, and later to discredit the ebullient Filippo del Giudice, who did more than any other to promote the production of national rather than cosmopolitan films in this country.

Shaw was the first to predict the power for good or evil of a medium that would have a global appeal. Mr. Costello reminds us that in 1914 he wrote:

> before printing could affect you, you had to learn to read; and until 1870 you mostly had not learnt to read. But even when you had, reading was not really a practical business for a manual labourer. Ask any man who has done eight or ten hours' heavy manual labour what happens to him when he takes up a book. He will tell you that he falls asleep in less than two minutes. Now the cinema tells its story to the illiterate as well as to the literate; and it keeps its victim (if you like to call him so) not only awake but fascinated as if by a serpent's eye. And that is why the cinema is going to produce effects that all the cheap books in the world could never produce.

Having such prescience, why did not Shaw, the ardent propagandist, recognize films as a direct channel of communication between himself and a public incalculably larger than he could command in the theatre or in print?

Authors should be duty-bound to veto mistranslation of their work to the screen. In fact Shaw and A. E. W. Mason were the only British writers to do so; most of their colleagues preferred to take the cash and let their credit and the quality of their work go. But the exercise of such a veto obliges an author to study the scope and limitations of this new medium. The shadows on the screen cannot hold the attention of an audience as can substantial actors on the stage. The task of the film director is to keep his audience on the alert by the rhythmic editing of film he has shot with that end in view. Shaw never really understood this and Pascal, in awe of his Master, sacrificed visual suspense for the flow of dialogue with catastrophic results.

18

'NO, BUT I SAW THE MOVIE'

COUNT DRACULA AND HIS BACKGROUND

IT IS BRAM STOKER'S singular misfortune to be remembered largely by films which have little or nothing to do with his original literary creation. 'No, but I saw the movie' might well be his epitaph. That is not to say that nobody reads *Dracula* any more: few books have been more readily, continuously available in popular paperback form. But for every one who has read the novel there must be thousands who have only seen films with Dracula as central character, and not necessarily the films—Murnau's *Nosferatu* (1921), Tod Browning's *Dracula* with Bela Lugosi (1931), or Terence Fisher's version with Christopher Lee (1958)—which have been directly based on the book, for the film Dracula has been as fertile as the film Frankenstein in sons, daughters and brides, not to mention returns, revenges, curses and even meetings with Abbott and Costello.

And where, in all this, does the poor author stand? Nowhere very much; when a first biography appeared in 1962, on the fiftieth anniversary of his death, it was even titled *A Biography of Dracula*, a curious instance of the author being apparently altogether lost in his creation. The fact that Stoker had to wait so long for a biography is also indicative. Though in his lifetime he knew a number of the great literary figures, and was even congratulated on certain of his writings by Tennyson and Gladstone, the enormous popularity of his most famous novel, and of those in a similar mode which followed it, made it increasingly difficult for him to be taken seriously as a writer. At the time of its appearance (1897) *Dracula* was at once recognized for what it was, the last of the great Gothic novels: the *Daily Mail* remarked:

BRAM STOKER: *Dracula*. 336 pp. 3s. 6d. *The Jewel of the Seven Stars*. 254 pp. 2s. 6d. *The Lady of the Shroud*. 192 pp. 2s. 6d. *The Lair of the White Worm*. 191 pp. 2s. 6d. *Dracula's Guest*. 192 pp. 3s. 6d. Arrow Books.

> In seeking a parallel to this weird, powerful and horrible story, our minds revert to such tales as *The Mysteries of Udolpho*, *Frankenstein*, *Wuthering Heights*, *The Fall of the House of Usher*, and *Marjery of Quelher*. But *Dracula* is even more appalling in its gloomy fascination than any one of these!

But in thus placing the book the critics were already writing it down, putting it at the tail end of a line long regarded with some patronage.

In terms of sales, Stoker never looked back; but it was virtually the end of his reputation as a figure to be reckoned with in literature, based at that time above all on his strange book of stories allegedly for children, *Under the Sunset*, and his Irish romance *The Snake's Pass*, the book which Tennyson and Gladstone had praised. Hardly anybody denied his abilities, as far as they went; but then hardly anyone would be willing to suppose that they went much farther than those of, say, Henty or Sax Rohmer. Even time has not really brought Stoker full revenge. Though no fewer than five of his books are readily available in paperback—all, that is, which touch significantly on the supernatural except *The Mystery of the Sea*—he is still, if he is considered at all, dismissed superiorly as a coarse-grained popular entertainer.

The trouble, it is usually said, is that whatever his gifts as an inventor of spine-chilling situations, he does not 'write well'. The phrase is used, generally, as though its meaning were self-evident. But any such assumption would be optimistic. It is a sign, perhaps, as much as anything, that we remain slaves of the intentional fallacy in literature, pathetically ready to accept writers according to their ambitions rather than their achievements. We will suppose, for instance, that George Moore must in some mysterious way be a better writer than Bram Stoker, even if Stoker is still read and Moore on the whole is not, because Moore spent a lot of time and energy carrying on about his dedication to high art while Stoker churned out best-sellers in the spare moments of an otherwise busy life. Moore, in his later books, writes with extreme care and self-conscious artistry, but the result is unreadable; Stoker, whatever else may be said of him, is still intensely readable. So which, in the final analysis, writes better?

The accusation of not writing well usually turns out on examination to be a judgment of kind rather than of quality. Though Stoker could, when he wished, write in a conscious, carefully wrought style, and uses one to some effect in *Under the Sunset*, his forte is the sort of writing in which the style is not noticeable at all. Brisk, strictly functional, sacrificing all evident graces to telling complicated and incident-packed stories with maximum efficiency. If Stoker's novels are not among the most imaginative in the literature of his time, at least they are among the most triumphantly inventive. He is never at a loss for telling incident which forwards the plot and keeps the reader on tenterhooks to know what will happen next. And his books are the work of a fastidious literary craftsman in at least one respect, that most vital to his purposes: they are constructed with great care, their big scenes built up to and elaborated with a sure dramatic flair which suggests that Stoker's years as Irving's acting manager were by no means so irrelevant to his literary activities as they seem at first sight.

For Stoker—and this is another thing which has tended to be held against him—was almost throughout his life a part-time writer only. He began his career in the law, writing dramatic criticism for the Dublin press in his spare time. A meeting with Irving led to his being offered the managing job in 1878, when he was thirty-one, and it was not until the next year that his first book was published—*The Duties of Clerks of Petty Sessions in Ireland.* From that time on his days were fully occupied with shepherding Irving's company through Lyceum seasons and provincial tours, as well as preparing for Bar examinations (he was finally called to the Bar in 1890). How he had time to write at all remains a mystery, and yet write he did, which remarkable regularity and application. From the appearance of his first work of fiction, *Under the Sunset*, in 1881, he was seldom idle from writing for long—there were short stories, non-fiction works like his *Glimpses of America* (1886), a by-product of one of Irving's American tours, which Stanley took with him across Africa and said had more information in it about America than any other book ever written; there was his Irish novel *The Snake's Pass* (1889) and a couple of less notable romances, and there were numerous articles and rewrite jobs—mainly uncredited—on plays added to the company's repertoire.

Then, in 1897, Stoker finally hit his stride with *Dracula*, an instant best-seller which at once made him a name to conjure with. It was the first of his novels which had tackled the supernatural directly, though several of the eerie short stories collected after his death in *Dracula's Guest* were written before. On the face of it, the material of his triumph seemed curious, for Stoker was the last man anyone associated with such flights of morbid fantasy. He was, in fact, one of those extravagantly manly, uncomplicated-seeming men, a hefty six-footer given to acts of bravery like plunging into the Thames to rescue a determined suicide or preventing fire-panic in the theatre by seizing the culprit by the throat and throwing him to the ground with the words 'It's cowards like you who cause death to helpless women'. And yet along with all this, and with an extraordinary organizing gift which caused many, Whistler among them, to attempt to woo him away from Irving as business manager, there was another side to Stoker. He was interested from early days in morbid subjects; there is extant, for instance, a long letter, printed by Harry Ludham in his biography, in which Stoker's mother complies with his request that she should give him full details of the cholera epidemic at Sligo which she lived through as a girl, and the subject of plague occurs gruesomely in one of the stories from *Under the Sunset*, 'The Invisible Giant', in which an orphan girl has a vision of death brooding over the city and is persecuted for her pains until the plague actually descends. Several of the other stories in the book are equally nasty, and surprisingly strong meat, even in the death-obsessed world of much Victorian writing for children.

What more practical, organized interest, if any, Stoker took in the occult remains somewhat mysterious. It has been stated that he was a member of the Golden Dawn, an hermetic society in which Crowley and Yeats, among others, played prominent parts; Mr. Ludlam, who got much of his information from Stoker's son, does not mention this, and it may not be so, though it is quite possible—Sax Rohmer, for instance, was undoubtedly on the fringes of the group. Certainly from the early 1890s, under the influence of his close friend Hall Caine (to whom, under the Manx pet-name Hommy-Beg, *Dracula* is dedicated), Stoker became increasingly involved in study of the occult, and his novels on supernatural themes contain a surprising amount of incidental erudition. Perhaps it is not unfair to take the hero of *The Mystery of the Sea* as a sort of idealized self-portrait: a man's man with all the conventional views of the period on honour, duty towards the weaker sex, and so on, he is at the same time gifted with second sight and therefore able to see in vision what is withheld from the more prosaic characters about the significance of Lammastide at Cruden Sands. This combination of the stolid, ordinary chap and the dreamy visionary seems to have been very much Stoker's own nature. But he was not driven, like his contemporary William Sharp (Fiona Macleod), to fence off the fey side of his nature and manufacture another persona from behind which he could give expression to it. Instead, in his best books he combines the two—hence the oddly haunting quality of his writing which at once puts him in a quite different class from, say, Dennis Wheatley, with whom he has often been compared.

A closer and fairer comparison, curiously enough, would be with Matthew Gregory Lewis, whose best works, *The Monk* particularly, have the same precipitate, stop-at-nothing narrative drive, and the same air of being unashamedly popular writing under which may be glimpsed clearly an essential basis of personal obsession. Though *Dracula* is undoubtedly Stoker's best book, he is much less a one-book writer than Lewis. It is unlikely that anyone now would find much of interest in such novels as *The Man*, *Miss Betty* and *Lady Athlyne*, light, silly ephemeral romances in the mood of the day, but even apart from his *Personal Reminiscences of Henry Irving*, a book of permanent value for the theatrically minded, and *Famous Impostors*, a diverting collection which might well be worth some paperback publisher's while, there are at least five works of fiction which still bear re-reading.

Perhaps that should be six, for *The Lair of the White Worm*, Stoker's last novel, has always been one of his steadiest sellers. This is hard to understand, though, for it bears every sign of being written (as it was) under great strain during Stoker's last illness: characters come and go, and change with no rhyme or reason, and almost everyone, after a spell of suspicious behaviour designed to make us wonder whether he or she can be the monster, turns out to be harmlessly but all too conveniently mad. On the other hand *The Jewel of the Seven Stars* is a straight study in terror in which Stoker abandons *Dracula*'s involuted form of narrative, learnt from Wilkie Collins, for a straightforward first-person narration leading to a climax—the attempted resurrection of an ancient Egyptian princess in modern Cornwall—which was considered so horrible at the time that Stoker's publishers persuaded him to soften it for later editions (though even the softened version remains nicely ambiguous). *Dracula's Guest* contains in addition to the title story, an episode cut from *Dracula* itself in revision to correct a structural fault, eight short stories with supernatural or horrific overtones, one of which, 'The Burial of the Rats', is a virtuoso piece on the subject of nightmare flight from danger in Stoker's very best style. And *The Lady of the Shroud* and *The Mystery of the Sea* both neatly dovetail the two sides of Stoker's nature. In the first the man-of-action hero finds himself falling, rather disturbingly, in love with a vampire, but then fortunately she proves after all to be a Balkan princess merely posing as a vampire to ensure her own safety, and the whole thing ends in a fine piece of aerial warfare which even today, when it has moved out of science fiction into hard fact, would make a splendid film climax. *The Mystery of the Sea* has, as well as visions, a quest for lost treasure, a cipher which even Conan Doyle found masterly, a fair amount of brisk, uncloying romance, and dastardly foreigners to be outwitted at the last.

But of course it is above all as the author of *Dracula* that Stoker survives. And it is a book that has to be read, since no film yet has ever done it justice. Indeed, the films always leave out the best parts, because, no doubt, even today scenes like that in which one of the two innocent young heroines, now undead, is cut off from her grave when she returned sated with blood and finally put to rest, would be a little more than the average audience is willing to take—not because of the elementary physical horrors but because of the imaginative effect created by the extreme character change in someone who has up to now been highly sympathetic. Nor has the fly-eater Renfield, the novel's most convincing and extraordinary character, ever received his just deserts in the cinema. There are few refinements in the book, certainly; but then there are more important things in literature than refinement. If Stoker had tried to write a *Turn of the Screw* he would probably have failed; but then he had more sense than to do so. He chose to paint in poster-colour because he knew he could do it well, and it would be foolish to reproach the bold and brilliant composition which resulted for lacking the delicacy of a pastel. In *Dracula*, after all, Stoker gave shape to a myth, and that is more than many more important writers can claim in a whole career devoted to the life of art.

19

CRISIS IN CRITICISM

THE PICARD–BARTHES DEBATE

IN A LEADING article published on February 3, we drew attention to a difference of opinion about the interpretation of Racine between M. Raymond Picard, a professor at the Sorbonne, and M. Roland Barthes, a lecturer at the École des Hautes Études. In a sharply-worded little volume, *Nouvelle critique ou nouvelle imposture*, M. Picard, one of the foremost academic experts on Racine and the editor of the dramatist's works in the Pléiade series, took M. Barthes to task in connexion with certain statements in his little book, *Sur Racine*. The gist of M. Picard's complaint was that M. Barthes is guilty of fanciful readings, which he puts forward with solemn assurance. This 'dogmatic impressionism', M. Picard added, is characteristic of a whole new school, *la nouvelle critique*, of which M. Barthes is one of the leading lights and perhaps the outstanding figure.

*   *   *

By attacking this movement at its centre, M. Picard claimed to be performing an act of intellectual hygiene, to be clearing the air of pretentious critical cant. In fact, he has set the cat among the pigeons. Not since the heyday of Sartre's quarrels with Camus and David Rousset has there been such a flapping of wings. Articles and letters have appeared in many newspapers and periodicals. *Le Nouvel Observateur* and *La Quinzaine Littéraire* have printed statements for and against the two protagonists. M. Barthes has answered *Nouvelle critique ou nouvelle imposture* with a no less mordant pamphlet

---

RAYMOND PICARD: *Nouvelle critique ou nouvelle imposture.* 149 pp. Paris: Pauvert. 3.10 fr.

ROLAND BARTHES: *Critique et vérité.* 79 pp. Paris: Éditions du Seuil. 4.50 fr.

SERGE DOUBROVSKY: *Pourquoi la nouvelle critique.* 257 pp. Mercure de France. 16.95 fr.

GUSTAVE LANSON: *Essais de méthode, de critique et d'histoire littéraire.* Rassemblés et présentés par Henri Peyre. 477 pp. Paris: Hachette.

Critique et vérité. M. Serge Doubrovsky has weighed in with quite a large book, *Pourquoi la nouvelle critique*, and this is only Volume I, *Critique et objectivité*. Volume II, *Critique et subjectivité*, is promised for the near future, M. Jean-François Revel, who edits the Pauvert series 'Libertés', in which M. Picard's little book appeared, has accused the 'new critics' of not answering M. Picard's objections. The 'new critics', for their part, maintain that this controversy is a fresh version of the quarrel of the Ancients and Moderns, and imply that M. Picard is hardly worth answering since, being an Ancient, he is too deaf and benighted to understand. M. Picard refuses to be classed as an Ancient and claims to be as modern as anyone.

In the resulting turmoil, almost all the themes of contemporary French intellectual life have been brought to the surface at once: Existentialism, Marxism, Freudianism, Structuralism (both linguistic and anthropological), the psychology of mythic substances, the nature of rhetoric and preciosity, the myriad approaches to the problem of being, and the relationship between criticism and creativeness—all of which, of course, can be subsumed under the single heading: What is truth? One can imagine Racine's bewilderment, if he could be made aware of these complexities, all of which are unrelated to the Christian conception of truth. The debate is taking place within the secular tradition, and its violence may be partly explicable by the fact that certain of the participants have a nostalgia for the satisfying mysteries of faith, or at least, like those strange bedfellows Mallarmé and Sartre, want to make the use of language a total act which puts the writer in an absolute relationship with the ultimate mysteries.

* * *

The 'Ancient and Modern' interpretation is an easy way into the controversy, even if it does not take the inquirer very far. M. Barthes is only one of a number of critics who are not, or were not, in the mainstream of French academic discussion of literature. Some of them converged on literary criticism from other disciplines; for instance, the late Gaston Bachelard, a most important influence, was an historian of science who nevertheless believed the pre-scientific categories of perception to be essential modes of the imagination. Jean-Pierre Richard, the author of an unorthodox doctoral thesis on Mallarmé, has so far preferred to pursue his career in French Institutes abroad. Maurice Blanchot is a rather mysterious recluse with no official function. Georges Poulet is a Belgian now teaching in Zurich; Jean Starobinski is a Genevan. These, and many others, can be thought of as innovators battling against the hide-bound traditions of the Sorbonne, with its emphasis on literary history, its prudent accumulation of 'factual' detail and its positivistic approach inherited from the nineteenth century, by way of Lanson and his successors. In fact Lanson's name has been quoted so frequently as a symbol of academic obtuseness that M. Henri Peyre, the leading French academic in America, has just reissued a volume of his essays for the express purpose of proving that Lanson is greatly superior to his reputation in literary circles. Whether or not one thinks that M. Peyre proves his point, there is, rightly or wrongly, a widespread feeling that Lanson is the patron of the old guard and that the concept of the avant-garde must be introduced into criticism as it has been in literature. M. Doubrovsky puts this point of view most forcibly:

> . . . la nouvelle critique n'est rien d'autre, dans ses divergences évidentes, dans ses disparates criantes, que l'ouverture, longtemps différée, de la recherche universitaire au monde moderne.
> . . . cette nouvelle critique, où Raymond Picard aperçoit tout juste quelques talents fourvoyés, c'est Sartre, c'est Bachelard, c'est Blanchot, c'est Poulet, c'est en un mot comme en dix, tout ce qui compte depuis trente ans, dans l'effort de rénovation de la pensée française.

* * *

One can, of course, comment that the concept of the avant-garde has done more harm than good in literature and art, and is now bedevilling criticism. It looks like a military metaphor, but in fact its overtones are political and scientific; it introduces into literature and art the idea of conscious change and evolution and of cumulative results, and this may be just as dangerous as the previous neo-classical concept of the respectful imitation of established models. There may be modishness in criticism as in art. Admittedly, each age, if it is true to itself, necessarily reinterprets the past in the light of its own emphases.

Lanson, and more especially his uninspired imitators, may have got stuck in a narrow, positivistic groove, and for this reason a good deal of what passes for the study of literature in university courses is sterile irrelevance and needs to be replaced by something else. On the other hand, in criticism as in art, it is not enough to be new to be convincing, because a new arrangement of the elements in the non-experimental pursuits is not equivalent to a new development in science, where each stage can be an objectively tested advance. A new arrangement may be a new mistake or a reminting of an old error. Yet it is interesting to see that the mass of non-academic intellectuals indignantly *assume* that M. Barthes is right and M. Picard wrong, because the former belongs to the avant-garde, whereas the latter holds a state professorship. A cognate assumption, which M. Barthes himself seems to be acting upon in *Critique et vérité*, is that the avant-garde is left wing while the opponents of the avant-garde are right wing. To the English observer both assumptions may seem doubtful. There is nothing specifically right wing in M. Picard's pamphlet, and the fact that some conventional bourgeois writers have sprung to his side because they think M. Barthes left wing and subversive is just one of the accidents of public controversy. What M. Picard is really concerned with is accuracy; he argues that M. Barthes, in finding obsessional patterns in Racine, is generalizing wildly on the basis of tendentious interpretations of individual phrases, that he falls into contradiction, and that he often puts his assertions into jargon which gives an appearance of profundity without a corresponding increase in precision.

* * *

M. Barthes's answer is that M. Picard has completely misunderstood his purpose and is resting his case on the obsolete shibboleths of 'objectivity', 'taste', and 'clarity', the first of which dates from the nineteenth century and the other two from the seventeenth century. The historical analysis is justifiable, but the accusation is slightly unfair to M. Picard, who sees that taste is relative, and specifically accepts technical vocabularies as valuable, if convincingly used. The crux of the matter is really the problem of objectivity. If M. Picard is old-fashioned, it is because he supposes that there is a certain 'truth' of the work, which is what Racine and his contemporaries supposed it to be; the critic's business is to define this truth as accurately as possible from the standpoint of his own period and to defend it against error. M. Picard is really a believer in that now hated thing, an essence. For M. Barthes, who is a Structuralist with Existentialist, Marxist, and Freudian overtones, there is no such thing as the essential truth of the work. There are as many truths as there are symbolic systems that the work can be fitted into. A critic is not someone who clarifies the objective nature of the work; he is a secondary writer who recreates the work as he discusses it (or creates something which is not the work but his reaction to it), just as the primary writer, starting from the phenomena of the world, created the pattern which is the work.

* * *

M. Barthes develops this attitude with great subtlety and talent, so much so that *Critique et vérité*, with its blend of concepts drawn from different disciplines, its emphasis on language as a cluster of symbolic patterns, its repeated assumption that form is more important than content, is a manifesto of contemporary French thought, almost in the way M. Robbe-Grillet's *Pour un nouveau roman* was a manifesto of the 'new novel'. Indeed, M. Doubrovsky points out that those people who resist *la nouvelle critique* also tend to be those who are doubtful about *le nouveau roman*, and it goes without saying that, in his view, they are doubly wrong. But is this certain? The 'old-fashioned' reader may not be as totally unaware of the problem of language as he is sometimes supposed to be, and he may suspect that both the new novel and the new criticism are vitiated to some extent by an ingenious, but perhaps ultimately mistaken, view of the functioning of language. It is true that all language is a system of referential signs, that words and books do not 'contain' a meaning, except metaphorically. Each reading is a vitalization, or a revitalization, in the subject of his own associational system, not the transfer of an objective content from one mind to another. But the shift from this assertion to the much more extreme one that 'the subject-matter is put in parenthesis' (as M. Barthes says in one of his essays on M. Robbe-Grillet) seems to be too rapid an acceptance of that solipsism which casts a blight of non-significance over so many 'new novels'. The repeated cry of the 'old-fashioned' reader, who may after all not be completely stupid, is that the 'new novel' tells him a lot of things he does not want to know, or does not need to know, or even cannot ultimately know, about the position of the 'character' in space, but omits the core of subjectivity which would change the 'character' from a vacant lot into a fully-inhabited identity. It is one thing to condemn the traditional analysis of this identity as being inadequate; it is quite another to remove the analysis altogether or to atomize it almost out of existence. Similarly, in criticism, one can accept the proposition that what is called subject-matter is really an ever-changing mass of different, linguistically stimulated, associations, and yet jib at the statement that the associational mass, being ever-changing, does not really exist, or has no possible overall coherence. It is the latter view that M. Barthes appears to be expressing in the following passage, where at least three concepts seem to converge: Mallarmé's theme of 'absence', the Existentialist rejection of 'essence' and the Structuralist view that music, for instance, 'exists' neither in the orchestra nor in the listener but in the inter-relation between the two:

Le langage n'est pas le prédicat d'un sujet, inexprimable ou qu'il servirait à exprimer, il est le sujet. Il me semble (et je ne crois pas être le seul à le penser) que c'est cela très précisément qui définit la littérature: s'il s'agissait simplement d'exprimer (comme un citron) des sujets et des objets également pleins, par des 'images', à quoi bon la littérature? Le discours de mauvaise foi y suffirait. Ce qui emporte le symbole, c'est la nécessité de désigner inlassablement le *rien* du *je* que je suis. En ajoutant son langage à celui de l'auteur et ses symboles à ceux de l'oeuvre, le critique ne 'déforme' pas l'objet pour s'exprimer en lui, il n'en fait pas le prédicat de sa propre personne; il reproduit une fois de plus, comme un signe décroché et varié, le signe des oeuvres elles-mêmes, dont le message, infiniment ressassé, n'est pas telle 'subjectivité', mais la confusion même du sujet et du langage, en sorte que la critique et l'oeuvre disent toujours: *je suis littérature*, et que, par leurs voix conjuguées, la littérature n'énonce jamais que l'absence du sujet. . . .

. . . La critique n'est pas une traduction, mais une périphrase. Elle ne peut prétendre retrouver le 'fond' de l'oeuvre, car ce fond est le sujet même, c'est-à-dire une absence: toute métaphore est un signe sans fond, et c'est ce lointain du signifié que le procès symbolique dans sa profusion, désigne.

The task of the critic, says M. Barthes, is not to 'explain' the supposed significant content, but to develop his own symbolism in a musical relationship of harmony with the symbolic system of the original. The critic does not judge content; he tests the coherence of symbolic systems:

On retrouve ici, transposée à l'échelle d'une science du discours, la tâche de la linguistique récente, qui est de décrire la *grammaticalité* des phrases, non leur signification. De la même façon, on s'efforcera de décrire *l'acceptabilité* des oeuvres, non leur sens.

* * *

All this is most seductively expressed, but is it 'true'? M. Barthes creates an abstruse siren song, full of tantalizing harmonics and which seems far more profound than M. Picard's brisk commonsense, but is the former in the right and the latter in the wrong? If one is a Barthesian, one says that M. Picard is mistaken, and at the same time that the concept of 'truth' is itself part of the crude sclerosis of the past. If one goes all the way with M. Picard, one is in danger of denying oneself the possibility of reinterpreting Racine's plays as aesthetic patterns of psychological tensions, independently of the legends Racine used, the neo-classical principles he respected and what he, consciously, thought he was doing. Perhaps the English observer may be allowed to compromise and to say that he has greatly enjoyed reading both *Nouvelle critique, nouvelle imposture* and *Critique et vérité* and that he does not want to make an absolute choice between them. M. Barthes and his fellow-critics are full of interesting suggestions, but M. Picard has served a useful purpose by objecting to their sweeping assertiveness. However ingenious M. Barthes's reply, M. Picard has got him on the hop in connexion with the interpretation of certain phrases. M. Barthes, indirectly, admits this, first by declaring that his book on Racine is several years old and that his views may have changed in the meantime, and secondly by resorting to the curious argument that criticism has to be dogmatic because all language is assertion:

> L'écriture *déclare*, et c'est en cela qu'elle est écriture. Comment la critique pourrait-elle être, interrogative, optative ou dubitative, sans mauvaise foi, puisqu'elle est écriture et qu'écrire, c'est précisément rencontrer le risque apophantique, l'alternative inéluctable du vrai/faux? Ce que dit le dogmatisme de l'écriture, s'il s'en trouve, c'est un engagement, non une certitude ou une suffisance: ce n'est rien qu'un acte, ce peu d'acte qui subsiste dans l'écriture.

Surely this remark is as wrongheaded as the affirmation that literature is *absence du sujet*, and in any case, if it is true, it is valid in the case of M. Picard, Lanson and anyone else, so that one finds oneself with a welter of assertions and no possibility of choosing between them, except as members of dogmatic series, themselves all equally valid. But we know, in fact, that although language has to operate assertively (even doubts are negated affirmations), the psychological reality from which the assertions are emerging is always, to some degree, dubitative. Our assertions may be contradicted by other assertions of our own, or by those made by someone else and accepted by us; why should our commitment (*engagement*) to the initial assertions, which can be altered by our assent to the subsequent assertions, be called *le dogmatisme de l'écriture*? Is this not a perverse kind of intellectual poetry, a way of giving excessive solidity to the form of language when that form is misleading? M. Barthes makes at least two further remarks which confirm the suspicion that he is falling into this trap. In one place, he says that there is no fundamental distinction between the 'critic' and the 'writer'. The critic is a writer. In another place, he says that all writers believe that the relationship between linguistic signs and their meanings is not arbitrary but 'natural':

La littérature est exploration du nom: Proust a sorti tout un monde de ces quelques sons: *Guermantes*. Au fond, l'écrivain a toujours en lui la croyance que les signes ne sont pas arbitraires, et que le nom est une propriété naturelle de la chose: les écrivains sont du côté de Cratyle, non d'Hermogène.

These statements are extremely debatable, but leaving aside their accuracy or inaccuracy, if M. Barthes himself is a writer and is 'du côté de Cratyle, non d'Hermogène', he must know that he is opting for a 'poetic' view, rather than a scientific one, and that, in so doing, he is moving out of the realm of discussion into what M. Picard, justifiably, refers to as vaticination.

* * *

The curious thing about a good deal of *la nouvelle critique* is that it gives itself scientific airs, while at the same time draping itself in a philosophico-poetic profundity, which is agreeable enough if one is in a fuzzy mood, without being ultimately satisfactory either as philosophy or poetry. In the worst instances, it fails on all three counts, as philosophy, as poetry and as science. It should be emphasized that one can take this view without believing in the possibility of a return to any simple form of *la clarté française*. So much of *la nouvelle critique* seems to be a form of secondary literature which takes itself more seriously than primary literature does, and which is often extremely speculative. Bachelard was right to look for the categories of the imagination, but he may have been wrong in supposing that they necessarily coincide with pre-scientific divisions. M. Goldmann is right to adopt a sociological approach to literature, but much of what he asserts in *Le Dieu caché* and *Sociologie du roman* is fragile assumption masquerading as science. M. Mauron is right to look for psychological patterns in literature, but a lot of his *psychocritique* is quite unconvincing. As for the lesser exponents, they can waffle just as tiresomely off the point as any of the dreary neo-

Lansonians. It is interesting to note that M. Doubrovsky, who sets out to show how wrong M. Picard is, has in all honesty to throw doubt on large sections of *la nouvelle critique*.

Yet one cannot simply conclude that *la nouvelle critique* should not exist; it is an attempt, albeit in some instances a rather immodest one, to insert the discussion of literature in a significant total discourse. Reversing Valéry's famous aphorism about man in general, one might say: 'La nouvelle critique est grande par ce qu'elle cherche et souvent absurde par ce qu'elle trouve.' If it were more humble, less prophetic, less inclined to postulate dogmatic totalities, less keen to rival the rumblings of *la bouche d'ombre*, it might serve its own cause and that of literature rather better.

20

BURSARS OF THE STATE

(*a*) ANTONIA WHITE

The Hound and the Falcon

ANTONIA WHITE was the only child of a scholarly father converted to the Catholic faith when his daughter was seven years old. Thus, although a Catholic from childhood, she suffered in the Church from a convert's malaise in a home atmosphere in which Catholicism was practised with an essentially Protestant rigour and self-consciousness. Seen in psychological terms (and of this the author, who underwent a Freudian analysis and remains grateful for it, is aware) her life might be seen as a drama of father and daughter: a child's adoration betrayed, in early adolescence, by her father's failure to support her when she was expelled from a Sacred Heart convent, an annulled (Catholic) marriage, a breakdown, an attempt to escape into sexual 'freedom', two more brief marriages, two daughters, a great deal of hard work, and finally while working for the B.B.C. in wartime London, a return to the Church.

These letters addressed to a correspondent whom she had never met, are in fact written to herself, in an attempt to clarify her thought. They cover the period of her return to the Church, which takes place, however, almost imperceptibly and without the slightest

---

(*a*) *The Hound and the Falcon.* The Story of a Reconversion to the Catholic Faith. 171 pp. Longmans. 30s.

(*b*) *I Hear Voices.* 218 pp. Olympia Press. 8s. 6d. *Tests.* 61 pp. *Green Julia.* 61 pp. Methuen. 15s. each. (Paperback, 6s.)

(*c*) *The Microcosm.* 289 pp. Hutchinson. 30s.

(*d*) *Loquitur.* 77 pp. Fulcrum Press. 35s. *The Spoils.* The Morden Tower Book Room. Distributed by Migrant Press. 5s.

(*e*) *A Christ of the Ice Floes.* 77 pp. Macmillan. 18s.

(*f*) *Walking Wounded.* Poems 1962–65. 63 pp. Eyre and Spottiswoode. 12s. 6d.

(*g*) *Trawl.* 183 pp. Secker and Warburg. 27s. 6d.

(*h*) *Langrishe, Go Down.* 271 pp. Calder and Boyars. 30s.

(*i*) *In My Own Land.* Photographs by James Bridgen. 139 pp. Douglas, Isle of Man: Times Press. 35s.

abatement of her stringent criticism. One day her 'doubts' (a Carmelite father said he found these 'quite an education', although another priest said that for every one she could produce he could produce ten more she had not even thought of) seem sufficient reason for staying 'out'; the next day they do not. If anything she is, as a Catholic, more critical, more anxious to put in order a house once more her own.

Miss White is as meticulous a thinker as she is a writer; and many of her criticisms of the Church (and 'Church History is *not* pretty reading') have since found expression in the Vatican Councils. Her correspondent had known von Hügel's friend Father Tyrrell, expelled from the Jesuit order for 'modernism'; and Miss White champions the cause of the rebel who paved the way to reform.

The 'Tony' of the letters was unfortunate in receiving her Catholic education at a time when apologetics and discursive logic had in practice become the objects of 'faith' to a degree approaching idolatry. No wonder she defends Freud, who in drawing attention to unconscious regions of the mind which, like Aquinas's 'truths of faith', may not contradict but certainly transcend reason, must have cut the knots of that religious snare of apologetic involutions whose intricacy Stephen Dedalus knew so well. Nor does she deny her indebtedness to Freud in the vexed questions of sex. It must seem to many 'outside' unfitting, almost indecent, that so great an issue as the acceptance of the Christian faith should be conditional upon rules of sexual conduct too minutely, rigidly, and unspiritually defined; rules much more stringent than in the Eastern Orthodox Church. Has not Rome been over-categorical about many secondary issues from which retreat is now absurdly complicated?

These are the letters not of one who doubts the spiritual realities but of one who asks whether the Church is in fact a means, or an obstacle to spiritual knowledge. Often she has been galled into feeling that 'the Catholic Church had no connection with the religion of the Gospels any more and had become a mere collection of meaningless formulae'; but this is only to judge the Church in terms of its own central teaching: with all its faults it continues to fulfil its mission as 'a link between the seen world and the unseen'. Miss White is aware that other traditions may also be valid as 'ways'; but granting the teachings true of Islam, Buddhism, or the protean Hindu system of mythology and metaphysics, Christianity cannot be denied an equal validity, to say the least; though the author might agree with René Guénon that the Catholic Church may be likened to a box of treasures whose key has been mislaid.

Finally it is a question of language; Catholicism is the author's native language, 'and though one may have become denationalized, one cannot help reverting to it and thinking in its terms'.

To say that there may be other languages in which spiritual knowledge may be transmitted is not to say that any and every set of terms is adequate. There are many too hasty advocates of adapting to spiritual realities the terminology of the quantitative sciences. All knowledge, Aquinas says, is necessarily in the mode of the knower; and without adequate terms there are truths which cannot be realized. T. S. Eliot once explained to a student of Indian metaphysics that he remained a Christian because, after a brief excursion into Indian thought, he had realized that it was too difficult to learn so foreign a language of discourse. There must be few Europeans for whom the Christian terms and symbols are not in the end the most viable; for Miss White there was no real alternative: 'One will probably go down with the old ship because there isn't another to embark on. . . . She has enough bread, if she'd unlock the cupboard and not put us off with stones.'

(*b*) PAUL ABLEMAN

I Hear Voices; *Tests*; and *Green Julia*

If the history of the postwar British *avant-garde* ever comes to be written one suspects that Paul Ableman will find a place in it as one of those useful shadow figures who are remembered less for their original talent than for reflecting the movements of their time. As Mr. Ableman is still a youngish writer this may be an unfairly premature judgment; but on the evidence of these three books, it does seem that his main gift is a barometric sensitivity to changes in the cultural climate.

Although his work spans a wide stylistic gulf it has all appeared in under ten years on the narrow platform open to British experimental writers. The novel *I Hear Voices* was first published in Paris in 1958, thus attracting the kind of esteem previously accorded to such Parisian imprints as *The Rock Pool* and *The Ginger Man*. Subsequently Mr. Ableman turned to drama, and the series of 'surrealist playlets' now collected under the title of *Tests* appeared variously on the Third Programme, as a part of the Royal Shakespeare Company's 'Theatre of Cruelty' programme, and as a late-night Edinburgh Festival revue, heralded with such testimonials as 'A Capital Entertainment' and 'I Laughed Till It Hurt' credited to Marx and the Marquis de Sade. *Green Julia* also originated in Edinburgh as a Traverse Theatre show last year; later it had a successful run in London at the Arts Theatre.

Read in sequence these works show a progressive change from defiantly minority writing to clear-cut professionalism. It is as though Mr. Ableman began by assuming that as few people were likely to take an interest in what he had to say there was no point in making concessions; and that as an audience began to appear he went out to meet them half way.

I Hear Voices consists of an uninterrupted stream of schizophrenic reveries. So far as one can be sure of anything in the book (where definite statements are made only to be instantly contradicted) it appears that the narrator shares a house with two women, a small girl, and his brother Arthur who confine him to his bedroom and keep him on a diet of eggs. This is the fixed material from which extravagant free-association fantasies develop. There are two key preoccupations in the fantasies: the narrator's fear of his protectors as authority figures; and his desire to obtain an identity of his own. According to which preoccupation is dominant, the other figures vary between threatening and subservient aspects. Arthur, who has some menial office job, periodically blossoms into a booming captain of industry; while Maria softens into a docile waif as the narrator triumphantly squires her round town in a taxi knee-deep in jewels. His ego goes in and out like a balloon. His only defence against abrupt deflation is to assert various arbitrarily chosen identities—at one moment an ex-plumber, at another a philosopher—none of which can finally withstand exposure even to fantasy life.

All of this is readily reducible to modern psychological terms; in fact the novel might have been written to exemplify R. D. Laing's theories of existential insecurity, the dread of 'implosion', and the false-self system. It also embodies Freud's principle that the unconscious is a great joker: the weird mutations and confrontations of unrelated elements in the narrator's mind often seem the work of a malignant *farceur*. And the language itself, full of half-remembered quotations and nursery rhymes, twisted clichés, and mesmeric nonsense, seems to have been dredged straight from the unconscious;

it has the quality of mysteriously significant inconsequence that comes in dreams. What lowers one's regard for the writing is that it fails to convey any sense of pain. One would not gather from reading the novel that schizophrenia is a condition of anguish and nightmare. The unconscious may be a joker; it seems that the author is one as well; and that the book springs less from expressive urgency than from the revived cult of fantasy which gave surrealism its second wind in the 1950s.

Tests strengthens one's doubts of Mr. Ableman's seriousness. There is some entertaining material in the collection: a calm love scene between a couple of anthropomorphic computers punctuated by human shrieks for help; an eve of battle debate in which an inquisitive awkward squad (each member called Johnson) drive their exasperated commander (another Johnson) into identifying the enemy as the Saracens ('That's hundreds of years ago.' 'Yes, but they're stirring again.') But on the page, as in performance, the writing is only as good as the gags. If it suggests Ionesco and the absurd, it also suggests Light Programme comedy scripts.

Green Julia—a farewell party duologue between two students, one of whom is trying to unload his girl friend on to the other—is a thoroughly stageworthy piece in the line of descent from John Mortimer's *The Dock Brief* and Edward Albee's *Who's Afraid of Virginia Woolf?*—quasi-domestic works which exploit the role-playing habits of ordinary life to multiply the range of characters and situations available for small casts. Looked at thematically it has several things in common with Mr. Ableman's previous writings: a sense of the impermanence of identity, and a rooted feeling that 'real' life is going on somewhere else (his characters are always looking for the action). But these are widely shared preoccupations; and although Mr. Ableman's fertility of invention and sheer command of language are impressive, he has yet to show any strong feeling or personal style that would make them his own. Reading his work you do hear voices; but they are not his voice.

(*c*) MAUREEN DUFFY

The Microcosm

Ruminating on her class of pubescent girls singing about the 'world's tempestuous sea', one of Miss Duffy's characters calculates that one and a bit among them ought to be lesbian, according to the statistics. A substantial minority, for whom Miss Duffy has written a long, hectic, impassioned apologia, cramming together in one book the material for half a dozen novels. The brave message which her book carries, for at least two of the women whose lives we are invited to try to understand, is that the world has grown so full of minorities—in fields of knowledge, as well as experience—that it is no use imagining that any group is a microcosm.

It is, as a rock-pool, however, full of its own peculiar different-coloured fish forming and reforming in couples to mate or fight, shut off from the world outside, that Miss Duffy presents her lesbian case-histories. They call the club where on Saturday nights no one asks questions about the sex of dancing-partners The House of Shades, and Cathy, who has run away from her foster-parents to become a bus-conductress in London, feels as soon as she sets foot there that this is the home she has always longed to discover. Steve, the gym mistress whom all her pupils like so much, wonders fleetingly whether the day will come when one of them walks down the stairs of the club and guesses her secret. Matt, who is throughout referred to as 'he', thinks with fond pity about her mate on the petrol pumps, the innocent long-suffering Alice 'with her skinny sickly old man and two thin kids like bundles of sticks', and gloats that Alice never knows what she's thinking. It is a secret, guilty world they inhabit, even if Miss Duffy shows us more than enough of it to make the case for more toleration and understanding both poignant and incontrovertible.

She is at her best when she allows the stories to plead for her. The minute-by-minute description of the school day, with clamouring questions, petty administrative quibbles and the undercurrent of enthusiastic interest in what goes on in the children's heads, gells into an admirably written character sketch of Steve, the lesbian teacher who is an obvious asset to any school. There is a rather breathless but moving Molly Bloom-like section about the young wife whose disastrous parents and brutish husband have so plainly driven her to a neurotic state in which only a lesbian relationship could possibly make up for what she has suffered. There is the devoted, pretty Sadie, the factory girl so anxious to gain her Johnnie's approval and scared she may not be bright enough to make it last much longer.

Where Miss Duffy has allowed the character and her tale to

impose some discipline on the writing she shows a quite outstanding talent—even the twenty-page pastiche of an early nineteenth-century biographical sketch, almost totally irrelevant and totally unexplained as part of the novel, is brilliantly authentic. But when Matt and his *femme* begin apostrophizing history—what about Joan of Arc, Queen Elizabeth, the Nightingale and so on?—and talking about what has become of the golden age, and the tremendous liberation of mental energy the world needs, or even about their own unending self-explorations, the whole book begins to sound like a pastiche of Mr. Colin Wilson at his most ambitious. Indeed, many readers, bewildered by the exertion of trying to work out in the first fifty pages not only the sex but the identity of all these urgent voices, may well find they lack energy to go farther.

(*d*) BASIL BUNTING

Loquitur and *The Spoils*

Put out more Bunting seems to be the order of the day, as though to fill in a missing era of English poetry:

> Landscape salvaged from
> evinced notice of
> superabundance, of
> since parsimonious
> soil . . .

When Mr. Bunting begins a stanza 'Nevertheless . . .' we know (and there are other like clues) where his tone comes from. Sometimes, as in the satirical 'odes' 13 and 23, the Poundian influence amounts to pastiche: these are acceptable imitation *moeurs contemporaines*. *The Spoils*, too, reflects the master's prophetic edginess on a quasi-economic theme realized in a collocation of personae from biblical and present-day Middle East. You track him everywhere in Pound's snow. The more circumspect reader may be forgiven for viewing with suspicion a poet who translates Louis Zukovsky (one of the 'two greatest poets of our age') into Latin. (Into *Latin*?) But should he be blamed for finding what is thus derivative in Mr. Bunting's style mannered? One knows that the English have always been accused of being Eliot-wise and Pound-foolish, but must they *now* apologize for neglecting this sensitive poet because his flexible, guarded, powerful voice was lured into a foreign and ambitious manner?

(*e*) DAVID WEVILL

A Christ of the Ice Floes

Mr. David Wevill is a poet of disconcerting surfaces. Wandering very consciously alone through an unfriendly universe, contemplating nature's violences in a manner neither deeply engaged nor yet detached and rigorous enough to seem impersonally wise, his open-ended meditations on man, beast and landscape run all the risks of inflation and vacuity. That these dangers are almost entirely avoided is due to qualities not always apparent at first reading: a real concreteness, verbal precision and emotional honesty under the upper layers of gesture.

Three of the shorter poems can serve as examples. 'Catkins' movingly juxtaposes the sense of impending death in the hospital room with the visitors' gift of catkins severed during frost ('wiry, March-stiff')—representing a *failed* symbol of life renewing. In 'Diagona', two people warm indoors in snowy weather watch simulated violence on the television screen (it 'flickers as the wind hunts its wires'), and are more conscious of that than of all the suffering asking compassion in the world outside. Yet the cold stands for a persisting guilt:

> the wintry earth goes deeper and survives
> whatever makes us glad but afraid to live.

The natural and the 'modern' images combine easily in a delicately poised and strangely immediate comment on personal comfort and wider responsibility. In a third poem, 'Death of a Salesman' (unclever title) the poet's ability to shake off a boy cyclist trying to outstrip him in his car is used as an image of the petty and somehow valueless advantages of adulthood:

> In the mirror I see
> Just the empty road behind me,
> The vanished boy, and the wheels loitering back slowly. . . .
> And the whipped heart retreats to pride, my loss.
> His victory will come when he owns a car.
> His loss will follow when he ends this race.

That fourth line almost moralizes; but a balance is regained by the final paradoxes.

It would be good to see the rather inexplicit personal elements behind some of these complexes of highly arresting imagery come forward more frankly. But in the meantime Mr. Wevill is exploring man's relationship with nature with a detailed and humane sensitivity.

(*f*) VERNON SCANNELL

Walking Wounded

Mr. Scannell gives the appearance of working harder for his effects [than Francis Hope, whose *Instead of a Poet* was reviewed earlier in the same article], though, to be fair, his range is wider. He shares with Mr. Hope a somewhat ruthless urge to moralize and a weakness for a flat ending, but he does not seem to achieve as much as the younger poet, in spite of a vigorous and not unsympathetic attack on 'up-to-date' and difficult subject-matter. Mr. Scannell's real failing is glibness, a confident facility for metaphor and colourful argufying. And this, too, screws those flat last lines into hair-clutching banality, simply because most of the time Mr. Scannell is going through lively motions and one really does wait for the pay-off. There are perhaps some lurking Dionysiac notions of an ex-Maverick to be found in this hit-or-miss method. What is needed is some restraint, some exactness and purity of language. It is worth noting that Mr. Scannell's publishers are able to produce more pages more pleasantly for less money than is usual.

(*g*) B. S. JOHNSON

Trawl

B. S. Johnson sees himself as an avant-garde novelist and at first sight *Trawl*—format, epigraph, opening page—looks as though its claim on our attention might be originality. The appearance is misleading; Mr. Johnson's sensibility is thoroughly traditional and the technical method turns out to be a simplification of that used by

Joyce in the Stephen Dedalus chapters of *Ulysses*. None of it presents any difficulty to the common reader, but it provokes a good deal of irritation at the sight of misused talent.

The narrator has taken passage in a deep-water trawler in the hope that this will help him to understand his sense of isolation. Scenes of trawling alternate with the lengthy, coherent chunks of recollection which he fishes up from his past. The metaphor of trawling is asserted with a determination that we shall not miss the point, a determination also manifested in the clear signalling of jumps from present to past. There is no harm in obviousness, but here it confirms the impression, derived from the touching evocation of the feelings of a lonely evacuee and the excellent descriptions of men gutting fish, that Mr. Johnson's real talent is for the traditional novel of character and narrative. His dallyings with experiment are irritating because they produce arbitrary gaps in what is elsewhere a coherent story. Most unjustifiable of all is his insistent echoing of the rhythms of Beckett, to whom he gestures self-consciously by naming the trawler's wireless operator Molloy. In Beckett the pedantic enumeration of trivialities is an index of desperation about the status of perceptions; but Mr. Johnson's narrator is no Watt and his mimicry merely leads to an unintended facetiousness and a feeling of the consciously literary which obscures the true nature which is elsewhere given him, convincingly and even movingly, by his creator.

(*h*) AIDAN HIGGINS

Langrishe, Go Down

That the self-regarding lethargy of Irish life which drives so many talented writers into exile still proves oddly irresistible and artistically rewarding to them is demonstrated once again by Mr. Higgins's first novel. The decline of the Langrishe family, shrunk to three spinster sisters, illustrates the decay of the Protestant gentry in the 1930s, and the love-affair between Imogen and Otto Beck, a wandering German scholar, underlines how far off-shore an island Ireland is. However, the author is really less concerned with this kind of point than with the textures and sensations of individual lives. The bulk of the book consists of episodes and fragments from Imogen's life with Otto: the whole presentation of this provincial woman's clutching at erotic happiness proves what life there still can be in the *Bovary* vein.

Mr. Higgins clearly feels his responsibilities towards prose rather acutely, but his style is sustained not so much by ambition as by an unremitting attention, and although his particularities can verge on the gratuitous, they do make you see. The relation of the bits of the novel to the whole piece is not always convincing (and never achieves that rhythm of organization so impressive in, for example, John McGahern's *The Dark*), but *Langrishe, Go Down* certainly reveals a promising talent.

(*i*) PHILIP CALLOW

In My Own Land

Impressions of people and places make up a curious book. Mr. Callow, no mean user of words, flings out his reactions to everything from a cinema to a cliff top. Mr. Bridgen adds arresting photographs. The book is nothing if not vivid but it is rather self-consciously unconventional.

21

OF TEXT AND TYPE

NEW CRITICAL ASPECTS

'WHAT IS BIBLIOGRAPHY?' says the jesting critic, and stays not for an answer. Is this a fair indication of the relationship between the critic and the bibliographer? The two disciplines have coexisted for years past, those who practise them subsisting on the same raw material, working and often living in the same place, and yet curiously detached —each tending to misunderstand or underrate the purpose and technique of the other. The critic is apt to stare in bewilderment at the bibliographer's algebra, wondering whether, and if so where, it contains a clue to his text. Sometimes he can hardly be blamed if he begins to feel that he is looking through a microscope at a life so minute that it can have no bearing on his own activities. The bibliographer is also uncomfortably aware of the microscope; if he looks back up it, he may be depressed by the magnitude of the subject at whose base he is scratching about. But again, he is apt to feel indignant at the cavalier way in which the critic makes assumptions about his text which are technically indefensible.

The point has now been reached where the spectator watches the contenders stalking each other, as it were, along different sides of the same hedge, each convinced that he is Feste, but looking down nervously from time to time to see if a pair of yellow stockings, cross-gartered, have found their way on to his legs. 'If this were played upon a stage now, I could condemn it as an improbable fiction.'

* * *

Criticism is as old as Alexandria: bibliography is a relatively new science. Moreover, it presents two faces to the beholder, which correspond with the divergence that has taken place in the older

---

FREDSON BOWERS: *Bibliography and Textual Criticism.* 207 pp. Clarendon Press: Oxford University Press. 35s.

study of manuscript texts. There one path has been taken by the palaeographers, whose first interest is the hand and not the text, and another by the textual critics, whose interests are in the reverse order. So in bibliography there has been on the one hand the palaeographical approach which descends from Mabillon (whose *De Re Diplomatica*, published in 1681, marks the beginning of modern palaeography). The course it has followed has been documented by Mr. Stanley Morison in his introduction to the first series of *Type Specimen Facsimiles*. Towards the end of the eighteenth century, F-X. Laire and Dom Placidus Braun both published independently catalogues of early printed books to which were subjoined, following Mabillon's example exactly, a series of plates illustrating the types of the books described. These are the first major bibliographic works to be based on accurate study of the physical make-up of their material. The example was not lost on William Blades, whom Mr. Morison has rightly called 'the founder of modern scientific bibliography'. His *Life and Typography of William Caxton* (1861), in which he combined scholarly research with his professional knowledge of printing, set a standard of bibliographic description which transmitted through Bradshaw, Duff and Proctor, and, on the Continent Holtrop and Haebler, has been canonized in the British Museum *Catalogue of Books Printed in the Fifteenth Century* and the *Gesamtkatalog der Wiegendrucke*.

* * *

The other aspect of bibliography, the textual side, has been more a development belonging to the English-speaking world, and has grown out of and revolved round the problems of the text of Shakespeare. The Shakespearian editors Capell and Malone occupy the same position in the history of textual bibliography as Laire and Braun in what may be called 'pure' bibliography. Textual bibliography has grown up more recently: the equivalent landmark to Blades's *Caxton* is, perhaps, the paper *Some Points in Bibliographical Description* given to the Bibliographical Society by A. W. Pollard and W. W. Greg in 1906, and subsequently published in the society's *Transactions*, with an important appendix by Falconer Madan, in 1909. The leading exponents of the principles of textual bibliography in the last generation were R. B. McKerrow and Greg; McKerrow was first in the field (*An Introduction to Bibliography*, 1927), but it is unquestionably Greg whose work, culminating in the great *Biblio-*

graphy of the English Printed Drama to the Restoration (1939–59), has been the dominant influence.

* * *

Large though his gifts were, this situation was not entirely of Greg's creating. Pure bibliography has been going through a period of consolidation. The application of palaeographical principles to early printed books has continued, but there has been no great advance in methodology. The reason for this lies largely in the material. To elucidate the work of the early printers, small and often itinerant businesses, with their own peculiar types, is a task very similar to the palaeographer's when he analyses individual manuscripts, and traces the centres of manuscript production, the development of hands and on occasion the identity of the scribes themselves. In the sixteenth century, although the construction of books did not alter much, what had been a craft carried on by individuals became a complex trade in which the stationer, bookseller, printer and typefounder became separated. Here the palaeographical analogy breaks down. The enormous increase in the number of books to be described requires a modification of technique, and the rules which will govern this modification can only be formulated by a close study of the altered circumstances; it is not until the trade in white paper and printed books, printing techniques and movements of types and ornaments have been properly surveyed that it will be possible to chart the further development of books and printing as clearly as it has been in the fifteenth century.

Much of the work already done has been undertaken under the impetus of textual bibliography, and because the output of a particular author is a convenient sample of the output of a whole period, and because the study of such a sample has an applied usefulness outside the realm of pure bibliography, textual bibliography has been very much in the ascendant since the war. All the same, the textual bibliographer is bound to use many of the techniques of pure bibliography, and so it comes about that his occupation is poised, rather uneasily, between pure bibliography and pure textual criticism, a position which has excited both explanation and defence.

Of Greg's disciples, none has followed him more closely, nor deserved more to be called his successor, than Professor Fredson Bowers. In 1949 he published *Principles of Bibliographical Description*, an exhaustive manual of the technique of bibliography, which owed much to Greg's work (although more was quite original, and Greg himself did not wholly agree with it). Fifteen years later comes *Bibliography and Textual Criticism*, the text of the Lyell Lectures for 1959, which is a logical extension of his earlier work, since its subject is the application of his earlier *Principles* to the establishment of a text. There is, then, a case for assuming that his latest work represents the summation of his views on the technique and purpose of bibliography, and it is interesting to see how well his earlier work has lasted and also how he himself would apply it to textual problems.

* * *

It should be made clear at the outset that Professor Bowers would not agree with the distinction made here between textual and pure bibliography. 'Every bibliographical study of printing has as its final justification the practical use in a textual study or descriptive bibliography of the information thus gained', he wrote in *Principles*, and he has stuck to that. He once in a lecture modestly suggested that he could provide irrefutable (because it depended on the mechanics of composition) proof that Shakespeare wrote 'sallied flesh', only to be told by a distinguished critic that he, personally didn't care whether Shakespeare wrote 'sallied' or 'solid', but that he had always read 'solid' and intended to stick to it. Professor Bowers has been hardly treated by those he is anxious to help, and he is scarcely to be blamed if he shows some acerbity against those critics who persistently ignore bibliographic facts which are as demonstrable as Euclid. But the introduction of mathematical certainty into textual criticism is a dangerous business. The light of *Principia Mathematica*, as reflected by *The Calculus of Variants*, can be an *ingis fatuus*.

All modern textual critics are descendants of Lachmann, in that they follow the 'genealogical' treatment of texts which he originated; where they succeed in demonstrating the 'dependence' of one on another, the evidence should indeed be as conclusive as an algebraic statement. When Professor Bowers says that 'the mechanical interpretation of the bibliographer, based on physical fact, *is* to be preferred to the subjective interpretation of the literary critic' he is laying down an axiom. Again, when he warns against the danger of what he calls 'metacritical evidence, sometimes masquerading as bibliographical', we are bound to agree. But he is restricting the bibliographer's sphere of operations too much, when he adds:

When there is insufficient evidence to support inductive reasoning, pseudo-bibliography will usually result if (as a substitute for specific evidence) we try to deduce an interpretation of textual phenomena from our general ideas about printing practice.

There are a number of reasons, some good, some bad, why Professor Bowers's views have not been universally accepted. The first is that suggested above. The aim of bibliography is not just to serve textual criticism; further, restriction to the study and analysis of those aspects of printed books which refer directly to the text may inhibit the study of other aspects which may in the end prove the more useful. One of the defects of *Principles of Bibliographical Description* that has become more noticeable with the passage of time is that, although it purports to be a manual of bibliography for all periods, it is only really authoritative as a guide to the textual bibliography of the sixteenth and seventeenth centuries, and more particularly the printed drama of that period. This limitation results in two cumulative difficulties. Since Professor Bowers is primarily interested in the text, aspects of bibliography, such as paper and typography, that are less textually useful than, say, composition or the order of printing, are superficially treated. But knowledge of paper and typography may be useful too, and it is in those periods which Professor Bowers does not specialize in that their usefulness is greatest. Let us look at an example.

There is a small octavo edition of Farquhar's plays with the imprint 'London, Printed in the Year 1710' that is almost certainly a later Dutch piracy of the first collected edition, genuinely published in London in 1710. Like its original, the piracy has separate pagination and separate title pages for each play. In several copies, *The Recruiting Officer* is found in a totally or partially uncancelled state, complete with the cancellantia. This reveals that the text runs from pages 1 to 96 in eights (A-F), ending half way through Act V, Scene 6, and that the job was completed with another full sixteen-page working, of which the outer four provided the prelims (title, verso, Prologue, and Dramatis Personae), the inner four pages 97 to 100 (end of text, Errata, and Epilogue), and the middle eight cancels for pages 57, 58, 61, 62, 63, 64, 7 and 8. Now, following *Principles*, the collation statement would run: π^2 A^8 ($\pm$A4) B-C^8–D^8 ($\pm$D5$-$D7,8 $+$D7.8) E-F^8 G^2. Clearly any bibliographer would record the full facts if he found them; but if only cancelled copies were known, the formula would discourage reference to a conjecture that the first and last signatures were worked off together as a half sheet, let alone with the cancels as a full sheet. This is indeed the necessary consequence of treating the formula as a statement of the 'ideal copy', but the lack of interest which the collational statement induces in a feature only indirectly associated with the text might lead the bibliographer, in a similar case, to miss an important *textual* point.

There can be no doubt that Professor Bowers would be the first to condemn any oversight of this sort, and he could point out that he has warned us against just such an omission: 'Yet even at its most mechanical, some very odd fortuitous hits may occur to warn a critic against over-rash assumptions on too narrowly based evidence.' *Naturam furca expellas tamen usque recurret.* Professor Bowers may deny it, but to say that 'analytical bibliography deals with books and their relations solely as material objects', that 'the function of textual bibliography is to treat these imprinted shapes, their selection and arrangement, without primary concern for their symbolic value as conceptual organisms—that is, not as words that have meaningful values—but, instead, as impersonal and non-conceptual inked prints'—this is really taking a pitchfork to bibliography.

* * *

Closely linked with the exclusiveness that demands the omission of what is irrelevant to the text is the inclusiveness that demands a uniform treatment for all works dealt with. Here again, Professor Bowers has anticipated the problem: 'the form and necessities of this description differ somewhat in various periods. . . . To a certain extent, also, the mere physical fact of the magnitude or relative wieldiness of the number of books to be described must be taken into account'. On the other hand, there is no real indication, either in *Principles* or elsewhere, of any method of varying descriptions. Yet the necessity of this has been acknowledged as early as Pollard and Greg's 1906 paper. 'There is no such thing as a standard bibliographical description applicable to all cases', they wrote; the purpose of the description has to be considered, whether 'as an example of the art of printing or as the material form of a piece of literature', and also the date of the books to be described: 'any attempt to treat books of all periods in the same way will be found to be impracticable and to lead only to complications and inconsistencies'.

These views were crystallized in the 'degressive principle', defined by Madan in his appendix as 'the principle of varying a description according to the difference of the period treated or of the importance of the work to be described'. The modern bibliographer is admirably equipped to deal with works of equal textual importance, but confronted with a vast amount of material of varying importance he has only the most primitive means of providing the necessary variation in the technique of description. A 'rationale of degression' is still very far off. Time spent on studying the printing and bookselling practice of the time and relating it to what one sees is always better spent than on forcing the evidence of one's eyes to fit a predetermined set of values. This is not to deny the value of subjecting each copy of every edition seen to the same set of questions; but it is not necessary always to record all the information thus derived, nor should it be thought that all the relevant information will be known once the questions are answered.

* * *

Now it is easy enough to criticize, but far harder to substantiate such criticism. One may feel that it is a little perfunctory to write of typography that it 'has no significance to students of literature but constitutes a part of the book's printing history, and on occasions the evidence may help to date a book or provide proof of irregularity of printing or of variant edition'; or that 'the paper and watermark may be of interest'; nevertheless all that Professor Bowers says is true, and one can hardly quarrel about a question of emphasis. Again, he is well aware of the problems created by periods other than his own. In *Principles* he wrote:

> Since it is not unknown for eighteenth-century editions of a book to copy earlier editions with astonishing faithfulness . . . a bibliographer must be considerably more alert to catch variations on much finer-grained evidence.

Yet, in spite of this warning, after fifteen years he can only report:

> But critics and editors of the eighteenth-century literature still make one despair occasionally when they exhibit a bland disregard for the intensive research and the clarified principles that have been characteristic of scholarship devoted to the editorial principles of the sixteenth and seventeenth centuries.

He goes on to quote some frightening examples, and here his anger seems a little pharisaical. What help may the eighteenth-century bibliographer (who must prepare the way for the textual critic) derive from his textbook? Little more than a warning that the evidence will be 'finer-grained', which can be construed to mean that in some cases little or no result will be achieved by the traditional means of accurate transcription and correct listing of contents and collation, and that other means, not so much 'finer-grained' as unfamiliar, must be used instead. Of these, two of the most important in the eighteenth century are paper and typography, on which, as has been seen, Professor Bowers bestows a rather guarded mention. It is perhaps a foul blow to recall his remarks on press-figures, that peculiarly eighteenth-century phenomenon, since hardly anything was known about them in 1949. At first he was inclined to allow, as minimum, that 'the description should state whether or not press-numbers are present' but he recanted in an addendum:

> The significance which now attaches to these figures as bibliographical evidence requires that they be minutely recorded in a shorthand manner for every forme and sheet of a book in an eighteenth-century bibliography which has any pretensions towards being definitive in its descriptions.

Nowadays, when one reflects that sheets from different impressions are found in the same copy, that on a long run sheets of the same impression can be found with two or more figures, the last demand seems as impossibly large as the earlier was dangerously low.

An indication of the limitations of the textual bibliographic technique described by Professor Bowers is afforded by a work which, although out of his period, has striven to observe his rules: Mrs. Norma Russell's recent *Bibliography of William Cowper to 1837*. In fairness to Professor Bowers, it must be said that it lacks something of the imagination and knowledge, the indefinable flair, which he would have brought to such a task. It is, however, a work of immense industry and its short-comings are revealing. The text consists mainly of descriptions, as laid down in *Principles*, of the works treated. If these err on the full side, it is a fault to the good. But a bibliography of Cowper extending thirty-eight years after his death should be not merely a detailed list of a poet's works, but the chronicle of a great best-seller, coming at the peculiarly fascinating point when the book-trade was changing from a hand-craft to a mechanized industry. Here *Principles* is an imperfect guide, and although Mrs. Russell makes an excellent job of both narrative and description, points are missed which, *ceteris paribus*, would never have been overlooked in a play quarto of a century earlier.

Take, for example, the nucleus of the bibliography of Cowper, the two-volume *Poems*. Originally printed separately as *Poems* (1782) and *The Task* (1785), the second edition of both called for by the success of the latter was brought out with some attempt at uniformity in 1786. This edition ran out towards the end of the year, and on January 3, 1787, Cowper wrote to Walter Bagot: 'I learn that my volumes are out of print, and that a third edition is to be printed.' During the period of derangement that followed from January to July, his friends saw this edition through the press, and it is demonstrably a more careful piece of work. The fourth followed in 1788, and the fifth, the first wholly uniform edition, in 1793: the sixth, which repeated the format of the fifth, came in 1794–95. In 1798 comes the first change of format (hitherto crown 8vo), four editions in all appearing in the same year. If, as seems possible, this represents the first attempt of Joseph Johnson, Cowper's bookseller, to exploit a growing market, his choice of format—foolscap 12mo, foolscap 8vo and two pott 8vo (or more likely two more foolscap editions)—is puzzling. But in 1800 a full range of editions, royal and demy 8vo, foolscap 8vo and 12mo, was issued, and from then on edition followed edition as the demand for Cowper's works grew.

Little is said in Mrs. Russell's entries for these books about press-figures or paper and less about type. The figures are set out in detail to distinguish the two issues of the second edition of Volume I, and sporadically elsewhere; where present, they are (to satisfy Professor Bowers's minimum requirement) noted. Of type, nothing is said until 1803 when two editions are noted as being 'good examples of the smaller volumes produced by Bensley in his early period. The title is set in small size Figgins fount specially designed for Bensley'.

Take the last point first. Not only the title pages but the texts of all editions published since 1800 are in Figgins types, the demy 8vo edition of that year being in his fine new pica roman with its Bodoni-esque italic. All these are 'Printed by T. Bensley', and it is a fair assumption that the two editions of 1798 (the foolscap 12mo and 8vo), which are entirely set in Figgins types, are also printed by Bensley, although without his imprint. Of the two, the 12mo may be conjectured to precede the 8vo. Printers in the eighteenth century, as Professor Bowers remarks, follow copy with surprising faithfulness, and the 12mo resembles in its typography the preceding edition (the sixth) more closely than the 8vo, which also includes a poem not in the 12mo. Both are printed in the earlier Figgins types with the descending J, the 8vo in long primer and the 12mo in brevier (presumably the types mentioned in the preface of Figgins's 1793 specimen, and perhaps shown in the lost 1794 specimen).

What then of the other two editions of 1798, the so-called pott 8vos? The first of these is a curiosity. The first and last two gatherings of volume I and the first of volume II are cancels printed on paper different from the rest of the book, in Figgins types. The prelim cancels are in the earlier type, on a good blue-white laid paper; that at the end of volume I is in the later long primer, one of the complete new series introduced between 1797 and 1798, and on a less good white laid. Both papers are superior to the paper (watermarked '1795') of the text, which is printed in Wilson's 1772 Long Primer No. 1. Scottish type? Paper marked '1795'? These are in fact the sheets of the uncanonical edition printed by James Morison at St. Andrews in 1797 on paper similarly watermarked, which must have found their way to Johnson, whether purchased to supply an urgent need, or confiscated for piracy—the double cancel is clearly designed to bring the old sheets in line with the later of the two authentic editions, which may have run out unexpectedly early. Finally, there is the last of the 1798 editions, demonstrably (as Mrs. Russell points out) copied from the composite edition. The text of this is set in the 'New Long Primer No. 3' of Fry's 1788 specimen. Now Bensley (as far as can be seen) never bought type from Fry; originally a customer of Caslon, about 1793 (possibly after a quarrel) he transferred to Figgins. The chances are, then, that if not printed by Bensley (who did so small a job as the cancels for the St. Andrews copies) it was not really published by Johnson: that the imprint is fictitious and this is, in fact, a provincial piracy.

So much for type and paper. What more can be deduced from press-figures? Up to 1803, Bensley's editions are, with two exceptions, figured. After 1803, figuring disappears, presumably because, in the words of John Johnson's *Typographia*, it 'disfigured the page'. Now Bensley's practice in the matter commands attention, because the printing office rules in Stower's *The Printer's Grammar* (1808), which include an injunction to work with a figure, are there said to have been adopted by 'the father of the present Mr. Bensley'. His Cowper editions indeed seem to show evidence of a regular custom. Of those seen, the majority are figured throughout, and not more than four and sometimes only two figures appear in each volume. This suggests that Bensley liked to see that the printing of any one book and successive editions of the same book remained the responsibility of the same pressmen. This is reinforced by the fact that the same figures, 1 3 6 7 8 (and, later, 5) recur in edition after edition. It is interesting to note that the spuriousness of the two odd editions of 1798 is further revealed by their figuring. The cancelled Scottish edition is figured only on the sheets which Bensley printed; the solitary figure, 7, is one of those regularly used by him. The piracy, however, is figured 1 5 2, of which only 1 was in regular use on the 'canon' editions of the time.

Bearing this in mind it is interesting to note the figuring of the two 'canon' editions (the fifth and sixth) preceding those which can be definitely attributed to Bensley. Both are restricted to a relatively small range of figures: in the sixth edition, volume I is figured 1 3 5 6 7 8—a complete set of the 1798–1803 figures—and II, 1 3 4 7 8; in the fifth, both volumes show the same four figures 3 4 5 8. It was noticed above that the fifth edition of 1793 is the first in which the two volumes are in a uniform style; the inference that each volume was regularly printed by a different printer up to 1788 is confirmed by the figuring of the first four editions. There are no figures in volume I, but a complete range from 1 to 12 in II (except in the first edition which has none).

From such neglected trifles as types, paper, and press-figures, a surprising amount may be learnt. Of the four editions of 1798, one is a piracy and the other is not what it seems; although no printer's name appears on any 'canon' edition until 1799, it is likely that Bensley had printed all editions since 1793. Small beer, perhaps; but these facts are not to be despised in considering the printing and publishing history of a best-seller; nor, perhaps, are they insignificant to the study of the text, at a time when it was continually changing, as new poems were added to the canon, and Cowper's friends tried to make it more 'correct'.

Mrs. Russell's knowledge of Cowper and of the publication of his works is profound and her facts are, as far as those of any bibliographer can be, right. But her work could have been more informative and illuminating had she known more of contemporary printing practice; one cannot but feel that she has been so distracted by the business of setting out all the facts that the authorities prescribe in the approved form that she has failed to notice those that are not demanded and for which no formula exists. 'This', says Professor Bowers of spelling tests and typographical analyses, 'is a world the critic never made, a world to which a sound classical education and a First in Greats seem to have little pertinence.' Here is a world that Professor Bowers has yet to reach, where something more is needed than the application of predetermined principles of textual bibliography.

* * *

Two final criticisms must be made before turning to the more agreeable task of praising Professor Bowers. The first concerns his style: never easy reading, it reaches a degree of opacity in *Bibliography and Textual Criticism* that slows the reader up almost unbearably. Academic prose is often deliberately dull, but it need not be obscure as well.

The second is rather more distressing. Hitherto Professor Bowers has shown himself a hard-hitting but generous controversialist. Much of his best work has had the effect of deflating old reputations or destroying long-held theories, and this he has done firmly but not unsympathetically; he has not spared the rod but his castigation has been without vindictiveness. It has been noticed earlier, too, that he has suffered much from the purely 'literary' critics.

But this does not excuse the curiously shrill and embittered tone in which he now recounts critical ineptitudes; least of all is it justified in speaking of the critic most often singled out for attack, Professor Dover Wilson. Admittedly many of his theories about the transmission of Shakespearian texts have been invalidated by bibliographical research, not least that of Professor Bowers. But it is hardly fair to blame the non-specialist critic for errors of technique which the bibliographer only demonstrates thirty years later. When one considers how much he has done to introduce scientific method to Shakespearian studies, a carping spirit seems exceptionally out of place in a bibliography whose work would be immeasurably harder and far less advanced if Professor Dover Wilson's had never existed. Once at least (over the altered date on the title page of Q2 *Hamlet*) Professor Bowers appears to be deliberately picking a quarrel, in a way which is equally absurd and unjust. This kind of criticism wakens a sense of injustice in the reader, and an irrational desire to find fault himself.

How unjust, in turn, this would be, the magnitude of Professor Bowers's own achievements can witness. *Principles of Bibliographical Description* was a brilliant, as well as massive, extension of the techniques advanced by Pollard and Greg in 1906, and in Greg's subsequent paper 'A Formulary of Collation' in 1933. It was firmly based on a wide knowledge of bibliographical reference books and an even wider knowledge of the source material. All this was assimilated and presented in a form that has dominated bibliographical work on English literature since the war.

It is clear that bibliography owes a great deal to Professor Bowers, and that alone should give pause to the critic. It is probable, too, that he would now agree with much of the criticism voiced here: a good deal has happened since 1949. It is even possible that he would agree that some aspects of the construction of printed books have been neglected at the expense of others, merely pointing out that it was a case of first things first, and that in his opinion it is the text that matters. Given such agreement, what may be hoped for?

* * *

One day there will be a World Union Catalogue of typographic material, a Hinman collating machine in every university library, a complete dictionary of printers, binders and booksellers, chemical dilating tests for paper, and many other aids to quicker, better bibliography. By then, however, bibliographical description will be fully computerized. The pure and the textual bibliographers (if they can tell each other apart) will hardly be able to quarrel even about circuitry.

In the meantime, nature will keep creeping back. Faced with the remorseless logic which demonstrates the priority of variants, frail humanity mutinies. From McKerrow to the recent reviewer of Dr. Hinman's study of the printing of the First Folio, bibliographers have been tempted to hope that the explanation of some anomaly may be due to no more logical explanation than that the printers got drunk. It is a hypothesis of no practical usefulness, but one that may provide both warning and comfort to critic and bibliographer. Does it all matter very much, anyway? This is the question the critic (and *a fortiori* the palaeographer or bibliographer who is anxious to help him) has had to answer many times.

So far as textual criticism is concerned the standard answer will have to suffice: a perfect text must be better than an imperfect one. It may not spoil *Hamlet* for us, but we ought to know whether it is 'sallied' or 'solid'. There is an equally standard answer for the pure bibliographer: any new fact discovered is an enlargement of knowledge. It is not necessary to have an ulterior purpose. The archaeologist can evaluate his discoveries in his own terms without feeling any need to subordinate his techniques to the need of the historian: the bibliographer who identifies the anonymous printer of a fifteenth-century reprint of a common eleventh-century text need not feel his labour wasted. Here all bibliographers will be at one, and none, however remote his province from Professor Bowers's occupation with the recovery of text, will dispute the importance of his achievement, both in his own particular field and to bibliography as a whole.

* * *

Sir,—As the reviewer of Professor Bowers's *Bibliography and Textual Criticism* in your issue of March 24 draws attention to my *Bibliography of Cowper* (1963), discussing a small part of it at considerable length, I hope you will allow me this opportunity of making it known that a Supplement, begun when the book was still in the press, is now practically ready.

Both the late Kenneth Povey, an acknowledged authority on press-figures and the history and practice of printing, and I suspected that some of the pre-1799 editions of Cowper's *Poems* were printed by Bensley and we hoped that corroborating evidence would in time be forthcoming. What your reviewer now tells me about Bensley's printing practice is evidently derived from specialized work on this printer in particular, and is therefore most gratefully received and all the more acceptable because it is just in time for the Supplement.

When, however, your reviewer turns to particular cases (to illustrate his thesis that a lack of knowledge of Bensley has led me astray) I am disappointed to find that his comments are neither so useful nor so timely. I am well aware that the first of the two pott 8vo editions of the poems published by Joseph Johnson in 1798 (no. 80 in my Bibliography) is something of a bibliographical freak, consisting of the sheets of the St. Andrews edition printed by James Morison in 1797 (in Wilson's Long Primer No. 2, not No. 1 as your reviewer says) with new titles and half-titles in both volumes, with the last signature of vol. 1 (sig. 2H of the St. Andrews edition) reprinted more compactly—and with sig. 21 added to accommodate the two new poems of that year. Your reviewer, by the way, is wrong when he says that the prelims of both volumes were printed by Bensley. In vol. 2 he will find on a closer examination that the 'Advertisement' and the leaf of Contents, both misbound in vol. 1 of the Bodleian copy, are of the St. Andrews printing. He will also find that some of the St. Andrews sheets are watermarked 1794. The presence of the St. Andrews sheets in Johnson's edition was detected by Kenneth Povey in March 1963 when the University of St. Andrews kindly deposited their copy of the dated St. Andrews edition—the only copy known to me—so that it could be compared with the Bodleian copy of Johnson's edition. The

Bibliography was then in the press and it seemed to us both that here was leading material for the Supplement which was already seen to be inevitable. Kenneth Povey reported his findings to St. Andrews at the time, mentioning that I should be using the information in my Supplement. One can only guess how Johnson came by the St. Andrews sheets. Your reviewer suggests that they may have been confiscated for piracy. But Morison was a highly reputable publisher with a strong theological bent (see R. H. Carnie, *Printing in Perth before 1807*, Abertay Hist. Soc. 1960) and it is known that he had widened the scope of his business by establishing connexions with several London publishers. He was getting into financial difficulties in 1798 and had begun to sell off part of his considerable stock. Johnson may well have taken the sheets off his hands at this point, or, alternatively, he could have commissioned him to print the text of the London edition, allowing him to publish part of it on his own account.

I cannot follow your reviewer when he asserts, first as a probability, and later categorically, that the second pott 8vo London edition of 1798 (my no. 81) is a provincial piracy because it is demonstrably not printed by Bensley. Why does he rule out the possibility that Johnson employed another printer for this small job, and why does he overlook the fact that the next pott 8vo edition, that of 1801 (my no. 88) bears the imprint of G. Woodfall (vol. 1) and H. Bryer (vol. 2) at a time when Bensley was certainly printing other editions for Johnson? The evidence of the type suggests that the same firm which printed the pott 8vo of 1801 had also printed the pott 8vo of 1798 (81), since both are in Fry's Long Primer No. 3 type (described as new in his 1785 specimen). 1801 is clearly set up from 1798 (81) and 81 shows corrections in the text of the composite edition (80) of the same year which one would not expect to find if 81 were a piracy. Finally, the evidence of a copy of a variant issue of the composite edition, now in the Povey collection at Princeton, containing sheets A–M of vol. 1 of 81, puts the matter beyond dispute and surely indicates that 81 as well as 80 was Johnson's property and accordingly authentic.

Your reviewer suggests that his remarks about the 1798 editions and the other editions printed, or probably printed, by Bensley between 1793 and 1800 'may not be insignificant to the study of the text, at a time when it was continually changing as new poems were added to the canon and Cowper's friends strove to make it more correct'. Recent experience in editing the text compels me to disagree with him. It is true that some of the corrections and amendments in the third edition of 1787 are likely to have been approved or suggested by his friends, since Cowper himself, having been mentally incapacitated for the previous six months, knew little about it. But there is hardly any evidence that they had anything to do with the correction of subsequent two-volume editions. Mistakes crept in, and Johnson's fine royal and demy 8vo edition published after Cowper's death in 1800, far from being the most correct, offers the worst text any modern editor could choose. Indeed an examination of all the two-volume editions of the poems published between 1793 and 1837 leads me to the exasperating conclusion that, apart from the new poems added from time to time, almost all are textually worthless.

NORMA H. RUSSELL.
7 Bradmore Road, Oxford.

⁂ Our reviewer writes:—I must disabuse Mrs. Russell of any notion that I have any specialist knowledge of eighteenth-century bibliography, let alone of any particular printer. I was merely anxious to show that the principles of bibliography which she had followed were not as useful from a textual point of view as for, say, a play quarto of the previous century; and that the establishment of the text was not necessarily the prime function of a work like hers. I am very glad to know that a Supplement to her *Bibliography of Cowper* is now nearly ready; it will no doubt put right the small factual points I mentioned, but it cannot alter the whole approach of the original work, which seemed to me misguided.

I willingly accept Mrs. Russell's corrections, for she writes, as I have said, with far greater authority than I can claim. I can only say that some copies of the cancelled St. Andrews sheets do exist, which are exactly as I described; I can only suppose that the Bodleian copy, with its misbound prelims in vol. 1, is a freak of a freak. I certainly withdraw 'piracy', although the possession of a 'strong theological bent' was hardly proof in the eighteenth century of uprightness in the matter of copyright—rather the reverse; at any rate, the relationship between Morison and Johnson is far from clear. As to the text, it may well be that the examples given were of no practical usefulness; but these later editions cannot be entirely ignored, while new matter was still being added. There are variants in the text of the poems added in 1798, and, if the text indeed shows a progressive deterioration, it is presumably useful to know which edition came first, a point which was not immediately clear in Mrs. Russell's work.

22

BABEL AND AFTER

SOCIETY AND THE STRUCTURE OF LANGUAGE

ONE OF THE PRINCIPAL revolutions of spirit during the past fifty years has occurred in our view of language: language, the act and nature of verbal communication, has moved outwards from immediacy. It has become objectified; awareness examines and seeks to circumscribe it as it does other phenomena. The exteriority is a special one: the study of language is itself a linguistic act, instrument and object necessarily interpenetrate (hence the various notions of 'metalanguage' as that mode of linguistic operation which deals especially with semantics, syntax, phonology, and communication as formal structure).

But although the relationship between ourselves as 'language creatures'—Aristotle's and Xenophon's φωνᾶντα ζῷα—and the language acts which we study is one of complex intimacy, that study has begun to alter our entire sense of the word, of man's singular linguistic determination, and of the relations between speech and society. It is a change, a making deliberate of instinctive perception, which has clear antecedents in Plato, in Leibniz, in Herder and Humboldt. But it has only recently developed the kinds of techniques, of professional conventions and psychological confidence, which we associate with a modern discipline.

If French symbolism and Mallarmé, who remains a crucial case for the application of modern linguistics to literature, mark the writer's new consciousness of his medium, his new concept of language as both the problematic means and end of the poetic act; if

---

GIULIO C. LEPSCHY: *La Linguistica Strutturale*. 234 pp. Turin: Einaudi. L. 1,000.

NOAM CHOMSKY: *Cartesian Linguistics*. A Chapter in the History of Rationalist Thought. 119 pp. Harper and Row. £2.

JEAN COHEN: *Structure de langage poétique*. 231 pp. Paris: Flammarion. F. 16.50.

HENRI LEFEBVRE: *Le Langage et la société*. 376 pp. Paris: Gallimard. 4.95 fr.

Wittgenstein and his contemporaries represent the turn of philosophy towards essentially linguistic topics, towards a critique and therapy of verbal statement; then one may confidently say that the works of Saussure and the Prague school mark a related transformation which entails the change from traditional philology and comparative grammar to modern linguistics. The fascinating question is: what common historical and psychological factors underlie the new vision of language at work in the poet, in the logician and in the linguist?

The seminal years extend from the publication of Saussure's *Mémoire sur le système primitif des voyelles dans les langues indo-européennes* in 1878 (a publication rightly termed by Signor G. C. Lepschy as 'una delle avventure intelletuali piú eccitanti dell'indo-europeistica') to 1939 and the *Études phonologiques dédiées à la mémoire de M. le prince N. S. Trubeckoj*. That these dates and titles should already have a certain mythological resonance, that structural linguistics should be producing its own histories and personal memoirs, points to the tremendous expansion of the field since the 1930s. Yet in actual fact the great moments are not distant. In the life and work of Roman Jakobson the adventures of intelligence and reorientations of linguistic feeling which lead from Saussure to Noam Chomsky have a living witness and master.

* * *

Signor Lepschy's *La Linguistica Strutturale* sets out to give an introductory history of the field and to indicate its most significant current trends. Himself a phonetician and Latinist, Signor Lepschy gives a concise summary of the main linguistic theories and problems from the original structuralism of Saussure to recent developments in machine translation and information theory. The bibliographical notes which follow each chapter are particularly useful though at times engagingly ceremonious ('Non è facile isolare . . . una corrente propriamente o esclusivamente "firthiana"; per quello che si chiama a volte "neo-firthianesimo" cfr. oltre.').

The drawback is that Signor Lepschy has not quite made up his mind about the level of his intended reader. Much of the book and the series in which it appears is directed at the layman. At various points, however, the argument is so allusive and compact that it requires a fair amount of previous knowledge (e.g., in the discussion of functional linguistics in Jakobson and Martinet). Nevertheless this is a useful primer and it is refreshing to see the work of Noam

Chomsky treated with both the admiration and partial scepticism appropriate to it.

Professor Chomsky's new book is an historical monograph on the linguistic theories of the Port-Royal *Grammar* and of such post-Cartesian linguists as Cordemoy, Beauzée and Du Marsais. Analysing the 'deep and surface structure' picture of the sentence developed by the Port-Royal grammarians, and the uses of *construction* and *syntax* in Du Marsais, Professor Chomsky shows important philosophical and practical antecedents to his own transformational grammar. Thus the Port-Royal view of inner mental aspect and outer physical aspect (the sound sequence) may be formalized

> by describing the syntax of language in terms of two systems of rules: a *base system* that generates deep structures and a *transformational system* that maps these into surface structures.

In its investigation of the 'role of internally represented schemata or models', current linguistics may be seen as 'a continuation of the tradition of Cartesian Linguistics and the psychology that underlies it'.

* * *

Professor Chomsky's treatment has its antiquarian touches, a scholarly delight in the resuscitation of names or books which have been unjustly ignored or misrepresented. There is something artificial about a discussion of seventeenth-century linguistic thought which passes over Spinoza and stops short of Leibniz. But what is important is the underlying direction of feeling: the view that the true foundations for a theory of language can be traced to the rational formalism of Cartesian logic and Cartesian psychology, with the clear implication that most of what came between Humboldt and Z. S. Harris is romantic digression. This has the necessary but striking consequence that the theory of the mind, of mental life, in a transformational grammar will differ radically from that of Freud. What needs clearing up now is the relation, if any, between notions of 'deep structure' and those of the subconscious as generative of linguistic patterns. Professor Chomsky's return to what Whitehead called 'the century of genius' connects transformational linguistics in a suggestive way with the anti-romanticism of T. S. Eliot, with the bias of stylistic feeling in the New Criticism, and with numerous tendencies in current political and philosophic thought. *Le grand siècle* is much in vogue.

Almost a contrary orientation marks Jean Cohen's *Structure du langage poétique*. His thesis is that the structure of poetry can only be analysed with rigour if we understand that the poetic idiom is not an intensified variant of prose, that it is not prose plus embellishment or elision. Poetry is *de l'antiprose*. The poet destroys ordinary language in order to reconstruct codes and conventions of communication on a higher plane. Poetics is, in essence, the study of these 'superior pathologies'—one almost thinks of *pourritures nobles*—of language.

M. Cohen selects a number of parameters with which to define and measure the 'poeticization' of speech, its estrangement from the prosaic norm. These are the divergence between syntax and prosody (*l'agrammaticalisme*); the use of epithets that modify the noun in some illogical, conventionally irrelevant, even oxymoronic way (Mallarmé's *crépuscules blancs*); the achievement of seeming inconsequence, the information transfer of the poem being deliberately redundant or elliptic or ambiguous when compared with the linear economy of ordinary discourse; and summing up all these, the dislocation from the habitual grid of both words and grammatical forms. Thus the difference between poetry and prose 'est de nature linguistique, c'est-à-dire formelle'.

Not much in all this is new. Similar conclusions are current in the work of Roman Jakobson and T. A. Sebeok. They are summarized in Sol Saporta's paper on 'The Relation of Language to Poetry' and, with particular incisiveness, in Ivan Fónagy's 'Poetic Language: Form and Function' (reprinted in *Problèmes du langage* in the Collection Diogène). What is valuable is M. Cohen's demonstration that French poetry becomes increasingly 'poeticized' as we proceed from classicism to romanticism, and from the romantics to Verlaine, Rimbaud and Mallarmé. Subjecting each form of linguistic abnormality to statistical tabulation, M. Cohen shows that the history of French verse from Corneille to Mallarmé is that of a progressively increasing distance from prose structure. Consequently there is a demonstrable meaning to the proposition that Mallarmé is not only a different kind of poet from Racine but also 'more of a poet'. This is an arresting thought, but what are its logical correlatives? Carried forward, M. Cohen's parameters of the poetic make of automatic writing or *lettrisme* a supreme poetry. What would appear as a statistical, neutral linguistic investigation in fact entails a characteristically modern aesthetic, an aesthetic which cannot give adequate recognition to the poetry of reason and drama of syntax in neoclassicism. M. Cohen's is, none the less, a stimulating book and one that leaves in the mind fascinating questions about the development of the image and adjective in the European sensibility and the reasons for that development.

Such questions are a legitimate part of that congruence of historical linguistic, psychological and sociological interests at work in Henri Lefebvre's *Le Langage et la société*. This is an exciting, many sided, often chaotic book. Starting out as a critique of structural linguistics, as an inquiry into the historical sources and validity of the contemporary treatment of language, it becomes in turn a very acute challenge to the 'linguistic economics' of Lévi-Strauss, an attempt to restore philosophic and social pertinence to current linguistic models, and finally a brilliant excursus on the applications of Marxist theories of value to an understanding of the role of language in society.

* * *

M. Lefebvre is one of the most resourceful of that distinctive group of French 'post-' or 'para-Marxists'. His writings embody a genuine attempt to fuse a Hegelian dialectic with the philosophic sociology of Durkheim and Mauss. This gives to his critique of structural linguistic models its particular focus. Models which do not include the dynamics of continual historical and social change in the functions of language, or whose mappings apply only to arrested, deeply impoverished cultures (Lévi-Strauss) are inadequate to the actual facts of our civilization. So far so good. What is much less clear is M. Lefebvre's own 'tridimensional' theory of language. Postulating language to be *la forme du contenu social* and assuming a fully dialectical interrelation between language and social structure, M. Lefebvre sets up a model of linguistic form and function which one reviewer, at least, finds no more lucid or comprehensive than the many abstractions rejected earlier in the book.

The finest thing in the argument comes almost as an afterthought. In its discussion of the extension of Marx's notions of alienation, fetishism and surplus value to phenomena of advertisement, propaganda, linguistic inflation and decay in modern culture, *Le Langage et la société* fully justifies its title. The short 'history of discourse' (*de la parole aux parleries*) which concludes the book embodies an audacity of historical imagining, a sheer intuitive gusto, reminiscent of Walter Benjamin, some of whose conjectures on language and the evolution of mercantile society it may in fact reflect.

Whatever the deficiencies of his own model, M. Lefebvre is surely on the right track. The thinness of traditional 'lit. crit.' and literary history is becoming apparent to all but the most entrenched academics. The next step must be the development of a genuine 'philosophy of language' in which linguistics, sociology, psychology, linguistic philosophy and the critical valuation of literary texts each play their part. What is needed is a direction of spirit flexible and adventurous enough to know that Sartre's *Les Mots* and John Cage's *Silence* are fully relevant to its purpose. That this intimation of a new approach to language is already effective is shown by such works as Mr. Helmut Gipper's remarkable *Bausteine zur Sprachinhaltsforschung* (indeed, *Sprache und Gemeinschaft*, the series in which it appears, almost exactly translates M. Lefebvre's own title).

There is need of a restatement and clarification of the recognition, so urgent in Leibniz and Herder, that man is uniquely conditioned by his linguistic heritage and practice. What Lévi-Strauss calls *la science de l'homme* is, centrally, a science or philosophy of language. To such a philosophy modern structural linguistics has a very important contribution to make. But it cannot do the whole job, because the habits of feeling and linguistic response which it necessarily cultivates will too often be antiphilosophic and indifferent to literature. Thus when one thinks about language in society, about the present erosion of verbal literacy and what this may mean in regard to the future of poetic forms, there will be many things to be learnt from Du Marsais; but even more, one suspects, from De Maistre.

23

TWO LINGOS

(*a*) JEAN FOLLAIN

Petit glossaire de l'argot ecclésiastique

ANY CLOSED SOCIETY is likely to produce its own, often barbarous, inbred horseplay, its tribalistic initiation ceremonies, and, above all, its own semi-secret language. When the brutal *bizutage* of Saint-Louis, Saint-Cyr, Grignon or Agro is safely a thing of the past, still to be evoked with sentimental nostalgia, something of the secret languages of adolescence is liable to persist, if only as a sign of recognition and mutual esteem—like a masonic handshake—and perhaps too in an effort to remain young and to combat obesity and family responsibilities. *Normaliens* will still speak of *caïmans*, of *archicubes* and of *thurnes*, when among themselves, or in the presence of the uninitiated, even if they are Ministers of State or *professeurs aux Hautes Études;* a *saumurois* of eighty will greet a surviving member of his *promotion* in the vigorous language of the young men in white gloves and heavy swords who go to bed, not alone and with their spurs on, and who, like Courteline's monocled dragoons, spend noisy evenings *chez Madame Irma*. The President of the French Republic tends, it is said, in private conversation, still to relapse into the vocabulary of the pre-1914 *cyrard*.

The *séminaire* and the *presbytère* are no exception; priests, in their world somewhat apart, have to rely on one another for company, for encouragement and for assistance, much more than any professional body or trade group. There is a feeling of red-faced fraternity, of knowledge and experience shared—and denied to others—about any social occasion at which *curés* and *vicaires* come together; and it would be hard to equal the almost schoolboy gaiety of those lunches or dinners to which neighbouring priests invite one another. In the Hôtel de la Croix Blanche at Avignon everything is on a somewhat monumental scale, even the pepper pots and the plates; its clientele consists largely of *ces Messieurs*. It is not, of course, a fantasy of

---

(*a*) *Petit glossaire de l'argot ecclésiastique*. 50 pp. Paris: Pauvert. 7.05 fr.
(*b*) *Lern Yerself Scouse*, 80 pp. Liverpool: The Scouse Press.

advertisers that so many *digestifs* (as so many patent medicines designed to relieve indigestion) should carry the names—and often the portraits—of thickset Gallican priests, their faces reassuringly rubicund above their old-fashioned white-edged bands; in the present glossary, the second word is *L'Ami du Clergé*, the bottle of calvados as it circulates among those in charge of souls in the lush pastures of Lower and Upper Normandy: 'Confrère, passez-moi l'Ami du Clergé'. This, like many others, is something of a private joke, *L'Ami du Clergé* being a newspaper addressed almost exclusively to the rural priesthood. And whether that most recent addition to the language of drink—*garçon, un kir!*—is in use among the Burgundian lower clergy, as well as among the general public, there is no doubt about the clerical origin of the drink itself (its inventor would be too old to qualify for the title *Ogino*, used, we are told, to designate those very rare canons nominated since the Council). In a country like rural France, where eating brings men together, *la mine couperosé* is a good image to put out; a vegetarian priest who drank water or *lolo* would make little headway among the *maqueux de Neufchâtel.* This is not to subscribe to the vulgar demagogy of *Clochemerle* or *Don Camillo*—both what French critics have described as *romans putains*. The very value of the present collection is that it represents exclusively the language in use among priests themselves.

It is a language which displays a healthy irreverence and an ability to speak of everyday priestly functions—'Grandeurs et Servitudes du Sacerdoce'—in most non-mystical terms. Irreverence towards the higher ranks—*les violets*, *le Harem*, *le Homard*, *le Protozoaire*, for respectively the bishops, diocesan administration, a Cardinal (M. Follain claims to have heard a Cardinal's chauffeur explain to a young chaplain: 'J'attends mon Homard')—and irreverence, mixed this time with some dislike, towards those who normally bar the way to these mighty personages; *le roquet*, for instance, designates the secretary and private chaplain of a bishop. (Outside the church it is, of course, used to describe any small dog with a loud bark.) It is reassuring to learn that priests describe as *entrer en piste* their passage from the sacristy to the altar, that *biner* is the verb used to indicate the celebration of two masses in one day, *triner* for three—there is also *binard* and *trinard*, people either to be pitied, or to be disliked for working overtime—that *faire la moisson* is used to describe a period in which a priest has a heavy load of funerals and masses for the dead. Perhaps the best of all is *extrêmiser* (to administer extreme unction). *Sucer le bonbon* is to kiss a bishop's ring. *Antibiotique* is apparently a recent (episcopal) addition to the language on the part of Mgr. Richaud: 'Savez-vous ce que chez nous gens d'église on dit des coadjuteurs: ce sont nos *antibiotiques*, ils nous prolongent.' *Entrer dans la Marine*, like *L'Ami du Clergé*, is regional. *Le Huitième Sacrament* is the collection.

The French clergy clearly have much in common both with the Army and with medical students and doctors. There is a pleasantly innocent, boyish quality in the irreverence of their metaphors; we even find an old English favourite to describe a certain type of shovel hat, long since condemned, blown away by the wind of change from Rome: *la T.S.F.* Nothing could be farther removed from the carping anti-clericalism of *La Calotte* or from the vulgar winks and nudges of *Le Canard* ('On sait, hein? On est au courant, hein? On connait les curetons?') with its insistence on the perfectly innocent *Mon Gouvernement*, *une Carabasen*, both words, the latter Breton, but in general ecclesiastical usage to indicate the elderly servant of a priest. This is the language of people who are matter-of-fact about their functions and happy in their vocation and who live in close harmony with their colleagues; it is gently irreverent, never iconoclastic or displeasing; it would not have displeased Saint-Vincent-de-Paul, whose language, one is told, 'ne manquait pas de verdeur'. It has a distinctly Gallican flavour, an ecclesiastical *bouquet de France*. M. Follain's little dictionary, which has a violet cover and is beautifully printed, carries an air of conviction, even though—and this is hardly surprising—it does not bear an *imprimatur*. It may shock the convert; it will certainly not shock the French clergy, many of whom could have greatly added to the collection. As it is, it is a welcome addition to *Le Petit Simonin* and other similar works on *argots*, *la langue verte*, and so on. The *argot* of this particular milieu might be described as *la langue violette*. M. Follain's work should be read with a kir, a benedictine or a calvados.

(*b*) FRANK SHAW, FRITZ SPIEGL, STAN KELLY

Lern Yerself Scouse

Last month the World Cup threw up one small by-product that is worth the attention of linguists and others. This is a booklet, produced ostensibly for the benefit of foreign visitors to Goodison Park, called *Lern Yerself Scouse. How to talk Proper in Liverpool.* It is the joint work of Messrs. Frank Shaw, Fritz Spiegl and Stan Kelly, has eighty oblong pages, and is published (at an undisclosed price) by the Scouse Press in that city. Scouse is Lobscouse, the mysterious stew-like dish favoured there, which Mr. Spiegl's erudite foreword identifies with the German or Norwegian *Labskaus.* The citizens accordingly become Scousers, and Scouse is what they not only eat but speak.

It is a language that links Thomas Creevey with Mr. Ken Dodd. 'Diddy', as Mr. Spiegl reminds us, was what Creevey's stepdaughters called him, 'diddy' still being the local word for small. Creevey was born in Liverpool and stood for Parliament in the Whig interest there; his use of such nicknames as Prinny and Sherry was entirely consonant with other modern local diminutives such as Ippy for Hippodrome and Lanny for Landing Stages. 'Dese are me bezzies' = *These are my best clothes.* 'Will yer send me to the ozzy?' says an item under the heading 'In the Doctor's Surgery'; a phrase translated with the authors' characteristic slight formality as *Do I have to go to hospital?*

The form of their work is that of a conversational phrase-book, progressing from 'Forms of Address' (Wack = *Sir;* Y'know like = *A useful but meaningless interjection*), through 'Dining Out', 'At the Outfitters' (Yer gorrup like a pox-doctor's clerk = *You are somewhat over-dressed*), 'In the Alehouse' and other useful sections, to a choice of verses from *The Rubáiyát of Omar Khayyám* rendered in the full glory of the Liverpool dialect and the *Weltanschauung* it expresses:

> De Ref no question makes of rights or wrongs
> Just makes de rules up as e goes along.
> And many a foul as penalised de weak
> While many an off-side rule supports de strong.

Football plays the expected prominent part in shaping the language. 'Ee's got both legs in one knicker' means *He is not playing well.* 'It im wid yer andbag!' *He is too timid when tackled.* Why it may be advisable for the spectator to roll up the football edition of the *Liverpool Echo* is discussed in a discreet note.

There is little rhyming slang here, or other London features, though certain expressions are certainly not unique to Merseyside: 'Moggy' for *cat*, for instance. The foreword quotes the old joke about

VAT 69, but this was used in Behan's *The Hostage*, and was familiar to Catholics from many parts of these islands. On the other hand, the southern reader is constantly being staggered by the splendour, sometimes of the sounds themselves, as with 'bur goo' for porridge, sometimes of the poetic vision, as when a coloured man is called a smoked Irishman. Birkenhead, across the Mersey, is the One-eyed City; Bootle is 'Whur de Bugs wur Clogs'; Walton gaol, for some unexplained reason, is 'Joe Gerks'.

'Gear', a term of approbation that has travelled south with the success of the Mersey Sound, is here related to the French 'de rigueur'. Seriously, or with the tongue in the cheek?—it is sometimes difficult to say. Such explanatory notes are not very frequent, but they are nearly always illuminating and apposite, adding much to the comic effect. Thus the section on 'Family and Friends', which begins:

Us	Yer, Yiz
I; me	*You.*
Yews.	Dem.
You (plural)	*They; these*

When a Liverpool teacher says "Stand up, Hughes!" to a boy thus named the whole class usually rises.

'Nallered' for *caught* is derived from a mixture of 'nab' and 'collar' (why not 'nail' too?); 'debbie' for *a derelict site* from the debris due to the bombing. It should not be forgotten that Mr. Spiegl is the former first flute of the Liverpool Philharmonic ('De Band of Hope Street'). 'I'll marmalise yer' for 'I will chastise you severely' is compared with Colette's text for the Ravel *L'Enfant et les Sortilèges*, where the teapot threatens the cup in an apparently home-made English: 'I punch your nose . . . I boxe you . . . I marm'lad' you!'

Observers of the Merseyside scene will note the recurrent aggressiveness of the remarks—aggressiveness that often develops to the brink of a real fight and then suddenly blows away—from the early 'Make yer name Walker, wack' (*Please go away*) to the whole section on 'Starting an Altercation' at the end. 'If yer can't fight wur a big at', as they say to the verbally truculent. Nowhere is a bigger one worn than at the football match, where threats vary from the facetious to the obscenely blood-curdling. And yet what could be more gently poetic than the expression for *wandering about thoughtfully* here attributed to the Liverpool dockers: 'I was moodyin'?

At a time when there are so many reasons for language to become tediously standardized it is heartening to feel that there are parts of England where words are so alive. The strong Irish influence in Liverpool is obviously a factor—or, even more, the general mixture of races of which this is only one part. It is no doubt the clash of such different national temperaments that helps preserve the citizens' verbal quick-wittedness against the erosions of standard English and spurious actors' dialect, and there is also the traditional local independence natural to an old trading and seafaring community. Local character *is* reflected in language, even in the language of the new Beatles songs, it seems, which is much superior to the old pop drivel. It will be interesting to see if the same features are to be found in the batch of works by Liverpool poets and novelists which are to come out in the next few months.

24

EXPRESSIONS OF THE NEW AGE

(*a*) *Communication and Language*

THE STUDY of science and technology as new sorts of languages, new codifications of experience, has come to seem a perfectly natural pursuit in recent years. It is not only in art and in literature that technique has come to be recognized as a means of discovery and of new perception. The authors of this book make it quite clear that new techniques of communication provide societies and cultures with new languages and new perceptions:

> Modern communications help to make us aware that we are the heirs of all previous history. They reveal the rich variety of human life and the great diversity of human societies; but at the same time they remind us that mankind is one. They make us realize that every man's past is nothing less than the whole human past, and that every man's present will contribute to the whole human future.

The great increase of critical self-awareness that this condition entails seems to point to the erosion, in some degree, of the unconscious, private and collective. The age of communication is perhaps in a special way the age of electric circuitry, and whereas merely mechanical communication tended to convey, or to transport, data from point to point, electric circuitry seems to fold the communicator entirely into the process of communication. This involvement in developmental processes favoured by an environment of electric circuitry inclines our time to be more concerned with making than matching. The sort of thinking that is natural to cultures of high visual orientation, and that Owen Barfield calls 'alpha' thinking in *Saving the Appearances*, is very much concerned with 'matching' as a means of determining truth. It is a kind of thinking that has long

---

(*a*) *Communication and Language*. Networks of Thought and Action. Edited by Sir Gerald Barry and Others. The Macdonald Illustrated Library. 367 pp. Macdonald. £2 15s.

(*b*) *Use of Mechanized Methods in Documentation Work*. 89 pp. Aslib. 36s. 18*s*. to members.

been accepted as the norm of discourse in the western world. It is based upon 'a point of view' and is necessarily fragmentary and analytic. It does not seem to have developed at any time without the direct technical aid of the phonetic alphabet.

What Owen Barfield calls 'beta-thinking' is not private but corporate and unconscious. It is the collective response of a whole society to new conditions of existence. When a new environment, created by a new technology, reprogrammes the entire sensory life of that society, its thinking and its outlook are totally altered by the new language of communication provided by the new environment. Each new technology provides this new pattern of 'beta-thinking' for entire populations. The sensory profile, as it were, of the entire population is modified and the body percept of individual and group alike is altered.

The authors of the present book make no claim to have studied all the effects of new communication techniques. They open the doors to such a study. They survey a wide range of communication techniques as they enable both animals and men to constitute themselves in communities. For example, when they describe 'Living Language' and 'The mechanics of speech' there is no attempt to present diverse languages as widely separated forms of perception and experience, any more than there is any sophisticated attempt to show how modern linguistics become possible through the tape recorder and related electric means for examining the structure of speech and rhythm. In general, the authors, in serving the world of media and the arts, content themselves with a descriptive rather than structural study. They observe:

> The effect of being able to copy books relatively quickly and cheaply was to take learning and the discussion of ideas out of the narrow confines of the clergy and to offer them generally to all who could learn to read. Within a few decades Europe was torn by religious wars and bitter controversies that lasted well into the seventeenth century—wars of ideas fought with books and pamphlets as well as with swords and guns. The Renaissance, the Reformation and Counter-Reformation, the growth of science and geographical exploration, the rediscovery of the classical past of Greek art, literature, and philosophy, would not have broken up the static outlook of the medieval world so surely and swiftly without the rapid spread of printed books.

Print, as a technology, created the Public in our sense. The Public was a new environment which eventually became related to uniform pricing and to markets. The ways in which print affected the means of production and the organization of markets was inseparable from its effect on individual sensibilities. Montaigne's response to 'la publique' was, in effect, the invention of the private man of letters.

> I owe a complete portrait of myself to the public. The wisdom of my lesson is wholly in truth, in freedom, in reality . . . of which propriety and ceremony are daughters, but bastard daughters.

What the authors seem inclined to overlook in this approach to 'mass media' is that they are less a factor of size than of speed. Electric speeds of information movement of themselves act as the new structuring forces as much in science and the arts as in politics and in entertainment. Whereas the slower speeds of print and wheeled transport permitted literacy and the public to exist in considerable quantity, the kinds of involvement and participation that were consistent with these media were very much less than those demanded of the mass audience created by an electric environment. Coexistence in space assumes a different character when it is also coexistence in time. Many of the arrangements made for spatial coexistence become embarrassing and irrelevant when instantaneous information exchange intrudes. That is to say that almost all of the existing arrangements in the educational establishment, for example, must seem bizarre to any young person today. Growing up in a world where all data and events appear integrally related, the student enters the educational establishment where instruction is in the main provided by means of classified data and separate subjects.

It is not surprising that our education should be organized on mechanical and fragmented patterns. In the pre-electric times, the rearrangement and accommodation of older patterns to new ones would have occurred over a generation or two. Under electric conditions, no such leisure is available. Since there are no precedents to indicate how we might meet the exigencies of instant speed, we tend to greet every new technology as a crisis, or ultimatum. Every such crisis conceals huge new potential. Speed-up of information ideally permits education to proceed by discovery and by pattern recognition rather than by instruction in classified data. The same speed-up that renders the economy obsolete also yields greatly more wealth.

It is a natural response to any new technology to set it at first to perform the older tasks. Even now computers are programmed to provide more quickly the data contained in catalogues and files. The same delusion besets those engaged in the educational uses of films, radio and television. They are inclined to repeat what has been or could be done in the existing classroom. This results in some confusion and in much delay in discovery of the real function of any new form. It would be possible to write the history of media in these terms. Among the mirages created by any new media is the nostalgic picture of the preceding period. Environments as such tend to be as invisible as they are invincible. As soon, however, as a new environment forms, it seems to have the power to transform the preceding environment into a clear, distinct and attractive image. The 'Elizabethan world picture' was of the Middle Ages. The nineteenth-century industrial image was of the earlier agrarian and handicraft world that we associate with the Romantic movement. The twentieth century has a clear image of nineteenth-century aims and goals. Whatever happens to be the current environment assumes the cloak of invisibility, like the Emperor's new clothes. Is there a natural fear of the environmental that makes us admire the preceding environments?

The present volume is lavishly illustrated with historical and contemporary images. The defect of the book may well be one shared by our entire culture. It tends to be a package and a tribute rather than a probe into the structure of new realities.

(*b*) HERBERT COBLANS

Use of Mechanized Methods in Documentation Work

It will be a long time before libraries and documentation centres have computer links as a matter of course, but their infiltration by automatic data processing equipment is already well under way. One consequence of this is that any distinction which ever existed between these two types of institution is likely to disappear in future, in face of the pervasive input-storage-output model. Dr. Coblans's book might be described as belonging to the post-first-flush stage of mechanized documentation. In the first flush it was assumed that containment of the information explosion was simply a tremendous chore, with trivial intellectual content, too vast for human beings to undertake, but not too vast for computers. That view has given way to another which finds typical expression in a single sentence in the

1964 Report on the National Science Foundation, 'The real difficulty in devising mechanized systems for organizing and searching large collections of scientific information is not technological, it is intellectual.'

It is for this reason, and not because of any shortcoming in the treatment, that to read Dr. Coblans's book is at times to receive the impression of being conducted on a peripheral excursion around the boundaries of important unilluminated central issues, which are logically and operationally prior to the punched tape, microfilm, peekaboo cards and other stock-in-trade of the data processing world. Tantalizingly Dr. Coblans speaks of the pitfalls of subject indexing and of the fundamental difficulty of assigning keywords, but, justifiably within the limits which he has set himself, takes us no farther. This situation is one in which we might expect a frustrated 'mechanical tail' to begin wagging a semantic dog, and indeed the author reports a complaint that it takes one third longer to find target material in the computerized *Index Medicus* than in the manually produced version, because the former has permitted the requirements of post-coordination computer searching techniques to influence its subject headings. It is also understandable that designers of computer produced indexes should have reverted to the crudities of title catchword indexing, thus sidestepping the semantic problem altogether. Historically the catchword index preceded the subject catalogue proper, and, in another context, it is possible to see the modern machine-oriented documentalists' preoccupation with thesauri as a re-enactment of the development of standard subject heading lists which started in the general library field (especially in the United States) half a century ago.

All these issues have to do with the use of computers and selectors for document retrieval, but Dr. Coblans sees a more immediate role for machines in library housekeeping activities—in application to such routines as physical production of catalogues and bibliographies, keeping track of the receipt of 'on order' material (especially serials), recording circulation, and the production of union lists of stock covering groups of libraries. One effect of mechanization will undoubtedly be to enhance the idea of individual libraries as units in a comprehensive information network. The book is highly successful in drawing out the essential pattern which lies beneath the patchwork of projects and experiments now being made to automate library processes. With its careful assessment both of the solid gains and of the pitfalls of automated documentation, it should be required reading both for the rockfast traditionalist and for the runaway mechanizer. Strangely, the author appears not to mention the overriding motive for mechanizing documentation work, namely, the short supply of the requisite human skill, which needs to be concentrated upon the tasks which human beings alone can do.

25

HOW MANY DIVISIONS?

THE POPE AND THE SECOND WORLD WAR

THE PUBLICATION of the first two volumes of *Actes et Documents du Saint Siège relatifs à la seconde guerre mondiale* not only marks an important innovation in the archival policy of the Vatican but also offers another token of the *aggiornamento* of the Roman Catholic Church. For centuries, the image of papal diplomacy as autocratic, secretive and even subversive has been a familiar one to the political and theological adversaries of the Roman Curia. The Vatican archives have been closed to all but historians of remote periods. The decision of the present Pope to allow publication of the official documents of the pontificate of Pius XII is therefore to be regarded as a very considerable step in the direction of liberal modernity.

* * *

There can be little doubt that these volumes owe their origin to a keen desire to refute the allegations widely bruited around since the appearance of Rolf Hochhuth's play *The Representative* some three years ago. The apologetic character of the publication necessarily

---

Le Saint Siège et la guerre en Europe: mars 1939–août 1940. 553 pp. *Lettres de Pie XII aux Évêques allemands, 1939–1944*. 453 pp. Actes et Documents du Saint Siège relatifs à la seconde guerre mondiale. Vatican City: Libreria Editrice Vaticana.

Die Briefe Pius XII an die deutschen Bischöfe 1939–1944. Herausgegeben von Burkhart Schneider mit Pierre Blet und Angelo Martini. 381 pp. Mainz: Matthias-Grünewald-Verlag. DM. 48.

SAUL FRIEDLÄNDER: *Pius XII and the Third Reich*. Translated by Charles Fullman. 238 pp. Chatto and Windus. 35s.

Der Notenwechsel zwischen dem Heiligen Stuhl und der deutschen Reichsregierung: Bearbeitet von Dieter Albrecht. I: Von der Ratifizierung des Reichskonkordats bis zur Enzyklika 'Mit brennender Sorge.' 459 pp. Mainz: Matthias-Grünewald-Verlag.

JENÖ LEVAI: *Geheime Reichssache: Papst Pius XII hat nicht geschwiegen*. 157 pp. Cologne: Verlag Wort und Werk.

MAXIME MOURIN: *Le Vatican et l'U.R.S.S.* 298 pp. Paris: Payot. 16 fr.

raises questions concerning the selection of the documents. Only when all the files are open to public scrutiny will every scholar be satisfied, but in the meantime the editors have produced these two volumes with excellent care and scholarly lucidity. The first, *Le Saint Siège et la guerre en Europe: mars 1939–août 1940*, is a selection of the official documents received or transmitted by the Vatican Secretariat of State during the first eighteen months of Pius XII's pontificate. The second, *Lettres de Pie XII aux Évêques allemands 1939–1944*, consists of all the official communications which were sent by Pius XII to the German bishops in the very difficult and dangerous circumstances of the war. Each begins with a long introduction, in French, and each reproduces the texts of the documents in the original language. The reader has to be conversant with the working language of the Secretariat of State, Italian, as well as with Latin, German and French. The critical apparatus is most carefully and meticulously put together. Photostats of some of the documents, showing the numerous handwritten corrections made by the Pope himself, are included. Every evidence of scholarly integrity is provided. The second volume is also available in a German edition, *Die Briefe Pius XII an die deutschen Bischöfe, 1939–1944*, appearing in a documentary series published by the Catholic Academy of Bavaria.

* * *

The value of this series of documents, when completed, will be enormous, and will enable scholars to study in their entirety the official policies of Pius XII in international relations during a period in which the Church was beset by radical challenges on a scale vaster than anything since the Reformation. Authoritative answers can then be given to those who, like Herr Hochhuth, have asked penetrating questions about Pius XII's attitudes towards the Nazis, the Communists and the Jews. It will also be possible to supplement the omissions and to correct the biases of those who have already attempted to answer these questions on the basis of a limited number of sources. Among the latter must be included M. Saul Friedländer, whose book *Pius XII and the Third Reich* has just appeared in an English translation of the French and German editions, though unfortunately without the sober assessment by the distinguished French historian, Alfred Grosser, appended in the earlier versions. M. Friedländer's main source has been the records of the German Foreign Ministry, particularly the files of its Vatican embassy, which was maintained right up to the collapse of the Nazi regime in 1945. M. Friedländer admits that to look at Papal policy through the eyes of German diplomats, often at second or third hand, is not the most satisfactory manner for an historian, and complains that the Vatican archives were not open to his inspection. Despite a brief note to the English edition acknowledging the recent publication of the first two volumes of Vatican documents, he has chosen not to revise his original text. But he has also overlooked, or decided to disregard, the numerous documents of the German Foreign Ministry which were mimeographed in the NG series at the Nuremberg trials, which give a very full picture of the many representations made by the Papal Nuncio in Berlin against the persecution of the Church by the Nazis. Even more striking is the omission of the strongest protests of all made by the Vatican, which were published in full at the time of the trials. His very partial selection of documents therefore throws some doubt on his admittedly tentative conclusion that

> the Sovereign Pontiff seems to have had a predilection for Germany which does not appear to have been diminished by the nature of the Nazi regime and which was not disavowed up to 1944.

* * *

Eugenio Pacelli possessed qualities of mind which had already marked him out even before his election to the Papal throne in March, 1939. His unparalleled diplomatic skill and his wide awareness of the political realities had been enhanced by his tenure for a decade of the Secretaryship of State. He knew seven languages, and had associated with the leaders of many nations ever since his first attempt to negotiate peace with Kaiser Willhelm II in 1917. It was no accident that, in the darkening climate of international relations, a man whose expertise lay in the resolution of conflicts should be chosen as the leader of the Roman Catholic Church. Many felt that the influence of the Church could best be deployed in the attempt to mitigate the clash of nationalist policies through mediation and diplomacy. Certainly Pius XII held this opinion himself almost too ardently. He saw his role not as a prophet calling his people and the world to repentance and a purer life, but as a diplomat calmly working to remove the causes of strife and to enhance peace between the nations. Pius XII was pessimistic about the position of the Church in a world beset by many radical and revolutionary movements in both thought and politics. He had seen the established tradition of church and state overthrown in many parts of the world, and believed, as he frequently wrote to the German bishops, that the Church would need to retreat into the fortress of faith and there to endure the attacks of its enemies until such time as it could once again take the initiative. For this initiative, peace would be necessary. It was his tragedy that during the first years of his pontificate the world was engulfed in war and his efforts to avert it were all in vain.

* * *

Despite their historical value, this series of documents, even when completed, is unlikely to alter the verdict of those who attack the Pope's judgment, and who believe that public and fearless protests would not only have enhanced the moral position of the Church throughout the world, but would also have been successful in deterring Hitler from his policies of terrorism and extermination. Most of the criticisms of Pius XII advanced by scholars such as M. Friedländer and Günther Lewy echo those of Herr Hochhuth in deploring the fact that Pius XII was the kind of man he was. He failed, they claim, to mobilize the whole Catholic Church in defence of human rights and freedoms, especially at the time of the extermination of the Jews. By his silence and refusal to name names, Pope Pius made the Church an accomplice in the most terrible crimes of this century. The reasons advanced for this silence are varied. Herr Hochhuth depicted the Pope as a superficial and ivory-towered opportunist interested only in enlarging the finances of the Papacy and taking subtle pleasure in the delicacy of his diplomatic web-spinning. M. Friedländer dismisses this idea and suggests that Pius's silence was due to his pro-German tendencies which made him favour concessions to Hitler even after the policy of appeasement had been abandoned by Britain and France. These tendencies were reinforced by the Pope's hope that Nazi Germany, if it were eventually reconciled with the western Allies, would become the essential rampart against any advance by the Soviet Union into western Europe. Above all his frequently expressed sympathy towards Germany, and his desire to protect the Catholic Church there, were responsible for his failure to denounce publicly the crimes of the Nazi regime about which he was well enough informed.

Professor Lewy and Gordon Zahn have previously made the pointed criticism, echoed by M. Friedländer, that another Pope would have acted differently. Yet it needs to be stressed that the

Pope's power was not nearly as effective as these critics imagine, and, indeed, one wonders whether they would not accuse the Pope of theocratical ambitions if such power had been exercised in any cause other than their own. The Pope's power to command the obedience of his bishops was slight, and slighter still to rectify the misdeeds of hostile totalitarian regimes. Even his admonitions were not very effective, as could be seen from the pro-Nazi attitudes of Cardinal Innitzer or Bishop Rarkowski. In writing to the German bishops, the Pope suffered from two handicaps: first, he sought to urge the cause of peace upon men whose parishioners were almost all willingly involved in the pursuit of military victory and who were critically divided in their loyalties to the Nazi government; secondly, he was rightly afraid that his words would be reported to, or captured by, the Gestapo. His official letters to the more nationalistic bishops, as printed in the second volume, are notably more formal than the much franker, but still reserved, remarks made to the staunchest anti-Nazi bishop, Preysing of Berlin. Even here he was careful not to use words which could give the Gestapo cause to brand the bishop as a traitor. For this reason alone, he believed, allusions and ambiguities were to be preferred to outright denunciations.

The Vatican documents now give a much clearer picture of Pius XII's policies than the second or third-hand sources which M. Friedländer has used to bolster his case, but they are unlikely to persuade the Pope's critics that he was right. On the crucial issue of his relations with Germany it should be remembered that Pacelli's close acquaintance with the German Government and people had extended over twenty years. It is undeniable that he was sympathetic to the best German traditions, but no evidence exists that he ever gave support to the ideas of Nazism, still less to Hitler and his upstart followers, from whom he believed only the worst could be expected. To be sure he had participated in the conclusion of the 1933 Concordat, but only in order to secure a recognized legal basis upon which Church-state relations could be established. These somewhat jejune hopes were to be increasingly disillusioned by the Nazi refusal to honour this agreement, and by the eagerness with which Germans, even bishops, were affected by the disease of Nazism. Again and again the Cardinal Secretary of State sent meticulous diplomatic notes to the German government deploring the increasing contraventions of the Concordat, in order to brand the perfidy of the Nazi regime. These Notes from 1933 to 1937 have now been published in a German edition by Professor D. Albrecht. *Der Notenwechsel zwischen dem Hl. Stuhl und der deutschen Reichsregierung* is the first of three volumes which are to carry the documentation up to the end of the war, and which likewise appear under the auspices of the Catholic Academy of Bavaria. Here is evidence enough of the Cardinal Secretary of State's resolute hostility to Nazi policies as well as of the refusal of the Berlin authorities to rectify his detailed complaints submitted through diplomatic exchanges. By 1937 the German bishops themselves asked for more outspoken measures, and in March the Papal Encyclical *Mit brennender Sorge* was smuggled into Germany and read from every Catholic pulpit. Pacelli played a very considerable part in its formulation, a fact mentioned by M. Friedländer only in a footnote. It was hardly surprising that at the time of Pius's election to the pontificate, 'a fanatical hatred filled the Nazi Party against Cardinal Pacelli', a fact similarly treated by M. Friedländer.

* * *

The results of the Encyclical were, however, disappointing. Hitler only stepped up his persecution of churchmen and church institutions. His popularity suffered no decline. And his aggressive moves against Austria and Czechoslovakia in 1938 only increased his hold over the German people, Catholics and Protestants alike. In March 1939, the senior cardinals of Germany, Bertram and Faulhaber, urged the new Pope not to take any measures which would brand Catholics as traitors to the regime, since this would play directly into the hands of the Nazi extremists.

By 1939, the need to maintain peace in Europe appeared to be the foremost requirement for Papal diplomacy, and this forms the thread of the first of the Vatican volumes, taking the account as far as August, 1940. Here is the full record, supplementing what is already known in outline from such sources as Ciano's Diary, and briefly summarized in a few pages by M. Friedländer, of the Papal diplomatic interventions in the search for peace. Following his election, Pius attempted to use his influence fully in this direction—an attempt made all the more urgent by the violent seizures of Czechoslovakia and Albania which occurred in the first month of his reign. To do this, however, he needed to cultivate the confidence of both sides in his impartiality. Encouraged by the advice of four senior German bishops, Pius resolved to begin his pontificate with gestures of accommodation towards the German government. Within two months of taking office, he suggested to the governments of Germany, Italy, France, Britain and Poland that an international conference be called which would tackle those issues apparently most likely to be the occasion for war, namely the German-Polish quarrel and Franco-Italian tensions. But at the end of May Hitler rejected this plan, stating that there was no need for such a conference since no danger of war between Germany and Poland existed. The Pope was obliged to see that his offer had been premature. He also drew the well-founded conclusion that Hitler's mind was closed to pressure from the Vatican. He concentrated his activities therefore on Mussolini and made repeated attempts to warn the Italian dictator of the dangers of war, urging him to use 'his great influence on Chancellor Hitler and on the German government in order that the question of Danzig should be treated with the calmness which the delicate international situation makes more than ever necessary'. These efforts were rendered void by the sudden announcement of the Nazi-Soviet pact, a combination between two anti-Christian forces which was as unsavoury as it was unwelcome. Not even the Pope's last minute intervention in favour of a negotiated peace—albeit at the cost of Polish concessions—could prevent the German decision to go to war.

* * *

Pius XII resolved, however, to continue his efforts for peace even after hostilities had begun, in the hopes of limiting the extent of the holocaust and of securing a negotiated settlement, as is described in the second half of the first Vatican volume of documents. Such aspirations for reconciliation were to be brazenly rejected by the Nazis, confident of total victory throughout 1940 and 1941, and were also thwarted by the Allies when in 1943 they adopted the policy of unconditional surrender. Throughout the first half of 1940 the Pope's efforts were tireless, if unavailing, in the attempt to prevent Mussolini from involving Italy on the German side. The documents make it clear that his expressions of sympathy for the Dutch and Belgian rulers in May 1940 were primarily directed as warnings to the Fascist Government, though they were treated by the Nazi press as evidence of the Pope's hostility to Germany. His refusal to be more explicit about the German aggressions was dictated by his hopes that an attitude of strict neutrality might enable him to use his influence in the direction of a settlement even at this late date. He was still hoping for a negotiated peace in his Christmas broadcast of 1943, which he believed, despite the propaganda attacks of the politicians, would find support among millions on both sides. For this reason too, as he confided to Archbishop Spellman in February, 1943, he still hoped that a coup d'état against Hitler and all his gang would be organized by the German generals whose efforts he had supported secretly as early as 1939. Understandably, however, the official Vatican records contain no documents on this episode.

The Pope was well aware of the danger that any Papal pronouncement would be used as a propaganda weapon by one side or the other in the attempt to enlist the Vatican as an ally. The Pope refused indeed to consider giving any religious approval to the acts of violence, because he was all too aware of the damage done to the Church before in blessing the guns of opposing armies. His public statements had, on the one hand, to be forceful enough to indicate his concern at the evils of war; on the other hand, they had to be general enough not to be exploited by either side for its own war-time propaganda. His Christmas messages were designed to emphasize his distress at 'the contempt for human dignity, human freedom and human life, resulting in deeds that cry to Heaven for vengeance', which deeds, he believed, resulted from the moral disaster of war affecting all the nations. His concern over the extermination of the Jews was forcibly expressed in an address to the Sacred College of Cardinals in June, 1943, which was not, as M. Friedländer states, a secret address, but was published in the next issue of the *Osservatore Romano*. In writing to the German bishops whose cities were destroyed in air-raids, he carefully avoided any mention of the R.A.F.—a fact which caused the Gestapo to denounce these expressions of sympathy as 'pessimistic and defeatist'. Nor did he agree, despite pressure, either to designate the German attack on Bolshevik Russia as a crusade, or to uphold the cause of the western democracies.

This attitude of impartiality was not easy to maintain. As Pius wrote to the Bishop of Würzburg in February, 1941:

At the present moment, we are assailed by countervailing forces: on the one side there are the overwhelming events in the secular field towards which the Pope desires to maintain a reserved attitude in accordance with his unimpaired impartiality; on the other side, the troubles and obligations of the Church compel him to intervene. The pressures run counter to each other so frequently and so ominously, more ominously indeed than in the former World War, that the successor of Peter can well apply to himself the words of Our Lord to the first Pope: 'another shall gird thee and carry thee whither thou wouldest not'—St. John 21, 18.

The second reason for silence was Pius's scepticism about the effectiveness of protest, either public or private. The representations made to the German Foreign Ministry by the Nuncio in Berlin after the outbreak of war met with no greater success than the protests submitted before the Encyclical of 1937. The Nuncio indeed called on the State Secretary, Weizsäcker, almost every month, and often more frequently, with lists of complaints which were forwarded to other agencies of the Nazi government, but almost always in vain. Nor were these protests limited to complaints about the numerous confiscations of Church property, as has been suggested. Far more important were the Papal interventions in various European capitals in condemnation of the ill-treatment, arrests, deportations, and incarceration in concentration camps of hundreds of prominent as well as lowly Catholic clergy, monks, nuns, and individuals, both Gentile and Jewish. In Berlin, the Nuncio made representations—which are not discussed by M. Friedländer—about the fate of hostages in France and Belgium, inquired about the expulsion of Slovenes in Serbia, pleaded against death sentences passed in France, and intervened on behalf of Provost Lichtenberg of Berlin, a Yugoslav consul, a captain in the Polish navy, an Amsterdam Jewess, and seventeen professors of Lemberg University who were 'liquidated' in 1942. As is made clear by L. E. Hill, the majority of these endeavours were rejected or politely side-tracked. And as Pius XII noted in a letter to Bishop Preysing in September, 1941: 'Up to now not a single answer had been vouchsafed to the protests of the Holy See'. Although these representations failed in their purpose, the fact that they were made refutes the view advanced by Rolf Hochhuth in the columns of this journal in October, 1963, that 'Pius XII did not even once make personal intervention for any one of the 3,000 nameless priests whom Hitler, his partner in the Concordat, caused to be murdered'.

The Nuncio's protests were carefully collected in Berlin—as Ribbentrop admitted at Nuremberg, he had a whole drawer full of them—in order that they could be used when the war was won, as prime evidence of the Vatican's hostility and as a pretext for the Nazi eradication of the Catholic Church from German life. There was no evidence that Hitler's mind could be changed by entreaties from Rome. On the contrary, there was enough evidence to fear that retaliatory measures would be taken not only against the Catholic Church but also against the victims for whom these intercessions were made. The Pope believed that if anything was to be done about the German atrocities it must be done from within Germany. For this reason he encouraged the activities of the German resistance, supported the German bishops in their protests to Hitler, urged Cardinal Faulhaber of Munich to make known the Pope's personal concern for the hundreds of priests incarcerated in Dachau, and applauded Bishop Galen's resolute challenge to the Nazi euthanasia programme. (Contrary to what M. Friedländer maintains, the *Osservatore Romano* did publish in December, 1940, the decree prohibiting euthanasia, obviously as a result of the events proceeding in Germany.)

* * *

Pressure from the Vatican could be effective only in circumstances where the government was responsive to humanitarian appeals as, for example, in Hungary. Jenö Levai's *Geheime Reichssache: Papst Pius hat nicht geschwiegen* is an account of the Catholic interventions against the deportations and ill-treatment of the Jews of Hungary in the months following the occupation by German troops in March, 1944. This makes available the documents Mr. Levai first published in Hungarian, and supplements the brief reference in the compendious volumes by R. L. Braham, *The Destruction of Hungarian Jewry*. This terrible example of Nazi bestiality, as organized by Eichmann and his henchmen, saw the mass transportation of Hungarian Jews to Auschwitz or other extermination centres—over 500,000 Jews being taken away in less than three months. Cattle trucks which were urgently needed for the provisioning of German troops on the eastern front were instead diverted to Budapest to be filled with Jews, allegedly being taken to Germany as slave labour in repayment for German military supplies for the defence of Hungary. Mr. Levai provides the documentary evidence of the protests made to Admiral Horthy and his Government by the Papal Nuncio and the Cardinal Primate, which were successful in obtaining temporary alleviations or ameliorations. The Papal envoy also succeeded, in cooperation with the Swiss, Swedish, Portuguese and Spanish diplomatists, in rescuing some hundreds of Jews from a death march to the Hungarian frontier about which Mr. Levai gives the gruesome details. Others found refuge in Catholic institutions. Such steps were insufficient to prevent the tragic fate of Hungarian Jewry. But they refute M. Friedländer's claim that the Pope was unwilling to promote measures to protect the victims of Nazi atrocities. One estimate is that as a result of Papal interventions throughout Europe no fewer than 860,000 Jewish lives were saved. This conclusion will doubtless be strengthened when the evidence of the efforts of the Nuncios in other European countries is published later.

A less favourable view of Pope Pius's diplomacy is taken by Maxime Mourin in his book *Le Vatican et l'U.R.S.S.* He views Vatican policy from the novel point of view of Moscow, and seeks to defend the Russian policies which over so many centuries have led to hostility between Orthodox Russia and the Papacy. He points out that the Bolshevik Revolution, while adding the element of a virulent ideological controversy, merely took over the long-established tradition in both Church and State of suspicion of Papal designs. In dealing with the period of the Second World War, M. Mourin seeks to draw a contrast between the Vatican's attitude towards the Russian aggressions of 1939 and 1940 and the reserve with which the German attacks were treated. Unfortunately, he has derived his views often at second hand and has failed to check the original sources. For example, both he and M. Friedländer (on pp. 94 and 52 respectively) give a quotation from the *Osservatore Romano* which does not exist. Nevertheless he too confirms the Pope's refusal to consider the German invasion of Russia as a crusade or to accept the advice of those of his entourage who undoubtedly longed for the complete destruction of the Bolshevik danger.

In Moscow, certain of the Pope's appointments to the vacant sees in the occupied areas, his attitude towards the Ustachi Government in Croatia, and his support of Franco Spain were readily interpreted as signs of an unholy collaboration between Christians and Nazis. On the other hand, the Soviet Government too was prepared to make accommodating gestures to the Churches in attempting to recruit the support of its own Christian citizens, and in its propaganda branded the Nazi regime as neo-pagan.

It was understandable that the Pope's refusal to endorse the pleas of Roosevelt in late 1941 for a strong stand against Germany was seen in both Washington and Moscow as a sign of pro-Axis sympathies. The suspicions of the Russians that the Pope was all along attempting to create an anti-communist ideological front led them to disbelieve the sincerity of his attempts to secure a just peace.

Similarly the establishment of official diplomatic relations between Japan and the Vatican in 1942 was regarded with astonishment, even though the Pope argued that this was the most effective way of securing humanitarian treatment of allied prisoners of war in Japanese hands. M. Mourin does not go so far as to claim with M. Friedländer that the Pope was principally concerned to reach a negotiated peace solely in order to prevent the spread of Bolshevism into central Europe. On the other hand, there is enough evidence of the fundamental anti-communist and anti-Orthodox attitudes of all the Vatican hierarchy to justify many of the Russians' suspicions, which indeed were to be reinforced by the postwar events and the increasingly outspoken hostility displayed by Pius XII in his later years, which M. Mourin describes as 'an obsession'. His thesis is that only after the lessening of the Cold War, the de-Stalinization of Russia, the increase in contacts between the west and the socialist countries of the east, the change of view of the Orthodox hierarchy, and the election of Pope John XXIII, could a more fruitful era of co-existence begin, in which hopes for a possible growth in mutual understanding can now flourish.

'How many divisions has the Pope?' Stalin is (apocryphally) said to have asked. According to M. Friedländer, Professor Lewy and Herr Hochhuth, the moral resources of the Papacy were never mobilized during the Second World War by prophetic utterances from the Vatican in defence of the persecuted races and the victims of German atrocities. According to Pius XII, as he made clear repeatedly in his letters to the German bishops, he was continually assailed with doubts about the effectiveness of such tactics. The Pope was deeply troubled about whether, in the actual circumstances of the war, this kind of specific protest would provoke harm or good. It is a legitimate criticism to suggest that in this matter his judgment was wrong. But no one familiar with the weight of the evidence now provided could doubt the difficulty of his predicament. His dilemma was succinctly expressed to Bishop Preysing in April, 1943:

> In constantly striving to find the right balance between the mutually contradictory claims of his pastoral office, the path ahead for the representative of Christ is becoming daily more overgrown, beset with difficulties and full of thorns.

Later volumes in the official Vatican series will doubtless give an even clearer picture of the dimensions of this dilemma. New documents, mislaid by the accidents of war, may yet be found. When all these have been published and evaluated, a more certain judgment may be reached about the subtle and complex diplomacy in which the Vatican was involved as the storms of war beat over Europe and engulfed the world in untold misery and tragedy.

26

PRIESTS AMONG THE WORKERS

THE EPISODE of the French worker-priests is not merely one of domestic interest for the Roman Catholic Church, although it represented a dramatic challenge to that Church's sense of responsibility for the millions of workers for whom religion has ceased to have any meaning. It needs to be seen in an historical context, in terms of a social revolution that is not confined to France and whose implications affect churches of every sort of allegiance. The episode itself can seem in retrospect a brief and brave experiment, soon brought to a close by ecclesiastical authority, and bearing with it human problems of a specially poignant kind.

There has been great need of an objective and adequately documented study of the origins of the movement, for, paradoxically enough, they matter more than the experience itself on which all the publicity has fallen. For what is really in question is not the propriety or effectiveness of priests engaging in industry as manual workers: it is the much larger problem of the huge and apparently unbridgeable gulf between the Church and a proletarian society. And the attempt of a few score French priests after the Second World War to establish communication between two separated worlds through their own heroic action is not an isolated phenomenon, to be judged either as good and necessary, or as naive and bound to fail. It has roots that are profoundly important and too little known. M. Poulat has provided for the first time the full background to the movement, and he confines himself to what led up to it. A judgment on the experiment itself and on its consequences deserves another book, and it is to be hoped that M. Poulat will provide it.

It was the publication of a book called *La France Pays de Mission?* in 1943 that concentrated French religious opinion on the gravity of the Church's task. The two authors, Abbé Godin and Abbé Daniel, gave facts and figures to justify the title of their book and perhaps to render the question-mark unnecessary. Abbé Godin in particular was

---

ÉMILE POULAT: *Naissance des Prêtres-ouvriers*. 537 pp. Paris: Casterman.

consumed with a sense of urgency. He had been closely connected with the Jeunesse Ouvrière Chrétienne (founded by Canon—now Cardinal—Cardijn), and increasingly he had come to realize the need for a special group of priests who would identify themselves with the workers of the industrial suburbs of Paris, not through a parochial structure but in a mission which would seek first to penetrate a society wholly estranged from the Church's traditional ministry. Cardinal Suhard, the archbishop of Paris, had read Godin's book with deep emotion and gave his full support to the new initiative of a Mission de Paris. A few days after the formal inauguration of the Mission (following a month of study sessions at Lisieux) Godin died (January 17, 1944). He remains the key figure to an understanding of the worker-priest movement, though he never lived to see it come to birth.

But he was far from alone. And M. Poulat provides much unfamiliar material to justify his claim that *La France Pays de Mission?* was only the culminating point of a movement that both in the efforts of individual priests and in the multiplying agencies of Catholic Action had reflected over many years a profound evolution in the French Church's conception of her missionary task. And, above all else, there was the experience of the war, the fall of France, the millions of French prisoners of war and, later, the terrible experience of forced labour and the concentration camps. What might sometimes have seemed an academic discussion, with all the French passion for intellectualizing problems that called for urgent action, was transformed by the experience of national humiliation and universal suffering into something very real. For the French clergy were conscripts, and in the German camps they were to be confronted with what had hitherto been a reality far removed from their experience—the almost total estrangement of the workers of France not merely from the practice of religion but from the very sense of religion itself.

Even more crucial was the experience of deportation, when priests who were involved in the Resistance or who had otherwise earned the hostility of the Vichy Government or its German masters went into captivity, and in many cases to death in the concentration camps. An identity in suffering, often with those who had no extrinsic share in their faith, gave to many priests a deep sense of the tragedy of the loss of contact between the Church and the common people of France. Deprived of all privilege, they were just men among men, and found new, often unlikely, ways to exercise a fundamental ministry of compassion. And when, in 1942, the German authorities began the massive movement of French forced labour into German factories there arose a challenge which was magnificently met. Many priests, with forged papers and with no outward sign of their priesthood, went to Germany with the workers, shared their toil and their agony, and established clandestine groups of Catholic believers which in turn drew others who had hitherto thought little of the Church and had never in any case considered priests as other than comfortably-off strangers. Nothing is more moving in M. Poulat's book than his account of this hidden work of devoted priests—in Berlin, Dresden, Frankfurt—forced to improvise, deprived of all the usual helps and sanctions of an ordered clerical life. As one of them wrote:

> Canon law, liturgy: we have had to drop them. All that architecture which piety and human respect have over the centuries built round the body of Christ. . . . That Christ who many of us have touched with our fingers, Christ the worker who has been sent into forced labour alongside us.

And Père Dillard, a distinguished Jesuit economist (whom President Roosevelt had invited to the White House in other days), found in this direct contact with a world that had hitherto been simply a matter of statistics and sociological research a terrible revelation of the truth:

> My Latin, my liturgy, my mass, my prayer, everything makes me separate, a curious phenomenon, like a pope or a Japanese bonze—a stray specimen left of a race that will soon disappear.

It was no longer a case of a few enthusiasts who had become aware of the pastoral problems presented by the loss of faith among industrial workers in a Paris suburb. A whole generation of young priests and seminarians (for they too had been rounded up for forced labour and of course had been conscribed for the Army as well) returned to France profoundly affected by the years of shared work and suffering with the ordinary working people of France. And return was not easy; the adjustment to wearing a cassock and living the bourgeois life of the conventional French priest seemed a return to the wrong kind of status quo. Yet such were inevitably the pressures of clerical life that very soon it became a matter of business as before. But not for all. And the emergence of the worker-priest owes much more, M. Poulat makes plain, to this tragic and yet invigorating legacy of the war than to any conscious response to the findings of the religious sociologists or indeed to the evolving mood of the theologians.

Perhaps this was the essential weakness, a certain impatience that looked for drastic remedies, and remedies that sometimes were applied without enough regard for the true facts of the case. The easy relationships under the stress of captivity, the necessary improvisation and indifference to law, could not be automatically transferred to life in the settled structures of France itself. M. Poulat is not concerned with judgment at all—it is the great merit of his magnificent book that he relies entirely on the testimony of the men themselves—but he says enough to show how certainly strain and misunderstanding were bound to follow.

The last part of his book gives a detailed documentation of the worker-priest missions as they evolved—in particular the Mission de Paris and the work of the Dominican Père Loew in Marseilles. Père Loew's importance is rightly stressed. He stands apart from the other worker-priests, perhaps because his mission had from the start been so closely related to the careful studies of Economie et Humanisme, which insisted on a scientific analysis of the social structures of the society that was to be reached. Furthermore, he (and the group he belonged to) was less absolute in the rejection of 'parish' as opposed to 'mission' which had been so insisted upon by Abbé Godin. Other religious orders and two or three dioceses (apart from Paris) gradually began to build up small groups of priests who were to work in factories. But their emphasis varied: some were only to work for short periods in order to learn about the true conditions, others saw in a priest's permanent share in the daily work of the people the only way of really identifying himself with their need. Hence the frequent insistence on a 'working class world', a reality apart which must be accepted from within.

M. Poulat ends with a chapter called 'Tensions', in which differences of opinion and approach are already evident, even though he ends his book with the first real worker-priests in 1947. It would be hard to overpraise a work of superb scholarship which for the first time makes available the sources for our understanding of an initiative that (in intention at least) reached to the central problem of our time. For what was—and is—really at stake is the truth about man: his freedom, his dignity, his ultimate hope.

27

SOME PEOPLE

(*a*) FRANZ JÄGERSTÄTTER

THE STUDY of mass psychology or mass psychiatry seems still to have a long way to go. The monkey, the parrot or the human child learns by imitation. Our species seems to share certain herd or ant-like inclinations. Usually these forms are harmless enough: wearing the same kind of clothes, keeping up with the Joneses over washing-machines and so on. The characteristic becomes dangerous when a tribe or nation develops it. The dividing line between cleaning your car in the same way and killing in the same way becomes obscured.

These and other disturbing questions will be raised in the mind of every reader of Dr. Zahn's outstanding book. Dr. Zahn is a Roman Catholic and a conscientious objector. He is also professor of sociology at Loyola University, Chicago. In the 1950s he produced a book called *German Catholics and Hitler's War*. It was in the course of his research for that book that he stumbled by chance on the amazing story of Franz Jägerstätter (the mis-spelling of this name on the dust-jacket should be corrected) which he now recounts to us. He dedicates his book to this man

> and to all the others who, like him, stood alone and said 'No'—many of whose stories have been completely lost to history, at least as it is kept and written by men.

Jägerstätter was destined by Power to be a non-person, and so he

---

(*a*) Gordon C. Zahn: *In Solitary Witness: The Life and Death of Franz Jägerstätter*. 277 pp. Geoffrey Chapman. 30s.
(*b*) *Diaries and Letters, 1930–1939*. Edited by Nigel Nicolson. 448 pp. Collins. £2 2s.
(*c*) *Faith Under Fire*. 383 pp. Leslie Frewin. £2.
(*d*) *A Late Beginner*. 261 pp. Michael Joseph. 35s.
(*e*) *Adventures with Authors*. 276 pp. Cambridge University Press. 35s.

might have come to be even among his remote Austrian fellow-villagers had it not been for Dr. Zahn. The professor arrived and brought to bear all the apparatus of checks and counter-checks on the stories of reluctant people. Gradually he established an outline and truth after truth emerged. There still remain some gaps. But he unearthed some of Jägerstätter's correspondence and various pieces of writing which he calls 'Commentaries'. They are written in untutored German which has been translated into plain English. They are a masterpiece of the human spirit.

The story of Franz Jägerstätter could be summed up in a few words. He was born in 1907, the illegitimate child of a father killed in the First World War. His birthplace was St. Radegund in Upper Austria, not very far from Hitler's birthplace. As a young man he was gay in the Austrian fashion. He married in 1936 and subsequently experienced a spiritual awakening. His favourite reading was the Bible and religious books and pamphlets. He does not seem to have been a conscientious objector quite in Dr. Zahn's sense. But after the *Anschluss* he answered the ritual *Heil Hitler* with *Pfui Hitler*, and announced that he would never fight in Hitler's wars which were unjust and against God's will. When he rejected his final call to arms in 1943 he was imprisoned, taken to Berlin, sentenced to death and beheaded on August 9 of that year.

Thus told, his fate might sound like that of thousands of other victims of our times. But there is something almost amounting to mystery about the serenity and unshakable conviction of this man who stood utterly alone. The village did not sympathize. Against his view was Dr. Goebbels's lie-machine (one of the most destructive ever invented) and the might of a totalitarian state. An uneducated man, he had to stand against the persuasion used by educated men, the clergy of his own religion who produced all the learned arguments that Christians have used for centuries to justify their own particular wars: that he was too ignorant to judge matters of state; that the war was liberating Europe from the Bolsheviks; how could he be right and eighty million Germans be wrong? What about his wife and children? And so on.

To all such arguments he answered with reflections on Christianity and holiness—and with shrewd common sense. There was no bitterness in his comments:

> However, let us not on this account cast stones at our bishops or priests. They, too, are men like us, made of flesh and blood, and can weaken.

They are probably much more sorely tempted by the evil enemy than the rest of us. Maybe they have been too poorly prepared to take up this struggle and to make a choice between life and death . . .

Or, from prison,

Let us love our enemies, bless those who curse us, pray for those who persecute us. For love will conquer and will endure for all eternity. And happy are those who live and die in God's love.

As a methodical sociologist, despite his sympathy for Jägerstätter, Dr. Zahn took trouble to verify that this opponent of mass-opinion had at no time shown signs of insanity. This is a question it is always good to ask about someone who seems socially unadapted—even to a society which is deluging the earth with blood. How did this peasant come to see and dare where universities or theological colleges either could not see or did not dare? We seem forced to the conclusion that mass-dementia cannot be cured by the intelligence alone: the learned may join the herd and accept the orthodoxy even if they do not write its apologia. It does not seem to be with our minds that we choose between what Bergson called the 'open' morality and the 'closed' morality. But there still remains the question-mark of how this peasant managed to commit that crime that no 'closed' society can endure—to be right at the wrong time, and in a supreme, indeed glorious, way.

(*b*) HAROLD NICOLSON

Diaries and Letters, 1930–1939

In 1930 Harold Nicolson resigned from the Foreign Service, which he had joined in 1909. He had been a success, he could look forward to becoming, like his father, an ambassador. He had managed to combine diplomacy with authorship. But his wife, V. Sackville-West, would not live out of England, and in order to lead the life they wanted in England they needed more money. Lord Beaverbrook offered a job, the Londoner's Diary on the *Evening Standard*, and the decision was made. A new pattern of life began; Nicolson spent Monday to Friday in London and the weekends in Kent where V. Sackville-West remained firmly planted, first at Long Barn near Knole, then at Sissinghurst. Nicolson continued to write to his wife every day when they were apart, as they had both done since their engagement in 1911, and he began to keep a diary. From this material his son Nigel has, with candour and tact, edited the present volume, the first in a series of three. It begins with the economic depression and ends with the outbreak of war; it sees the transformation of Sissinghurst from a ruin among cabbages to a rare and famous garden; two boys grow up; books are written; and as many lunches and dinners are eaten at the tables of the the great as ever Henry James consumed in his palmy London years.

3rd March, 1931

Lunch with Enid Jones. Find myself between Margot Oxford and Violet Bonham Carter who both abuse me for my review of Elizabeth's novel, for joining the Mosley Party, and in fact for being myself in any way at all. Feel as if I had been massaged by two Kurds.

Such brushes with the famous abound. Ramsay MacDonald shows off the Turners at Chequers and speaks fondly of his own Turner and his Richard Wilson. Deaf Lady (*Golden Bough*) Frazer appears at dinner with a wireless slung on her bosom which gives out jazz and a talk about poultry. Housman, 'a *bon bourgeois* who has seen more sensitive days', does not talk much except about food. The Prince of Wales, at the Savoy Grill, gazes critically at the soft collar and flabby tie which Nicolson has donned for 'comfort and an A. J. Balfour look'. Churchill stretches out great arms on Nicolson's first day in the House of Commons and booms a welcome across the smoking-room: his charm is overwhelming, 'but I would rather it had occurred in greater privacy'. But the book is much more than a record of classy hob-nobbings. There is a strong dramatic interest, with three connected themes: the drama of public affairs, the drama of Harold Nicolson, and the drama of a family.

Through his Foreign Office experience, through his own friends, through his fellow-guests at the tables of Mrs. Ronald Greville, Lady Colefax and all the other hostesses who were delighted to have such a desirable single man for their parties, Nicolson was an insider in politics long before he entered the House of Commons in 1935. His speculations and comments on the rise of Hitler, the reoccupation of the Rhineland, the Spanish Civil War, the Abdication, Munich, are those of a man close to Ramsay MacDonald, Eden, Churchill. They will be of continuing interest to historians, but perhaps their most fascinated readers will be those who themselves lived through the decade, but as outsiders. These will learn much about the circumstances and personalities surrounding the decisions which reached them through the newspapers and the B.B.C.; about, for instance, the resignation of Eden in 1938, with his successor Halifax telling a Cabinet colleague only three months later, 'Anthony was right'. Such readers may well be startled to discover how far the governing class continued to be deluded about the dictators' intentions. Nicolson belonged to this class, if often uneasily (combining, his son tells us, 'a liberal intent with an aristocratic disdain'), but he grew ever more disillusioned about its nerve. After the Czech crisis of May, 1938, he writes:

> We have lost our will-power, since our will-power is divided. People of the governing classes think only of their own fortunes, which means hatred of the Reds. This creates a perfectly artificial but at present most effective secret bond between ourselves and Hitler. Our class interests, on both sides, cut across our national interests. I go to bed in gloom.

The record of September, 1938, is of particular if melancholy interest. On September 11, Nicolson dines with Oliver Stanley, whose point of view is 'typical of the better type of Cabinet opinion'. Stanley sees that Britain may have to fight, but

> at heart he is longing to get out of it. Thus he loses no opportunity of abusing the Czechs and of reviling Benes for being tricky and slippery. At the same time any reference to Russian assistance makes him wince, and at one moment he sighed deeply and said, 'You see, whether we win or lose, it will be the end of everything we stand for'. By 'we' he means obviously the capitalist classes.

On September 29, Nicolson attends a meeting of some who have not lost their nerve:

> . . . Winston, Cecil, Lytton, Arthur Salter, Wickham Steed, Walter Layton, Archibald Sinclair, Arthur Henderson, Liddell Hart, Norman Angell, Megan Lloyd George, Violet Bonham Carter, &c. Lord Lloyd makes the first speech. He says that Chamberlain is going to run away again and that we must stop him.

Churchill has made his first appearance in the diary in 1930 as 'incredibly aged . . . an elder statesman'; at the end he has stepped vigorously to the front of the stage.

Woven in and out of this unfolding political drama is a private one. What and who is Harold Nicolson? Diplomat, journalist, writer, politician? Why is he for ever 'promising'? Why is he not graver, solider, deeper? Why does he sometimes like to cause pain? Why, in spite of going to the best tailors and shirtmakers, does he lack elegance? Why is his latest book so disappointing? Gloomily he sums up 1931:

Of all my years this has been the most unfortunate. Everything has gone wrong. I have lost not only my fortune [he means his good luck] but much of my reputation. I incurred enmities: the enmity of Beaverbrook; the enmity of the B.B.C. and the Athenaeum Club; the enmity of several stuffies. I left the *Evening Standard*, I failed in my Election, I failed over *Action*. I have been inexpedient throughout. My connexion with Tom Mosley has done me harm. I am thought trashy and a little mad. I have been reckless and arrogant. I have been silly. I must recapture my reputation. I must be cautious and more serious. I must not try to do so much, and must endeavour to do what I do with greater depth and application. I must avoid the superficial.

Yet in spite of all this—what fun life is!

It is to the accompaniment of such Boswellian self-scrutiny and self-scolding that we watch his career or, as it often appeared, 'the perennial problem of Harold Nicolson's future'. With hindsight, his first plunge into active politics in 1931 as a candidate for Mosley's New Party seems bizarre indeed; hardly less so his decision to contest West Leicester in 1935 as a National Labour candidate. He would not call himself Conservative though he supported Baldwin, he repudiated the MacDonald Government of 1929–31 though MacDonald now led his party. Once elected (by eighty-seven votes) he enjoyed being in the House of Commons more than he enjoyed party politics. He won respect by his speeches on foreign affairs, he did what he could to wake up the country to the dangers from Hitler, and this gave him satisfaction:

When I feel that I have done nothing in life, I shall always remember this quiet but resolute agitation.

This was his main contribution to the world of action. But all through the 1930s he was also writing books—*Public Faces*, *Peacemaking*, *Curzon*, *Dwight Morrow*, *Helen's Tower*—and book reviews with an enviable ease and punctuality, lecturing, travelling, and making the garden at Sissinghurst. It strikes one that for all Nicolson's worries about spreading himself in too many directions, his talent was for just this active diversity.

In general, it is the wives of professional men who are expected to keep several balls in the air at once—household, children, sociability, intellectual interests, perhaps a profession of their own. With Harold Nicolson and his wife the roles were reversed. V. Sackville-West concentrated firmly on her writing and her garden, ruthlessly cutting out irrelevant activities, whether being a member's wife at Leicester or dining at Buckingham Palace. In their creation of the garden, their son tells us, his was the classical planning of lines and vistas, hers the romantic planting; but in nearly everything else she appears as rational, realistic and firm in her convictions, while he is enthusiastic, wayward and volatile. Fascinated by Mosley, he rushes to join the New Party; she thinks it a great mistake, and Mosley gives her the creeps. He unfolds a glittering future when he will ride through Delhi on an elephant; she has fallen asleep. He is all for a warm measure of domesticity; she can't abide it, and the only way he can celebrate their silver wedding, an occasion she refuses to recognize, is to 'say a little private prayer of thanksgiving to Demeter, who I feel is the most appropriate person to receive it'. He is easily companionable; she, immensely reserved. She, disinherited from Knole because of her sex, is fiercely feminist; privately to his diary he affirms 'women are not fulfilling their proper function unless subservient to some man'. Such differences of temperament and outlook might wreck a marriage; beneath the Nicolsons' differences was a rock of mutual devotion and dependence. There are some deeply moving letters in which she expresses the feelings which she could not bring herself to speak, in which he conveys his tenderness and his reliance on her: 'When I get puzzled or angry or frightened, I want your old shaggy wisdom and your love.'

The other characters in the family drama are V. Sackville-West's mother who plays (off-stage) the role of a baleful fairy godmother, and the sons Benedict and Nigel Nicolson, whose development and changing relations with their parents we follow in some striking passages of the diary and letters. Such revelations about a family could be embarrassing; here they never are. Harold Nicolson respected his sons', as his wife's, independence and privacy; there is concern, but no prying; affection but also objectivity. And affection and objectivity have gone to the editing of this volume and have created, from the formidable mass of material, a work with a shape and with a deep personal as well as a public interest.

(*c*) CANON L. JOHN COLLINS

Faith Under Fire

Canon Collins opens his *apologia pro vita sua* with the question, 'Why don't I get out of the Church?'. From this record of more than thirty-five years of patently sincere, conscientious and often courageous Christian ministry it is initially difficult to see why this question should be put. Canon Collins is no heretic. He believes insistently in an immanent and transcendent Godhead, and in the historical Jesus of Nazareth as the human incarnation of that divine reality. The fulcrum of his faith is the Cross and Resurrection, and he declares his devotion to the great Anglican churches and the potential splendour of their ritual, in particular to the Cathedral of St. Paul in the City of London where he is Preceptor and Canon Residentiary. But he also writes:

Of one thing I feel convinced: to offer the New Testament Gospel of love as anything other than a realistic way of life for this world is to put Christ into the clouds, and reduce the Christian way of life either to an escapist's dream, or to a feeble prop to established privileges, an opiate for the dispossessed.

In implementation of this conviction he has been busily active over the past twenty years 'putting religion into politics'. Christian Action, the organization which he founded in 1946 for this purpose, has since embroiled itself in a succession of worthy causes, reconciliation with the German people after the war, defence and aid for the victims of apartheid, and of course the Campaign for Nuclear Disarmament. Canon Collins gives a very full account from his viewpoint of the inception and development of these campaigns and at times can tell a good joke against himself.

But with all the patent sincerity and ardour behind Canon Collins's activities, there is an uncomfortable tone of patronage, particularly towards fellow-Christians, which irritates the reader even when he is most in sympathy with the opinions expressed. There is a revealing paradox in Canon Collins's stated decision that 'it was in cooperation with semi-Christians, non-Christians and even anti-Christians that I was likely to find most of my colleagues in the things I felt I had to do'. Again, at the time of a peace conference in Accra: 'The British delegation . . . was by no means united in its attitude towards my position and viewpoint in the conference', and later, 'I declined the offer of being chairman or a member of the committee . . . partly because I could not see any very useful future for it.' Canon Collins is no humble worker in the vineyard. He leads from the head of the column or not at all. And this is perhaps the clue to that initial question. On the face of it there would seem no reason at all why Canon Collins should get out of the Church, which has provided him with headquarters for Christian Action, a pulpit from which he can declare his views without restraint, a position and background which command worldwide respect, and the freedom and time to travel extensively in the exercise of his personal vocation. But his style of writing begets an uneasy feeling that he resents the very facilities with which he has been provided. He is so insistent on being considered a turbulent priest, a persecuted rebel. Of Archbishop Fisher he writes with typical patronage, 'I have a certain sympathy with him in his attitude towards me', but gives very little insight into what that attitude might be. But it might well include the suspicion that the Canon is intellectually somewhat muddled, and that not all of his paradoxes are intentional: he uses words like 'existential' in a number of different ways, not many of them in the way usually understood; he uses 'agnostic' where others would probably have preferred 'sceptic'. 'Man, I believe', he concludes, 'if he is to fulfil himself happily and adequately, needs to travel through life unhampered by certainties, untrammelled by authority'—one is tempted to add, 'unless it is mine'. In the light of this conclusion and the general tone of this book, it is significant to note that when the split came in the leadership of C.N.D., it was not on the side of civil disobedience that Canon Collins was found but on the side of law and order.

These criticisms must not be allowed to detract from all the extensive and varied good work done by the organizations in whose leadership Canon Collins has served, nor from the simple good sense of his main proposition and his own steadfast devotion to it. Perhaps by writing a little less, the author would have done himself more justice, nor did we really need *all* those photographs of the Canon.

(*d*) PRISCILLA NAPIER

A Late Beginner

This is a triumph. Mrs. Napier's book is worthy of a place on the shelves of the discriminating reader next to Mrs. Raverat's *Period Piece*. There are perhaps three reasons which cause it to shine out from the slow-moving but steady flow of present-day autobiography or of what might be called books written now about then. The first reason is fortuitous. Mrs. Napier's childhood was largely spent in

Egypt, where her father was financial adviser to the government; and Cairo in the closing years before 1914 makes a fascinating but unfamiliar setting for books of this kind. The reader senses with the author the abrupt change from peace to war, from order to chaos, from the security of the confident world to the casualty lists from the front. 'Facts can be kept from a child but an atmosphere never can be.'

Her story turns on Cairo unruffled by what was developing in Europe and unconscious of Egypt's stormy future. The reader learns to love the Egyptian servants—the ponderous Mohammed and the spirited Almud ('we shall never have such a good second suffragi again', sighed the author's mother), the children of other English officials in Egypt—Goschens, Rowlatts, de Cossons, Blunts, and the family of Russell Pasha; and above everything the endless sunshine of an Egyptian childhood. Even youthful church-going seems bright and gay with the great imperialists—Kitchener, Wingate and Allenby—marching to the eagle to read the lessons. We shudder with the grown-ups when Mrs. Napier, tempted by the detestable son of a colonel, scooped up the waters of the Nile and drank, to the dregs, what her hands contained. She assures us that the draught did her no harm—though she has to confess that the water, in its progress, had drained several thousand villages.

The other two reasons are not fortuitous. The chief is Mrs. Napier's skill in drawing character—done simply and deftly without elaboration. The picture of her nurse is a brilliant recovery of a forgotten personality. She seems to catch every prejudice of the Englishwoman abroad—those prejudices which by sharp-tongued critics are invariably but mistakenly attached to the 'better-to-do'. 'Nanny, what happens to the Egyptian babies when they die?' 'In my father's house', Nanny said crisply 'are many mansions.' She was thirty-three, but each of her observations reflects the wisdom of antiquity.

The other reason for the success of the book is a certain tartness of style, which fixes the attention of the reader on what the author is saying. 'Sing the gloria, dear—you know that', murmurs her mother in church. But did she recognize what she knew under that pompous title? When she left off the eternal white muslin of early childhood she pranced under the leboc avenues—'I am blue, I am blue, in a blue linen dress, I am five, I am blue, I am five. I am Me, in a blue linen dress. WITH BLUE LINEN KNICKERS TO MATCH'.

There are two trifling slips which Mrs. Napier will forgive the Devonshire pedants (if such still exist) and the railway sentimentalists for noticing. The delectable and once secluded bay to the west of Sidmouth is Ladram, and it is pronounced by those who know as 'Lardr'm'. The London, Brighton and South Coast Railway was adorned with umber-coloured engines and umber and white carriages. 'The beautiful blue engines and crimson coaches' which her memory attributes to the L. B. & S. C. R. are more difficult to identify. Perhaps the Caledonian? But more likely she is thinking of the Somerset and Dorset Railway, with its carriages of royal blue. But these are irrelevancies. With Mrs. Napier as travelling companion we enjoy the journey to Sidmouth, with her brother—the present Warden of New College—babbling of the salmon-pink glories of the South Western. For when the heat of Egypt became intolerable the family spent high summer at Sidmouth in company with light-hearted Slessor cousins and with the true Devonians whose forbears had once seen the mighty Duke of Kent striding across their cliffs. One of the children's friends among the boatmen made a salty and characteristic comment on the bourgeois fancy for bathing: 'Mere idle bravery I calls it, with neither mirth nor comfort in it.' But in Mrs. Napier's delightful book there is plenty of both.

(*e*) S. C. ROBERTS

Adventures with Authors

Sydney Castle Roberts, who died this year shortly after completing this autobiographical memoir, was a man of many parts. He went up to Pembroke College, Cambridge, in 1907, and in 1911 he joined the Cambridge University Press as its assistant secretary. Eleven years later he became Secretary (i.e. director) of that Press, a post he held with distinction for twenty-six years. In 1948 he was elected Master of his old college and, a year later, became Vice-Chancellor of the University, filling also, both then and thereafter, a bewildering variety of public posts. He was in addition an authority on Samuel Johnson, on the University of Cambridge and on Sherlock Holmes; his original writings range from a history of the Press with which he was so intimately associated to the definitive biography of Dr. Watson.

A man so versatile naturally possessed many friends, and his position with the Press ensured that he should likewise make the acquaintance of many distinguished people, both in this country and in America. It follows, therefore, that his book is full of unexpected glimpses of the eminent or the near-eminent, almost all of whom are revealed to the best advantage, for Roberts was essentially a genial man and one who (at least in his own portrayal of himself) was quite unlike those Cambridge desperados whose lineaments have become familiar to us in the writings of C. P. Snow.

There is, perhaps, good reason for this disparity: 'Mr. Roberts', said an American publisher to him on one occasion, 'I believe you're a better man of business than what you are literary!' The revealing part of the story is Roberts's comment on it—'which I took as a high compliment'. This being the case, it is only natural that the most interesting pages of his book are those which deal with the business minutiae of the C.U.P. During Roberts's reign they published many important scholarly volumes, but also a number of more general ones of high quality in which he obviously took particular interest: the Cecil Torr 'Wreyland' series, George Sturt's *The Wheelwright's Shop*, Eric Benfield's *Purbeck Shop*, Margaret Penn's *Manchester XIV Miles*. At the same time, persons of quite unusual distinction were working for the Press: that remarkable printer, Walter Lewis; Frank Kendon, the assistant secretary and author of that little classic, *The Small Years*; George Sampson, whose single-volume condensation of the *History of English Literature* proved such an unexpected triumph. To these, and to many like them, Roberts pays well-deserved tribute.

His anecdotes, told with commendable pith and brevity, are numerous and excellent. There is de la Mare, for example, expatiating on book-collecting: 'Some men are born with a library, some acquire a library, others become reviewers'. More perfect still, in form, was the crushing observation of A. B. Cook on a particularly inane examination-question—'What were the recreations in the Viking Age of (*a*) men, (*b*) women?'—'Mr. Chairman,' he asked in his high-pitched voice, 'would a candidate receive full marks if he answered (*a*) women, (*b*) men?'

Sir Sydney Roberts's life was long and useful; it is sad he should not have been spared to receive the applause which this accomplished and good-tempered résumé of it so fully merits.

INDEX

This index, in addition to referring to articles and reviews in the present volume, also shows other major reviews of the year which have appeared in the T.L.S.

Date references and page numbers *in italic* are to articles and reviews in the T.L.S. not reprinted in this volume. Page numbers in parentheses are given only where the reference is not immediately obvious from the article.

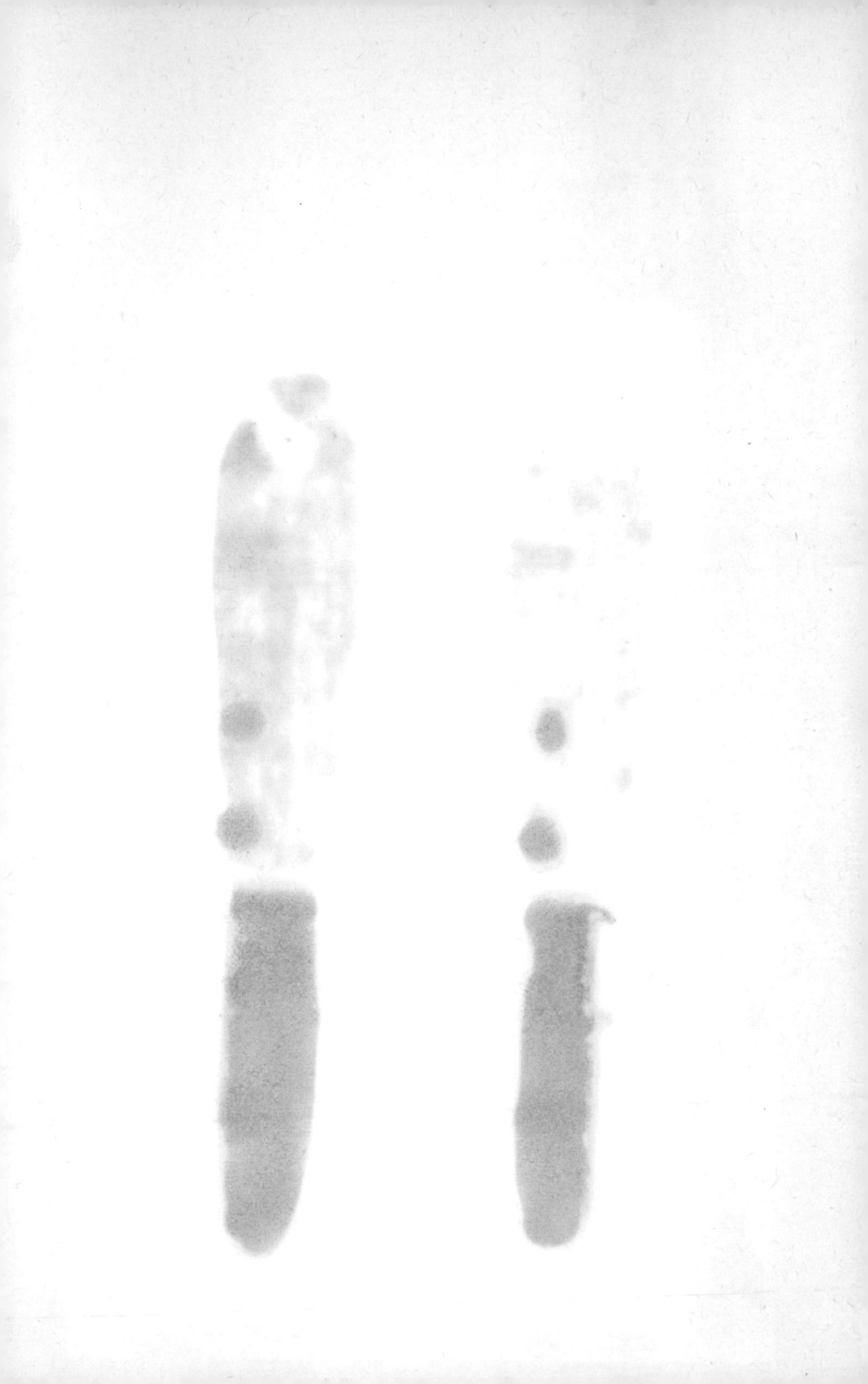